Going S

Af... ...e ... Punis... nt

Angela Devlin is a writer and broad... ... r v... ...ce the success of her first book, *Criminal Classes* (Wate... ...er... ...) has been in regular demand as a speaker on criminal justice matters. ...ne has written three further books since then: *Prison Patter* (Waterside Press, 1996: a dictionary of prison slang and jargon); *Anybody's Nightmare: The Sheila Bowler Story* (Taverner Publications, 1998: with her husband Tim she led the campaign which in 1997 brought about the release, retrial and subsequent acquittal of Sheila Bowler, wrongfully convicted of murder); and *Invisible Women: What's Wrong With Women's Prisons* (Waterside Press, 1998: she spent five years visiting prisons and interviewing women prisoners and staff).

Bob Turney was released from Wandsworth prison in 1979. Twenty years later, he completed a full-time university degree course and qualified as a probation officer. He has written about how he turned his life around in *I'm Still Standing* (Waterside Press, 1995) since when he has appeared on numerous TV and radio programmes. Bob is dyslexic. He lives with his wife and five children in Reading and works for Berkshire Probation Service. He spends his spare time helping people with alcohol or drugs problems, and writing, lecturing and speaking about his experiences at both ends of the criminal justice process.

Going Straight
After Crime and Punishment

Published 1999 by
WATERSIDE PRESS
Domum Road
Winchester SO23 9NN
Telephone or Fax 01962 855567
E-mail:106025.1020@compuserve.com

ISBN Paperback 1 872 870 66 X

Cataloguing-in-Publication Data A catalogue record for this book can be obtained from the British Library.

Printing and binding Antony Rowe Ltd, Chippenham

Cover design John Good Holbrook Ltd, Coventry. Front cover illustration by Peter Cameron. Peter Cameron, who is featured in *Going Straight,* started painting whilst serving a ten and a half year prison sentence and came to terms with his imprisonment by making it the subject of his art. He is now a freelance artist and can be contacted at The Hub, 9-13 Berry Street, Liverpool. Telephone 0151 709 0889.

Royalties All royalties from this book are being made over to UNLOCK, the National Association of Ex-Offenders run by ex-offenders.

Going Straight

After Crime and Punishment

Compiled by

Angela Devlin

Bob Turney

Foreword

The Rt Hon Jack Straw MP, Home Secretary

With contributions by

His Honour Sir Stephen Tumim

Roger Graef

WATERSIDE PRESS
WINCHESTER

Going Straight After Crime and Punishment

CONTENTS

Going Straight: Tales of Hope and Regeneration

(handwritten: focus — Bob Cummines ✗, Mark Leech ✗ on case study — 204 → check on internet — 222 → case study.)

With additional contributions by
His Honour Sir Stephen Tumim at p.233 and p.266

Acknowledgements

The authors would like to thank the Berkshire Probation Service, the Governor, staff and prisoners of HMP Wandsworth, Sue Turney and Tim Devlin for their support throughout this project.

Above all, they would like to express their gratitude to those who agreed to be interviewed for the book.

The authors' royalties go to UNLOCK, the National Association of Ex-Offenders run by ex-offenders. We hope that this contribution will help many others to go straight.

Angela Devlin
Bob Turney

February 1999

Foreword
The Rt Hon Jack Straw MP, Home Secretary

The stories in *Going Straight* concern people who have been able to mend their ways—to stop being offenders and to lead law-abiding lives. Some of the people involved say that they cannot now imagine circumstances in which they would be drawn towards crime. They are doing what any Home Secretary hopes offenders will do—leading honest and fulfilling lives free from crime.

What is particularly encouraging about the stories in this book is that 'going straight' is seen as something very positive by the individuals concerned. They are proud of their achievements and in several cases are actively using their past experiences to enhance their own communities.

The book draws together factors which, on the basis of the accounts, are likely to influence an offender to the extent that he or she makes some permanent commitment to a new way of life. In the final analysis, a degree of personal motivation on the part of an offender is essential before other, sometimes necessarily punitive, strategies for dealing with crime will fully succeed. The individual accounts contain other signposts indicating what is most likely to bring about that motivation and in the process to cause an offender to realise that a life of crime is an empty existence and ultimately counter-productive.

As can be seen from the accounts in the book, the individuals know the many risks they run, including a further prison sentence, if they offend again. Relationships, family, personal achievements, the respect which they have earned from others are among the things which the ex-offenders have come to value and which they know would be lost if they returned to crime. The more people have a stake in society the more they appreciate the devastating effect which crime can have. Similarly, the better our understanding of why people offend—and what causes them to stop—the more effective we can make our efforts to achieve this outcome in every case.

The stories in *Going Straight* show all of us involved in the administration of criminal justice that it is possible for a life to be turned around. Of course, not every offender will be turned away from crime. That would be unrealistic. But these accounts show what individuals can achieve. Whatever one's reactions to these accounts they are certainly worth reading.

The royalties from the book are being donated to the charity, UNLOCK, the National Association for Ex-Offenders run by ex-offenders, formed in 1998—whose members seek to give each other mutual support. Their President is Sir Stephen Tumim who was formerly HM Chief Inspector of Prisons and who has annotated two of the accounts: that by Mark Leech, chairman of UNLOCK; and that by Peter Cameron, the artist, who discovered his latent talents by winning an award from the Koestler Trust of which Sir Stephen is patron.

Angela Devlin and Bob Turney, the compilers of this book, and Roger Graef who wrote the *Postscript*, are to be congratulated for this valuable perspective on crime and punishment.

INTRODUCTION

Leaving Crime Behind

The idea for this book came from a chance remark by a police officer:

> We read an awful lot about crime and criminals ... but we never hear much about people who've given up crime – people who've gone straight.

The policeman is right. The long-standing success of films and books about the Kray twins, the Great Train Robbers and countless American gangsters bears witness to an enduring public appetite for and fascination with stories of criminal lives. Inevitably the focus of such projects—and indeed of most media coverage—is on crime and *its rewards*, and sometimes on graphic accounts of prison life. Prison-based films, plays and books are frequently about 'tough guys', 'likeable rogues' (people too clever for their own good who have sailed too close to the wind) 'prison intellectuals' (forever capable of outwitting the system), 'survivors' (who can endure whatever adverse treatment comes their way) and 'prison bosses' (who call the shots inside jails and outside where, remarkably, they still hold sway!). It is a world of fear, power, ludicrous escape plots and, as part of this celluloid sub-culture, the occasional smoked salmon served by prison officers. Perhaps this is the way viewers and readers have come to prefer their images of prisons—and maybe some prisoners do try to act the part. Life can begin to imitate art.

Prisons in reality
In our experience, real prisons bear little resemblance to those portrayed in popular culture. There may be an unnerving sense of violence in certain jails, and what can be described, loosely, as a 'pecking order', but most prisoners—their crime and sentence apart—are *ordinary* people. This often surprises those who have not been inside a prison before: 'But they're just like you and me!'—which of course they are (and this may provide one of our first clues about the influences likely to help offenders go straight). The minority apart, prisoners are often shocked, isolated, vulnerable people, sometimes denying the fairness of their predicament and just about coping as their world, such as it is, falls apart without their being able to do much about it. Many would readily exchange this powerless situation for a crime-free existence on the outside, but do not know how to set about it, and do not have the wherewithal to do so. Rather, their lives are attuned to basic, more mundane and precarious triggers which may cause them to return to prison, sometimes again and again.

Film and television coverage thus risks creating spurious role models by glamorising the criminal: witness the current fashion for ultra-baggy jeans worn low on the hips—a fashion which started in America in emulation of prisoners whose belts have been taken from them. Why should a group of New York rappers call themselves 'Fun Lovin' Criminals' if crime is not considered cool? Why are movies like *Goodfellas* so popular? This book makes no such contribution to the iconography of crime. The stories told in the accounts which follow show that criminal offending and imprisonment are not glamorous, only sordid and destructive. As one of the interviewees points out: 'In crime there are no winners, only victims'.

EVENTS AND EXPERIENCES

Going Straight focuses on people who have succeeded in moving away from criminal offending—or who, in one or two cases, are making a determined effort to do so. The individual accounts allow the reader to search for clues about life experiences and events which can trigger change. Why is it that some people *are* able to leave crime behind? How do they continue to remain 'crime free' despite a range of pressures and temptations? The accounts are not presented as if they provide some scientific or finite answer (and we doubt whether any amount of analysis can do that), but it is possible to identify certain recurring features which seem to point the way.

In the remainder of this *Introduction* we have tried to discuss the process of change under the headings *Getting Into Crime, Getting Out of Crime* and *Staying Out of Crime*. First, however, some of the more common factors affecting interviewees' decisions to stop offending can be identified, broadly, as follows:

- what might be described as a compelling one-off experience: some 'life event' or 'awakening'—a powerful, single and distinct occurrence which the individual can identify as a turning point and without which he or she would almost certainly have continued to offend. This event varies from individual to individual, and it seems to occur in a random kind of way, but it acts as a catalyst for what then follows

- sometimes a personal relationship is the trigger for change (family, romantic, intellectual or maybe with someone responsible for teaching, training or supervising a prisoner, who makes a strong impact). The relationship may have to contend with the existence of 'old' associations which, unless handled with resolve on the part of the ex-offender, can exert a strong pull in the opposite direction. Many of the interviewees speak of having had to break away, or to distance themselves from a circle of detrimental influences

- some offenders discover a creative impulse or way of rechannelling existing skills, energies and enthusiasm. This then becomes a powerful driving force. It is often linked to achievement, recognition (also themselves positive and recurring factors) and in some cases the wherewithal to earn a living

- not infrequently, there is a religious base for change, or some other similarly powerful 'supernatural' force seems to affect people. The individual concerned may 'develop a conscience' as a result of some incident, and this can also lead to remorse for victims or others whom the offender has treated badly in the past. Many of the interviewees comment that, in this sense, they will never be able to escape their past; others speak of it taking up to 20 years before they come to terms with the wrong they have done. 'Conversions' of this kind may be one way in which the spectre of the past can be dealt with

- closely linked with the last point (and with or without a religious base) is the sense of putting something back into the community, making up for the way the individual used to be. Again, this links to the benefits of achievement, self-respect and recognition. It may carry the double plus that the ex-offender is able to capitalise on his or her experiences on the wrong side of the line in order to inform or educate others about the ills of offending

- often criminal offending, or its origins, may be directly linked to some addiction (the most obviously destructive addictions being alcohol, drugs and gambling). Seemingly, from the accounts, crime itself can be addictive (though whether in the technical sense we do not presume to understand). But certainly offending can provide a strong 'buzz' and there often needs to be an equally strong alternative or substitute to wean someone away from it

- offending can give people a spurious kind of status. There is then the difficulty of being 'a nobody' outside the individual's peer group, so that an ability to reconcile ordinary, non-criminal behaviour with status and achievement can be a crucial factor for certain people looking to change their way of life. Closely connected with this, a strong indicator of potential success in going straight (and a point already made above) is the extent to which offenders can distance themselves from associates who are still involved in criminal activities or from other situations which draw them back into crime

- finally, for a significant proportion of offenders, there comes a point at which they simply decide to give up offending, having 'tired' of crime and all the problems it brings. Sometimes this is the maturing process at work: help may have been at hand but the offender was not until now ready to receive it. Others seem to reach a point when further crime becomes too great a risk; the older people become, the more reluctant they are to contemplate spending their few remaining years behind bars

- as part of the process of getting out of crime, then staying out of it, most ex-offenders will have acquired *something to lose*. This has a rare value: having something of real value (a home, partner, family, self-respect, personal achievements) may be something quite alien, and this may become an unusually powerful driving force. A determination to protect the status quo can stop people committing crimes and can give them a new zest for life.

These ingredients do not exist in tidy compartments; and together with more individual and personal factors they may be present in a variety of recipes. The fact of imprisonment may or may not be part of the overall mix, and it may play a part in the causal chain that leads to decisions to stop offending (as opposed to serving the purpose of containment). From the perspective of the interviewees, prison has a range of effects, and we illustrate these with extracts quoted at the end of the *Introduction*. Some, though relatively few, accounts place the fact of going to prison high on the list of catalysts which led to change.

Some interviewees realise very acutely that life is changing—and this, in turn, seems to 'energise' their efforts to keep things moving in the right direction, at least at the start. Yet as several of the accounts show, even when individual offenders have found their own formulae for change they may still fear that—in certain circumstances—they could re-offend, even many years on. Leaving crime behind *permanently* can, for some, be as fragile a process as making the change in the first place.

THE INTERVIEWS

Within the accounts which follow, there are, then, certain clues and signposts about those factors which may make an offender change direction. These show how and why 'damaged and damaging' people can become valued and valuable members of society. As well as being of interest to people who work with offenders, we believe that prisoners and other offenders may also find inspiration in these stories.

Prime minister Tony Blair has often said that his government intends to be 'tough on crime, and tough on the causes of crime'. To help people stop offending, we need to be aware of these causes, to understand how people came to be involved in crime in the first place. During the interviews we asked ex-criminals what led them into crime—as well as what led them out of it.

Between them, the people we interviewed have committed a wide range of offences, from dishonesty and drug trafficking all the way through to serious assaults and even murder. We did not interview sex-offenders to whom, we believe, quite separate and specific considerations apply which are beyond the scope of a general work. Some readers might feel that the same applies to offences of violence, but we are prepared to let the interviews themselves testify as to whether our decision to include such offenders was justified. Violence is often interwoven with other crimes, and we do not believe that it stands apart from the general run of offences in quite the same way. Naturally, what works with one type of offender in terms of change may not work with another.

The interviewees are now mostly in work and they come from all walks of life ranging from business to the theatre, from writing and television to the church, from probation work to plumbing. Several are now employed in what can be described as prison-related occupations (and we comment on this later). The key importance of employment cannot be overstated and, as many stories illustrate, ex-prisoners often experience considerable difficulties when trying to get into legitimate forms of work.

All the interviewees have been in trouble with the law, and most of them were sent to prison. All have found their own ways of coming to terms with their offending. Their stories are set out in the central section to the book, *Going Straight: Tales of Hope and Regeneration.* We hope that, like us, you will find them both moving and inspiring.

GETTING INTO CRIME

The reason why someone starts offending may point the way to the reason why he or she might stop doing so. Tony Blair has said he is convinced that family problems are at the root of social breakdown. Bruce Reynolds, one of the Great Train Robbers and now a writer and occasional *Guardian* film critic, says in his interview:

> Everybody I've met in prison has nearly always come from some sort of disturbed background. The families have broken up, there's marital discord. There's not many of them come from happy families.

This is true of almost all the people we spoke to, ranging from those with criminal fathers they had been brought up to regard as heroes, and those who were victims of childhood abuse, to those with no families at all.

Social background of the interviewees

Quite often, interviewees had criminal associations or what might be described as a criminal lifestyle: these became either a regular feature or a factor due to some random contact. Bruce Reynolds recalls:

> ...I met a guy that I'd call a wide boy: he wasn't a crook but he knew the ways of the streets. He was street-educated and when I started going out with him, he showed me how to get by on the Tube without buying a ticket, he showed me how to get into the cinemas by going in the back doors. Then we did a couple of minor robberies—we smashed a couple of kiosk windows and stole some lighters.

Pentecostal minister Terry Mortimer explains:

> ... I grew up with a bit of shame, a bit of a chip on my shoulder. I think that created the aggression in me. Because there was a clear distinction between me and our lot, and those toffee-nosed twits down the road. Other kids would get presents and go on holidays and they lived a normal life, with a decent home, mum and dad working.

Tommy from Northern Ireland has a similar explanation about his own, somewhat singular, background:

> From a very young age I felt I didn't fit in. I didn't fit into the family, and I never felt part of things at primary school. I never felt very confident in anything I ever did from an early age. My lack of self-esteem was caused by certain things at home, and I always felt I wanted to be part of a different family. I don't know why, because this was even before things went wrong in my family. I battled with that for years upon years, all my life. I think I had a lot of ability, but low self-esteem and low self-confidence hindered me a lot, because the way that I felt about myself influenced the way that I did my school work.

Tommy suffered active rejection from his peers, who even took to informing him in writing of his lack of worth. His later involvement with a sectarian mob, where he admits to getting 'a buzz', seems to have been, at least in part, a reaction to this earlier exclusion—though he remained a rebel, to his later cost. Chris Sheridan (now a probation officer) was *born* in prison, so that little about his institutional lifestyle growing up in care and going to approved school and then prison was likely to appear odd to him at that stage.

Self-made millionaire Michael Fraser describes how he now confronts his one-time criminal associates:

> The people I was hanging around with at the time we were doing the burglaries went on to do armed robberies and bank jobs with shotguns and everything. They're still doing it now. I see them occasionally when they come out of prison. When I meet them they say, "Oh God, Mike, look at your Ferrari, look at your Bentley". I try and say to them, "You could do it as well". I say the same thing to people when I go into the prisons. I say "You can do it if you want to do it".

Overbearing relationships

Sometimes there is evidence of overbearing or domineering behaviour on the part of a parent or other significant individual in the life of the offender, which creates an inescapable role model or, in other cases, ultimately leads to rebellion. This may result in a sense of repression, of not being a free agent, or in a need to emulate. 'No, the piano's for poofs, you're not doing that. I'd rather you go boxing', Bob Cummines was informed by his father. 'Being a man' later involved Bob in a life of misplaced loyalties and considerable violence until he began his own quite remarkable process of change. It was the same with Hugh Collins:

> I remember feeling rebellious but never really knowing why at first. Then I knew I was different because of my old man. I started wearing army belts and I had a lot of fights when anyone said anything about my dad. If somebody slagged him, I'd be up the back of the school with them. Then I started to take pride in the fact that I felt different. I started hanging round with the fighters in the yard. My father was a hard man so I felt it was expected of me to follow in his footsteps.

Feelings of isolation and loneliness

In view of the tragic family backgrounds described above, we found it particularly poignant that, with few exceptions, the interviewees nevertheless felt that their best hope of continuing to remain crime-free after their sentence lay in the family, in relationships, usually with partners and their own children though sometimes by keeping in touch with someone who had affected their life. Thus, according to video director Mish Biberovic:

> Now my relationship with my girlfriend helps me as well. She's what you call straight, very straight, the way she's been brought up, she's never got involved in any criminality. She's often said to me, 'Do you know anyone who isn't a criminal?' Because a lot of people I see even now are bent in one way or another. Or former-bent or prospective-bent! So she says 'Don't you know anyone who's straight?' She and her family are the only straight people I know.

Often because of family or other circumstances, the interviewees are people who when growing up felt different or isolated from their peers, particularly at school. They use terms like 'oddball' or 'outcast'. Being an outsider, being excluded (not being picked to join school teams, being pushed out of the house by their parents), suffering from extreme forms of loneliness or sensing a void in their lives is a strong common thread which runs through many of the stories, though the roots of isolation can sometimes also be traced to other anxieties, such as learning difficulties or confusion about sexuality. Whatever the cause, being different can sometimes lead to being labelled disruptive and being disruptive can mask other problems. As Michael Fraser notes:

> I think being disruptive was just a cry for my father's attention. I think I craved attention and the only way I could get it was by being bad. I think I had a relationship with my father where I felt that every time I copied anything he did, he sort of praised me for it, whether it was good or bad. As a youngster I think I was probably like my father. That was important to me. I felt I was a mirror image of him when he was younger. My father got killed in a car crash when I was about 16. I didn't find out for a year, and I had no relationship with my mother till years later, when I was in my twenties.

People can be labelled as disruptive even when the reason for this seems totally unjustified: Anita O'Connell got into fights as a result of being singled out and bullied and she also suffered because of her own intelligence:

> . . . I felt resentful that I couldn't really talk to anyone, and I never felt I belonged. I was in the top set for English and maths, but the trouble was that I always finished the maths work too quickly for the teacher. He'd give us enough work for half an hour's lesson but I'd get it done in ten minutes then I'd walk round the class giving other people a hand. So though I was speeding ahead, I was labelled disruptive and I was put in the remedial group for maths. I was all right at school till I was about 14: that's when things started to go wrong.

Carole also notes that intellectual loneliness and a measure 'superiority' led to isolation and an inability to make friends. Feeling isolated can make less desirable and potentially damaging overtures attractive to someone young, vulnerable and anxious to be included or cared for. Marie had good reason to feel 'different'. She was born and brought up in the 'wrong' sex. Again, deep-seated feelings of rejection plagued her early years.

Mark Leech tells how his life was firmly turned in the direction of crime because of an overwhelming sense of rejection, disillusionment and lack of trust. Abused by a teacher, he discovered that his was by no means a special, caring relationship when he found his abuser with another eight year old boy:

> It was a real turning point in my life. From that moment on—and I mean from that *second* on—walking into that room and finding it, and recognising what it was, my life changed completely. In that one single second my life changed and it never went back again. From that moment on, when I found that situation, all the illusions, the relationship that I thought I'd created, just fell down around my ears completely. And I swore blind that nobody in authority was ever going to do that to me again.

Drugs, alcohol gambling and addiction

It is perhaps unsurprising that so many of the interviewees began offending or abusing alcohol and drugs at a very young age in a misguided attempt to gain acceptance, to belong or to patch over damaging experiences. Jim Smith, who is now a social worker, followed this familiar path by committing thefts to fund his alcoholism, and was remanded to Brixton prison, where he made friends with criminals and moved on to yet more petty offending on release. He recalls:

> There was a direct connection between my alcohol abuse and my offending behaviour—a very direct connection. Once my drinking took off, I just had to have more and more. My earning capacity wasn't great, so I would steal. I wanted and I needed more alcohol, and I didn't have any money—so I stole.

It was the same for Mark Haines:

> Alcohol certainly gave me the old fashioned Dutch courage to carry out the violence that I was later to get involved in. I certainly used alcohol to be violent. But though it may seem hard to believe now, I was violent before I started drinking—not to the extremes I was with alcohol, but I was always a punch-up merchant even without a drink, even at school . . . By this time my drinking was getting me in a lot of trouble: violence, ABH, drunken brawls, assaults on the police, loads of stuff. All my offences were caused by alcohol.

Sadly, by embracing a life of crime, Jim and Mark only succeeded in isolating themselves even further. It is therefore heartening to read how many of the interviewees have finally found their place in society and now feel they do 'belong'.

For many, this attempt to belong meant misusing drugs and alcohol, which also helped them to block out the pain of rejection or abuse by parents and other people. Cameron Mackenzie recalls:

> I continued to drink alcohol because I liked it. It made me feel good. I started with wine and beer, and then moved on to vodka and lager and super-lagers, whatever was in fashion. If it was vodka we'd drink vodka, if

it was Carlsberg super-lager we'd drink ten of them and get out of our minds. Drinking always went on till you were steaming. It was never just a couple of drinks until you had a buzz. It was six or ten or 12 or 14, whatever it took to get you nigh on unconscious.

Most believe crime to be just as addictive—a habit as hard to kick as heroin or crack cocaine, because of the excitement, the 'buzz'. Perhaps the only antidote to addiction is to find some alternative to put in its place—and so it appears to be with crime for some people.

Criminal behaviour may be inextricably entwined with other types of addiction, such as gambling on fruit machines, as in Peter's case. As Jim Smith says:

> I feel now that my offending had to happen, because that's the path I was on. It was connected with the disease of addiction, alcoholism, and it was all kind of wrapped up in the way I was.

John Bowers is an ex-burglar and now edits the prison newspaper *Inside Time*. He agrees:

> I've always likened crime to an addiction and when people say to me "You're an intelligent man, why didn't you just stop?" my answer to them is "Go and ask any smoker or drinker or drug addict or gambler why they don't just stop!" We all know very intelligent people who smoke. They're slowly killing themselves but you just try stopping them! You try stopping the alcoholic! They can't just stop, and with criminals it's the same—just like any other addiction—you can't just stop committing crime. Sadly the only way to stop the alcoholic may be to tell him that if he takes one more drink he's dead. And if you're lucky he'll stop. But like the criminal, he needs an alternative.

Whether or not crime itself is sometimes properly described as an addiction, a recurring feature of the early lives of our interviewees is the lack of legitimate money to continue with a life of drink, drugs or other unaffordable aspect of a 'locked in' existence.

Drifting into crime

Laureal Lawrence's mother always wanted her children 'to be something'. Laureal describes a world in which she felt constantly obliged to please people—first her mother, then her teachers, and later the inhabitants of a murky world of night-clubs and drugs. She continued trying to please when she was in demand as a dancer and then as a 'clean' courier. Laureal always felt different, initially because of her National Health spectacles, being a 'swot', being the last to be picked for games and having a mother who was divorced.

The use of drugs seems to have been a major factor in translating rejection into offending. Laureal is one of a number of our interviewees who label their experience 'drifting into crime'—arguably a different, less definable entry route from that travelled by people regularly surrounded by truly criminal associates or offending purely to sustain a habit. Laureal was arrested on her second drug couriering trip (the first was abortive) and sentenced to four years—a complete shock to her and her family. It is also possible that she was rebelling against pressure to achieve. The need for acceptance, the need to please has, it seems, not left her. Similarly with Mary:

> I just drifted into this: I hadn't started to do it with criminal intent, more as a challenge really, but once I'd started it was very difficult to stop. In the end I had defrauded [my employer] of about £4,000 which was a lot of money in those days, the early 1980s. I spent the money on more and more expensive clothes, things like that. I knew perfectly well it wasn't legal. I did think I ought to stop, but the more money I took, the more I became trapped. I think I was addicted — addicted to spending money at that time.

Mish Biberovic explains:

> Offending was just something I sort of slipped into. The drugs scene was a lifestyle, and in West London, the area I come from — the Portobello Road, Ladbroke Grove area — it was rife. Everyone in the area would do it, and it became like it was acceptable. If you didn't use drugs you'd be considered strange.

We do not wish to labour the many potential causes of crime: this book is chiefly about *leaving crime behind* and going straight. We simply wish to make the point that the entry and exit points are by no means unconnected. It is also possible that, as certain interviews seem to indicate, there is no rational explanation for some offending.

GETTING OUT OF CRIME

The need for an 'alternative to crime' for people who are already enmeshed in criminal activity or criminal cultures emerges as a strong theme of this book. The stories contain accounts of a wide range of catalysts for dramatic change in the life of the story-teller. Thus, for Mish Biberovic it was as straightforward as an apology from the Governor of HM Prison Blantyre House:

> For the Governor to have the courage to admit he'd made a mistake and to shake my hand made a radical change. From then on I just looked in a different way at prison and at my life.

Such events teach us about the cascading effects of qualities such as humility and respect for the dignity of the individual. John Bowers was influenced by a negative experience:

> ... the catalyst in making me change my attitude to crime was the Governor of Dartmoor. He fined me a week's wages for self-mutilation. When I got back to my cell I determined there and then that I wasn't going to let these people continue doing this to me any more. I wasn't letting them have any more of my life.

In reality there is a consensus that crime, like any other addictive or habitual behaviour (if these are proper comparisons), can become a way of life to which people will keep returning unless they find something equally powerful to put in its place. Some discover a creative gift of some kind—painting, sculpture, writing, music. Others find spiritual support—whether in formal religion or the disciplined life-support systems of self-help groups like Alcoholics Anonymous or Narcotics Anonymous. Yet others find their salvation in work—or as actor Stephen Fry explains; in helping other people—and become motivated by achievement and well-earned praise. It has to be said that for certain people the solution can become as addictive or habitual as the criminal lifestyle it replaces, and among the interviewees there is a sprinkling of workaholics, midnight-oil-burners, and proselytising preachers. Others admit to succumbing to the temptation to replace the buzz of crime with the rush of adrenaline they get from speaking to the media or on public platforms.

Does a prison sentence help or hinder personal reform?
Sometimes people discovered their alternative to crime whilst they were in prison. But this is not a 'prison works' book. 'Prison didn't cure me', says John Bowers:

> When Michael Howard said "prison works", he should have added, as a rider to that, the word "temporarily". Prison stops you for a period of time and then you come out and you carry on again.

Prison can sometimes give individuals 'time out'—a chance to take stock of what has happened in their lives so far. Mish Biberovic says that when he was given a ten year sentence he was 'plucked out of a lifestyle which was destructive and made to have a rethink about everything'. The life of Cameron Mackenzie, now a Church of Scotland minister, was changed when, after two years in prison, he re-offended and expected to return to jail:

> Then I was let off and I first glimpsed mercy. I didnae deserve mercy, but it was that wee bit of mercy that made all the difference.

Marie is one of the few interviewees who believes that prison did stop her offending: it may be that incarceration can have that effect on people who are not from what might be called a criminal background:

> Going to prison had the most significant impact in stopping me offending. It meant I could stop and think about my life. When I got caught after that car chase, I was relieved because I realised by then that—though I didn't come from a criminal family—I was in danger of being trapped in a downward spiral of crime.

Mary too felt that her prison experience demonstrated to her the pointlessness of offending (she had committed what appears to be an equally pointless £4,000 fraud on her employer):

> I think being in prison did change me, seeing what happened to other women. I now think it's disgraceful that I should have been involved in fraud the way I was. But as I said, I do think fraud is addictive and in a way it helped me to go to prison and see the way prison was destroying so many people and I decided this was not for me. That fraud was my one and only crime.

Mish Biberovic thinks prison saved him from drug-induced disaster:

> For me prison was a positive experience. I know—I'm thoroughly convinced —that if I hadn't gone to jail at that time there would have been some sort of disaster waiting for me. Because I was up to my eyeballs in gear, I was taking sulphate, everything to try and blot out my father's death, my job loss, my daughter going, everything. And I didn't care—I became reckless because of it. The crime thing didn't matter to me, it was something that gave me a buzz, this getting involved in crime.

Therapeutic units

Writers Hugh Collins and Mark Leech, who both served part of their sentences in therapeutic units, certainly regard their time there as vital to the process of change, though both identified the catalyst for that change as their relationship with one particular individual. As Collins says,

> Art therapy provided an avenue to pour out all the anger, but being handed a paintbrush didn't change my life. Only people have the ability to invite change in someone else's circumstances.

Unlike traditional prison regimes, those in the therapeutic units provided a fertile ground in which such relationships could develop. Frank Cook, who like Mark Leech went to Grendon prison, confirms this view:

Grendon Underwood[1] was the first place that began to change me, and then the Special Unit at Hull Prison. Grendon kind of opened me up and modified me, though I was far from an angel. A guy called Joe Chapman was an officer on the YP wing and he gave me a lot of help. But all Grendon really did to me was take a truly dangerous young man out of the conventional prison system which wasn't doing him any good: in fact it was making him worse.

There are analogous accounts of the 'Special Units' at Barlinnie and Hull where interviewees discuss the effects of being trusted and given a chance to change. But few of the other interviewees saw prison as the solution. In fact some recognized that prison can itself become an addiction, habit, safe haven or sheltered world. For many years, prisons have been criticised as 'universities of crime'—but perhaps the most telling and insidious effect of a prison sentence is the damage it does to the prisoner's sense of his or her own value. Conversely, imprisonment confers upon some people a spurious status which they never managed to achieve outside, and the most difficult adjustment they have to make on release is the realisation that back on the streets they are, as one man put it, 'just a nobody, signing on'. Others, institutionalised after years of dependency and lacking even the most rudimentary coping skills, actively seek to return to jail where at least they have a sense of belonging and some idea of their own value or position (albeit in terms of a highly distorted moral code). Hugh Collins, jailed for life for murder, says:

In prison I had power, I had a reputation, I was a somebody. And then—wham! I'm on the street being treated like some arsehole. That first day outside I was full of heroin by nightfall, desperately trying to figure out a way to get myself back into jail.

Prison-related employment and activities
Some, although they are now free, have not strayed far beyond the prison walls. Many of our interviewees work in some capacity with ex-offenders. This is, of course, in part a pragmatic response to a society that demands that past convictions be declared in job applications. Serious challenges to this legal requirement can be expected as a result of the formation of UNLOCK, the National Association for Ex-Offenders run by ex-offenders. The charity's aims are discussed in Mark Leech's story and the additional material provided at the end of it by His Honour Sir Stephen Tumim. Whatever UNLOCK's position, we

---

[1] Now HMP Grendon. The address remains Grendon Underwood, Buckinghamshire. For an account of the regime, see *Murderers and Life Imprisonment: Containment, Treatment, Safety and Risk* by Eric Cullen and Tim Newell, Waterside Press, 1999.

emphasise that the rehabilitation and restoration of offenders to the community can only work if the community itself is prepared to give in equal part. About 98 per cent of offenders will eventually return to the community and they cannot be treated as a race apart.

Personal determination

For many, change comes from a power within themselves. As Chris Sheridan puts it:

> What made me change my life? The only person to influence my offending behaviour was *me* — because I never ever felt comfortable committing crimes. I never thought that this was the way my life should be. I thought I had more in me than just that . . . One of the things that helped change me was this: I remember when I was growing up people would say to me, "You'll be no good, you'll always be the same". That was repeated to me again and again throughout my life: "You're just a waste of space, you're a waste of time". Lots of people have said that . . . And I suddenly thought "Why should they dominate and run my life? Why should they tell me how my life is going to turn out and what I'm going to do?" I thought the only way I could beat them was by not allowing myself to be what they'd scripted me to be — just another con.

Carole 'found herself' when her grandmother died—the only person who seemed not to have abandoned her:

> The event that changed my life and made me determined to get out of Broadmoor was when my grandmother died. This was the grandmother I used to stay with in Brighton as a child. Gran used to come to Broadmoor twice a year by taxi all the way from Brighton. One day we were told we were allowed to have televisions in our rooms. This was while I was still in touch with my mum and dad, and I asked them for a black and white TV set. They said they were broke and couldn't get me one. But my gran came all the way up from Brighton in the taxi with a black and white TV on her lap. It meant the world to me that she did that.

Such determination and strength of character comes through time and again in certain of the interviews.

Coming back into the community

For some people there is a strong attraction in continuing relationships with those who have shared the experience of imprisonment. Some do voluntary work in this field or may be fortunate enough to be paid for their involvement. The relatively new organization UNLOCK provides one means by which ex-offenders can keep in touch with other people who have been to prison and with issues affecting prisoners, particularly matters which are pertinent to going straight, at the point of an offender's release back into the community. One effect is to allow people who have left crime behind to provide mutual support to one another in times of stress. Such mechanisms allow ex-offenders to feel that they belong, without the hazard that the people they are associating with will draw them back into crime.

The need for a stake in society

Others, particularly the women we interviewed, emerged from prison with such a sense of guilt and shame, feeling unworthy to rejoin society. Also, as ex-burglar John Bowers says:

> A lot of ex-offenders feel they can never take their place fully in society because of the person they once were. I've found it very difficult to laugh properly in company because I didn't think I had the right to be there.

Is it too obvious a conclusion to say that people who have no stake in society and nothing to lose are more likely to reoffend? All the interviewees are making a success of their lives, but many are still haunted by guilt and regret, some of it very bitter, about their past lives. They express deep regrets about ruined childhoods, disrupted education, fragmented relationships, missed chances—and the misery they have inflicted upon others (ranging from victims of their crimes to their devastated families and associates). Most of the story-tellers admit that while they were committing crimes they had *no concept at all* of the feelings of their victims. Ex-gangster Bob Cummines uses the chilling expression that at the time of his offences he regarded them as just 'bits of work'. He prided himself on giving an estimate for a shooting as professionally as a builder measuring up for a new kitchen extension.

Putting a human face to the victim is a crucial element of change, which is why recent experiments in restorative justice are proving so successful. John Bowers again:

> I'll be out on a stroll and there'll be a guy out doing his front garden and he'll nod and smile and I'll think "Christ, there was a time when I would have burgled that guy and I wouldn't have known him from Adam!" There wouldn't have been anything personal in it. It would have been deeply personal to him of course—but not to me. He was just another anonymous victim.

Most people we spoke to had begun breaking the law when they were very young—on average at the age of 15, though some were as young as ten. But the age when they stopped varied enormously and depended, as their stories show, on many different factors. As John Bowers says,

It's all about the penny dropping, it really is. You suddenly realise what you've lost in the past and what you want now. You suddenly start being receptive to help.

This surely is the key—the readiness to stop offending. If we agree with so many of our interviewees that criminal behaviour is addictive, habitual or the result of some unmet need, then punishment is not an answer to crime. Chris Tchaikovsky, Director of Women in Prison, has written: 'Imagine trying to punish individuals out of their dependency on alcohol or smoking!'

Equally, there is a need to look at more subtle, perhaps sometimes deeper roots of change. One of these can be trust, especially trust in someone who is not expecting it. Being trusted seems to have perplexed Bob Cummines. He recounts a quite remarkable tale of being allowed out of Maidstone prison to attend his mother's funeral. Bob's pride would not allow him to attend in handcuffs, but:

> ... this old guy called Bev Bingham suddenly came along and he said "I'll take him". He was head of the Education Department at Maidstone Prison and he said to me "If I can get permission to take you to see your mum, will you promise me you won't have a mob waiting there to take you out?" Which I certainly could have done . . . I said "What are you saying to me?" And he said, "Give me your word". I said "I can't do that, because if I give you my word, I'll have to stick by it".

But finally Bob did give his word, and his former associates seemed equally stunned that he did not want to take advantage of the situation and be sprung from prison:

> So I gave him my word and I went out of the prison with him in his car without any cuffs or anything. As we pulled up in the street where my mum lived, a couple of people saw us, and as we got out the car they said "You all right?" and I knew they were really saying "D'you wanna go?" . . . I said "Yeah, I'm fine, we'll be going back". And that was it. They knew then that I was going back to prison with this guy . . . I owed this guy too much. At the end of the visit we drove down the bottom of my road and the stallholders gave us a load of fruit to eat on the way back . . . We got in the car and he said "Are we going back?" and I said "Yeah, we're going back". Then I felt a real buzz because he said "Right, now I can tell you this: all the prison officers have been having bets in the officers' mess that I would be wrapped up and found somewhere and you'd be gone!"

Bob Cummines is not the only one of our interviewees for whom trust played a significant part in their decision to leave crime behind. Just as loneliness can lead people into crime or criminal relationships, change can be 'the loneliest thing in the world' as Cummines puts it.

Discovering a creative ability linked with a sense of achievement and, in some instances, public recognition, is a strong force in enabling offenders to come to terms with their lives. There are several such accounts in the interviews, including those of Frank Cook (now a sculptor, artist and journalist), Peter Cameron (artist) and Hugh Collins (writer). For Mary, achievement takes the form of educational attainments. She is attempting a course which many people might say was impossible—to qualify as a solicitor:

> My priorities now are my marriage and my husband—to get Jim out of prison so we can live a normal life—though I know we'll have problems with him readjusting . . . And my law studies are important of course. I don't think I'll have any problem becoming a solicitor. I contacted the Law Society and apparently it will be all right as my conviction is spent.

Financial achievement and security are somewhat unusual in the interviews. Michael Fraser's conclusion is instructive because he realised that Bentleys, Ferraris and a chauffeur cannot themselves bring happiness:

> Nobody believed in me. I wanted to prove to myself and to everybody else that I was capable of doing something—though I didn't know what. At that stage I didn't know what I was going to be, or how successful I was going to be. I didn't have a clue. I just wanted to do something that was positive. I wasn't motivated by money—I was motivated by the fact that I'd achieved something. Luckily I was in a market that needed something and I found the niche in that market. And I was motivated by that.

Hugh Collins sums up the mental pressures of leaving crime behind:

> I look upon each day as a bonus . . . This in itself is the future. That's all I want, to continue. I'd love to wake up not remembering, but I think that'll take another five or ten years, if I live that long—just to get rid of 16 years' experience, just to get rid of it. I don't think I'll ever forget what I've done, it's just I want to move away from it. And I'd just like to wake up one morning not remembering.

Blinding lights
Another feature of some instances of stopping offending is what might be called the 'blinding light' or 'sudden revelation'.[2] Cameron

---

[2] Author Bob Turney also describes two incidents in his own life of a similar kind. The first was the impression made on him by a dire warning about his future from a Salvation Army woman at Wandsworth prison. He also recalls waking up one morning at a rehabilitation clinic as if in a different world and with a renewed sense of purpose: see *I'm Still Standing*, Waterside Press, 1996.

Mackenzie, former gang member, now a minister of the Church of Scotland describes one such event:

> This woman got in my taxi, about four or five weeks before I lost my taxi badge because of taking drugs. She was a perfect stranger and yet she knew so much about me. Incredible. She knew more about my life than anybody should have known. And she put her finger right on it when she said "I see a great darkness over you, and the only person that can take that away is God. You must see God". That was Chinese to me! That was really a crazy thing to say to me, because I'd never had a religious thought in my life.

Terry Mortimer recalls a comparable experience when his energies all seemed spent and doctors were writing him off. Laureal Lawrence who 'drifted into crime' through a need to please people and perhaps in order to rebel, sees the way out of crime as the result of 'conscience' inspired by her mother:

> It was really because of my mother I stopped offending. My mother supported me—I knew she would—but it was the shame and the hassle of going through it all. My mum knows why I did it and it's because of her I haven't done it again. I don't want to let her down again, put her through that again. I think now I've always got that angel on my shoulder, that conscience. It's really my mum, and even when I was breaking the law I used to think "Gosh, if she really knew what I was doing, I know she wouldn't be happy". The last person I want to let down again is her.

STAYING OUT OF CRIME

As already indicated, getting out of crime is one thing but keeping away from it is quite another. Some of our interviewees have experienced such a radical psychological change that for them, in the words of John Bowers, crime is simply 'no longer on the agenda' whilst others still view themselves as failures because of what may have happened many years ago. Some ex-offenders still see themselves as at constant risk of reoffending or can visualise a situation, however remote, which could cause them to re-offend, although by the very nature of things such fears are likely to remain hidden.

For Cameron Mackenzie change came at the age of 27 when he became a Christian: 'My whole personality, my whole way of thinking, my whole way of living, was radically transformed'. Others, like Bruce Reynolds, whilst expressing remorse, are more pragmatic:

> I think that like an old soldier, you look at criminal reports in the newspapers and you think "Is there anything to admire in that? Do you feel the buzz?" There was no magical conversion on the road to Damascus for me. It's been a steady thing all the way along the line. The game basically

ain't worth the candle. The sort of time you get rules it out. I haven't got the years left to spend any more time in prison.

But for Mark Leech:

> If I had nothing left and nowhere to go, crime would be my very, very last option in order to survive. But that's what it would be—the last option. The final, ultimate resort.

Laureal Lawrence is less certain:

> But then again, when people talk about offending behaviour, I think to myself "Crime's crime, and if I see an opportunity, I can't honestly say I wouldn't do it again, if I could work it out and see that it made sense to do it". I don't think you ever really change your offending behaviour . . . A lot of people are criminals, if they see an opportunity that suits them, with a gain to their advantage.

But 'keeping busy' and 'working 16 hours a day at two jobs' helps Laureal and, above all

> . . . the opportunities aren't there now. I don't know the people, I don't have the contacts. I'm not in that circle any more, I've never been in that circle here in London.

Others have crossed a far greater divide, not only keeping busy, out of crime and in employment, but working for the system rather than against it. Mark Haines' life of alcohol abuse and violent crime was replaced, initially, by self-help groups—and then by his work in the Probation Service:

> I've now been working in the Probation Service for about four years, and I still feel quite privileged to be working in probation, having led the life I've lived. I like my job here at the hostel. I'd like to think that I would perhaps go on to do an NVQ in probation studies, but I'm not really an ambitious sort of person. I don't think I'm anything special. I just feel very fortunate in what happened to me. I know lots of people that I drank with did end up going to prison and if they're not in prison they're out there leading lives that I wouldn't want to swap with them.

Often, going straight is linked to 'going to' something after prison, most notably a stable home environment. Prisoners who remain in contact with their families are six times less likely to reoffend on release. Employment obviously provides the wherewithal to survive and also that sense of achievement which many ex-prisoners identify as a critical factor in their transition to law-abiding citizen. But getting into work is very difficult for most ex-prisoners. They must often survive on a paltry allowance pending their first state benefits. Many of those interviewed told of fruitless attempts to find employment; of solid prospects turning sour when employers learned of their convictions; of rejection following honest disclosure (which sometimes led to later applications being more economical with the truth). Rejections can begin to make ex-offenders think about returning to former, 'more comfortable', immediately gratifying ways. As Jane says:

> Luckily I have plenty of interests to keep me busy, so it's only the lack of finances that I'm finding difficult, and the need to support myself. These elements are difficult enough, and problems like this don't help if you're trying to "go straight". But people do need to get themselves more or less immediately into paid employment after release, not only for financial reasons but for a sense of achievement and the satisfaction you can get from work. But if my qualifications can't get me a job, after all that hard work I did in prison, what chance has any of us got?

Several of the interviewees felt compelled to beat the system by fair means or foul, including Bob Cummines:

> ... in the end I created my own past—like I used to do when I was on the run. I was quite good at it, I could do my own letterheads and stuff like that. I created this history of work and soon I landed a very good job as a purchasing manager and stock control manager. From there I went into a management position with a Dutch company. I made lots of money, we got lots of presents, they really looked after us. I never declared my form. And then I was made redundant.

The dilemma is graphically described by Mark Leech:

> The first thing that happens when you want to go straight and go for a job is they say to you "Where have you been?" And at that point you've got to make a decision. You either tell the truth—which carries with it the likelihood that you're not going to get the job—or you tell lies. And if you tell lies, then you're really on your way back to prison again . . . I've had many jobs. I used to hide my criminality and get jobs on the basis of a false pass. I've done that with a whole range of things from a bus conductor to an ambulance man, right the way up to head of security for the United Kingdom for *Toys R Us*—all based on lies and deceit and false background.

One important lesson is that ex-offenders ought not to be placed in such a position. In 1999, NACRO began a series of meetings with employers designed to bring about greater understanding of the problem.[3] There is

---

[3] *Going Straight to Work*, NACRO, March 1999. A central aim is to persuade employers to consider ex-offender job applicants on their merits and to eliminate unfair discrimination in recruitment practices. The idea is to work with a group of leading employers towards this end.

also good reason, as UNLOCK has pointed out, to alter the Rehabilitation of Offenders Act in this regard.

Again, for some, religion, or what Mark Haines describes as 'a higher power', can be a vital or further key to staying out of trouble. According to Cameron Mackenzie:

> . . . although I'd stopped the violent behaviour around the age of 20, when I started doing the drugs, I would say that the real change came in my life at the age of 27 when my whole personality, my whole way of thinking, my whole way of living, was radically transformed. Not just to the extent that I wasnae going to jail any more, but to the extent that I was able to get off drugs without any problem. I was able to stop sleeping around. I was able to start for the first time in my life believing in a God who loved me.

For Marie:

> The Church is what keeps me away from reoffending now. I love my church, and the thought of people praying for me gives me a buzz. There is nothing now that would make me return to crime. These days I am happy, especially with my sexuality. I like to think of the Shirley Bassey song *I Am What I Am*. I live on my own and I admit I do get lonely. I do get easily led and, as I've said, I've been in relationships in the past where I have been led astray.

Even Tommy from Northern Ireland found support through the church and his faith in Jesus Christ, which he found in Long Lartin prison. The interviews disclose a desparate need for support mechanisms for ex-offenders. We have already mentioned the work of UNLOCK, but the importance of a mix of family and other support structures cannot be overemphasised. As Frank Cook puts it:

> Now I have the support of certain organizations — the New Bridge in particular, which befriends prisoners during their sentence and after release. I've been with New Bridge now for nine years — and I phone almost every day, though sometimes I'm working and I forget — I'm only human. I've also got a lot of support from my wife and children. And I've got the support of positive individuals. I work very hard at mixing with people of a healthy mentality, good people who are valuable to society, themselves and myself.

And Jim Smith has discovered a new life through a mix of factors:

> Today I see myself as a responsible person in the community. I'm a social worker — I qualified a few years ago. I still attend alcoholism groups, as I have been doing for the past 22 years this year, and I "sponsor" a lot of newer members, specially the younger ones. But they help me too. It's not just a one-way process . . . I'm married with three daughters, and my family is very important to me . . . I believe the alcoholism group's programme of recovery has helped me become a better person and to strive for values I

didn't even dream possible. And now I've got some idea of a kind of spiritual power, a God. I'm not a religious man but I'm a spiritual man, and I try and enjoy my life, because life goes all too quickly.

Fragile lives: but no lack of determination

It is impossible to read the stories which follow without being aware of the poignant fragility of some of the success stories. For many people, *staying straight* depends on external factors beyond their own control: 'I can't guarantee I won't reoffend', they seem to be telling us. 'I can't say what I'd do if anything happened to my family, if I lost my job, if I had big financial problems, if I lost my faith'. Not one of them pretends leaving crime behind is easy. Bob Cummines, the ex-gunman confirms: 'It's the loneliest thing in the world when you choose to change'. Yet, for Bob, crime is definitely no longer an option:

> I don't think anything could make me go back to crime. I've always tried to understand why I felt so different from everyone else. It was because I didn't belong. Now I've actually found where I belong, and that's why returning to crime is not in the equation.

It is obviously vital for offenders to recognise the significance of the harm they have done and many are looking to put something back into their community. Tommy expresses a fairly common sentiment:

> A lot of what I have done I regret—the pain and the hurt that I put people through. The things that led me to commit offences were rejection, not being accepted, feeling like a square in a circle. I don't feel that now, not at all. From my own point of view, I can look at my past offending as a bonus. It's a plus to me, because it means I can go and talk to young people. I can relate to others who are leading the same lifestyle as I did. I hope that in the future I can be both a deterrent and an encouragement for young people like this, and show them there is hope at the end of the line.

Some ex-offenders are also aware that they still retain vestiges of the impulsive behaviour that led them to commit crime in the first place, and they speak honestly of the temptation they might face if 'the big one'—the chance of a lot of easy money—should suddenly come up. Perhaps the most important lesson, and the hardest one to learn, is that—as the title *Going Straight* suggests—leaving criminal offending behind is a continuing, not a finite process.

Something to lose

On a more positive note, it is clear that the more people have to lose and the more they become stakeholders in society—not just in monetary terms but by being valued in their work and in their relationships—the less likely they are to reoffend, and moving away from crime becomes a cumulative process. John Bowers sums up the feelings of many:

> Now people say to me "What keeps you out of prison? You must be terrified of going back to prison!" Actually I couldn't give a toss about going back to prison. The deterrent for me is what I would lose if I went back inside. It isn't prison itself, it's all the things I have got now in my life: a job, a relationship—things I don't want to lose.

Ambition and achievement

Similarly for Anita O'Connell there is a sense of achievement, obligation and family responsibility:

> The one person that really made a change to my life was my probation officer, who had a lot of time for me. The staff in the probation hostel I stayed in also talked to me a lot—they just spent a lot of time listening to me ... What keeps me from going back to offending now? My pets—I've got a dog and a cat, and if I did anything and went back into prison I'd have to leave them—and I just couldn't leave them with anyone else. Then there's my work with MIND. And my mum relies on me now for support. I help her by sharing the expenses with her, and I bring in some money.
>
> The most important things to me today are the people who depend on me, my family, specially my mum, and my pets, my godchildren, my friends. I think the only thing that would make me kick off and offend again would be if someone hurt my family, specially my mum.

Cameron Mackenzie refers to the importance of personal relationships and, in his case, the power of his religious beliefs:

> The important things in my life today are faith, worship, service, love of my family, my wife, my child, my brothers and sisters, my mum, my friends, I've got loads of friends that I love deeply and they love me deeply—we have relationships that really are important . . .   I stopped committing crimes when I was 20 except for using the illegal substances. But I only stopped *being a criminal* when I was saved.

For Jim Smith:

> My sobriety is the most important thing in my life today—just keeping clean and sober, living a drug-free and drink-free life, one day at a time. And trying to live a good life, along the lines of values that I aspire to, trying to help people wherever possible, and to learn from everyone I meet.

And for Mish Biberovic:

> The most important thing to me now is my family, without a doubt. I know this is probably clichéd and corny but it's true. That's what keeps me together. I've often thought about what would make me go back to crime

and do what I did before. If I lost all that, I suppose, if I lost my family, I can't say with my hand on my heart, 100 per cent, no, I would never commit another crime.

Peter, a former fruit machine addict and university undergraduate from a respectable background, found that because of his natural abilities he could be 'quite useful' to other people in prison, helping them in various ways with their correspondence. His anchor now is his wife, his young family, his work in the computer industry and his own personal code which would 'not allow me to lie anyway'. Even for the largely pragmatic Bruce Reynolds 'Without a doubt I would say my family and my friends are the most important things in my life today . . . I've lost a lot of friends that meant a lot to me and they're irreplaceable because obviously you haven't got the years left to make those sorts of friends again'.

Energy and enthusiasm

There is far more in the individual interviews than we could hope to summarise here. We have both enjoyed compiling this book and hope that readers will find much of interest in these compelling stories of people's lives.

Interviewing people who have overcome disaster and survived it, travelling with them through the traumas and triumphs of their lives, is always an affecting experience. When we embarked on this project we certainly did not expect to have such enjoyment. Shining through all the interviews is an energy, a *joie de vivre*. The average age of our interviewees is 42—an age when many people who have lived unimpeachable law-abiding lives are approaching their middle years with a growing sense of disillusionment, a feeling of 'Was that It?' These people are not like that. Without exception they seem to have an extraordinary zest for life. Having sunk into life's troughs, they are now reaching for its peaks and are excited about the future. So we end this *Introduction* on a few notes of optimism:

> I love life. Now I love waking up in the morning: Marie

> There's a lot on the horizon—there's more in front of me than has gone behind, and I'm quite excited about the future: Jim Smith

and John Bowers, whose words speak for so many others:

> I'm living now as I think deep down I always wanted to live, and I have peace of mind. I sleep all right now.

If people working with prisoners are able to consider and reflect on individual accounts of what caused ex-offenders to change, then it ought to be possible to create an environment where change is more likely and in which prisoners might discover for themselves a route to their own crime-free existence. The accounts in this book cannot be read, we would suggest, without our becoming acutely aware of the fact that personal determination is ultimately the single most important agent for change, whatever other individual, situational or chance factors come into play. The more that this determination, potential energy and enthusiasm to change can be harnessed, the better. With this challenge in mind, we leave the last word to Terry Mortimer:

> I'm a real optimist. I'm an enthusiastic person about life. I have an energy and a vitality . . . I can see the potential in anything, anyone. There is no such thing as someone beyond hope. There is no such thing.

Going Straight

TALES OF HOPE AND REGENERATION

The interviews

* Additional material contributed by
His Honour Sir Stephen Tumim

Anita O'Connell

Anita is 27: nine years ago she committed arson and narrowly missed being sent to Broadmoor. An exceptionally talented sportswoman at school, Anita looked set for a career in athletics. But she had problems getting her mother to accept that she was gay. In her early teens she drifted into drink and drugs, gave up sport, and at the age of 18 was jailed for setting fire to her mother's flat, serving her sentence in Holloway's notorious C1 psychiatric wing. She is now a worker for the mental health charity, MIND, and a qualified plumber.

I was 18 and in prison before I told my mother I was gay, and even then I had to write it in a letter to her.

My mother was always saying I ought to be getting married, and when I was nearly 18 I met this guy about ten years older. He was really besotted with me and he wanted me to marry him—and I was so desperate to please my mother that I went along with it. She was a very powerful woman in those days, and I always felt I had to try and please her. So I went out with this guy for about six months, and I eventually moved in with him. We never had any sort of sexual relationship, and I carried on seeing my girlfriends.

All the arrangements went ahead for the wedding—the church, the dress, the reception, everything. Then, literally the day before the wedding, he came back early and found me in bed with a woman. There was me and him in the front room and he called me all the names under the sun, then he ran out of the house crying.

My mum was in a state, asking why the wedding was off, so I told her it just didn't work out. He couldn't bear to tell her why and I certainly wasn't going to shatter her dreams by telling her.

So I moved back home. But my mother had just remarried and decided to move out, taking all the furniture with her except the bed. And one day I went back into the flat and set fire to the place. I think the reason I did it was anger. I was angry and I couldn't show it any other way. It was the place I'd lived in and I wanted to burn it down.

I could easily have been sent to Broadmoor because I'd committed arson. I saw four psychiatrists: two of them said I was a nutcase and two of them said I was OK. When the case came to court the judge gave me three years' probation with the stipulation that I should see a psychiatrist once a week for a year. He said I came from an appalling home background.

• • •

I was born in south-east London, the middle one in a family of five kids, with an older brother and sister, and a younger brother and sister. I was always a very self-reliant child, perhaps because my sister, who was one year and 12 days younger than me, was very demanding and got a lot of attention from my mother. I think I did resent it at the time. It seemed to me that if you were bad you got lots of attention, but if you were normal you were shunned.

When she was 12 my sister was put into care and she stayed there till she was 17, though she used to come home on visits. Though she was so naughty I did miss her. My elder sister had gone into care as well—that was for truanting from school.

I've never been close to my mother till recently. It was partly my fault because I closed myself in. I couldn't talk to anyone. Emotionally I didn't get anything from my brothers and sisters. My dad left my mum when I was two, so I don't remember him at all and I've never seen him since. He wasn't the father of my older brother and sister.

I just remember sitting quietly all on my own while my sister got all the attention. I think I did play with the neighbours' children—all the mothers in our street used to chat together and all the kids used to play.

• • •

The main thing I remember about going to school was getting loads of attention from the teacher. In fact I wasn't the only one—all the new kids got attention, but this was something new to me. My sister got all the attention at home and she had to be naughty to get it. Now I was getting attention without having to do anything and I wasn't used to it. I loved my first teacher—she used to read us *Winnie the Pooh* and do all the different voices.

My mum was supportive to some extent. I was very good at spelling and my mum was very proud if I did well in tests—my younger sister wasn't so bright academically. But I always found it very hard to accept compliments. I knew I was bright and I knew I was always very good at games. But I had very low self-esteem. I thought other people didn't think much of me.

I always felt different from the other children, and I didn't know why, and this feeling went on throughout primary school. All the girls used to run round playing skipping and kiss-chase, and I always wanted to play football and climb trees. It really annoyed my mum because I hated wearing dresses and skirts and used to come back all muddy and grass-stained. But my sister used to love dressing up in my mum's dresses and shoes.

I can't say I felt particularly happy about going on to secondary school. But when I was 11 I went on a school trip for a week to the Isle of

Wight. I shared with the other girls and I loved every minute. They were all homesick and crying for their mums every night, but I loved being away from home. It meant I could be on my own, I could get away from my sister.

The other girls in my class were all a bit stuck up for me. It was because they all had a mum and a dad. So I started going round with people from single-parent families—most of them had a mum but no dad.

I used to get bullied by kids from the gypsy site who would pick on me and beat me up. I soon learned how to fight back and later on I had lots of black and Asian friends and I used to get in lots of fights sticking up for them. Our estate was really racist. So I expected to have to fight.

I was very good at sport—discus, javelin and shot-putt. I was in the athletics team and my two records are still unbroken at that school. We had two really good women sports teachers. At 14 I was throwing the javelin 47 metres and in the athletics club I was in, even our adult javelin throwers were only throwing 60 metres. I was in the county championships for the club, and I was also automatically entered for all the inter-school championships. I competed against the British shot-putt champion Judy Oakes and came second against her. I did take a pride in myself then, and my mum was proud of me too.

But all the same I still felt resentful that I couldn't really talk to anyone, and I never felt I belonged. I was in the top set for English and maths, but the trouble was that I always finished the maths work too quickly for the teacher. He'd give us enough work for half an hour's lesson but I'd get it done in ten minutes then I'd walk round the class giving other people a hand. So though I was speeding ahead, I was labelled disruptive and I was put in the remedial group for maths. I was all right at school till I was about 14: that's when things started to go wrong.

• • •

I started drinking when I was about 14. By this time I was hanging round with friends who were the same age as my older brother, and with girls from our street who were going out with older blokes. At first it was drink from off-licences that we used to drink sitting in the streets—it was lager and cider at that time. And because I was drinking, I stopped doing sport. Also at this time I started sniffing glue and Tippex thinner. We used to sniff the thinner at the back of the class and you'd sit there with a blank expression. Other kids were doing it so I tried it too. I was also getting very verbal and loud by this time with the teachers I didn't get on with, like the maths teacher and the geography teacher.

The estate we lived in, the Thamesmead estate, was quite new when my mum moved into it, but it had nothing for teenagers to do, so drink and drugs seemed the perfect alternative. I did speed and marijuana and cocaine—the powder not crack. I liked cocaine because it made you feel nice and easy, not having to think. But I didn't carry on with it because I could see it was too easy—it could make you brain-dead. I tried acid once or twice—I'd try anything once. I liked not having to think, not having to be responsible.

Five or six of us used to bunk off school and go and drink and sniff butane gas in the ruins of this old abbey. Butane is terribly addictive and if I could get the money for it I'd be using five or six cans a day, at £1.20 a can. I carried on using it from when I was 14 till when I was over 17. The effect only lasts about five minutes but I loved it. It really freaked me out, but I liked that feeling, because it allowed me to be out of control for a while. I was always very controlled, so what I liked was the lack of responsibility the gas gave you. For instance, I remember I took it while I was watching TV and it seemed as if the screen with the picture on it fell right off the TV on to the floor in little jumbled-up bits.

Though all this was going on while I was bunking off, I still did well in my mock O levels—I passed six of them. But I couldn't be bothered going to school for the actual exams—I was drinking so much by this time. I left at 15, just before the exams. My mum found out when she had to pay for all the exams I hadn't gone in for. Still, she wanted me to carry on in school and finish my education but I wouldn't. I really regret it now.

● ● ●

Butane gas was why I started thieving from cars. I'd take radios and personal belongings—to get the money for the gas. There'd always be somebody on the street who'd buy the stuff I'd nicked. I used to do the thieving with a couple of other kids. You needed somebody to keep an eye out while you did it.

When I was 14 I was convicted of stealing from cars. I was trying to nick a car stereo but that car park was under observation from the police. I was with a boy a bit younger than me. All the girls were too prissy—they weren't into nicking things. I was caught with all the equipment on me to break into cars—a centre punch, screwdrivers etc. I was a year older than this boy and he blamed me. I was actually quite an honest child by nature and I admitted everything to the police.

I got a caution and I didn't tell my mother. Next day she went out to work as usual and I was hiding round the corner, waiting till she'd gone so I could get back into the house and bunk off school. But one of the other mothers told her about me getting in trouble with the police and she came back and went ape-shit. She beat the shit out of me. She didn't beat me very often.

But none of this stopped me doing cars. I must have done hundreds before and after that incident.

• • •

By the time I was 13 I'd got my first girlfriend and I knew straight away that I was comfortable about the way I felt about her. But I didn't tell anyone else. My mum was always telling me I had to get married and have kids, though when I was as young as 14 I told her I was never going to. This girl's family knew about me and her and they accepted it, though they didn't like it.

When I was 14, this first girlfriend was killed in a car crash. Though I wasn't even with her, I blamed myself for years. I never told anyone about it, I never talked to anyone. I just kept it secret and turned to drink and drugs. I was self-destructive and I wanted something to deaden the pain. *reppressed*

I did try going out with boys. One boy asked me out and I went out with him because he had a decent football—the only one on the estate! There was another guy that I slept with too—he was about five years older than me.

Then I got into a very destructive relationship. When I was about 16 I started baby-sitting for a woman in her thirties who was married with two kids. It turned out she was bisexual. I had this relationship with her for two years. I think I carried on with the relationship because I was getting attention from somebody older than me.

At this point I was drifting from job to job. When I left school I got on a YTS course, working for British Rail. I used to clean the trains and work on the stations in the ticket office. I stuck it out for a year, then I went from job to job, a week or two at a time. Jobs like packing in factories. I was still drinking and using butane gas during the day if I wasn't in work. I might be with my mates or on my own. There were plenty of places to drink, in some local ruins or on the estate, in places like under the garages.

• • •

When I was 18 I was sent to prison. At the time I'd just stopped working at Casey Jones, the burger place. I'd enjoyed the work there and I got to be supervisor. I'd also been in a relationship with a female supervisor two years older than me.

Then there was all that trouble over me nearly getting married, and I moved back home. My mother had decided to re-marry. In the months leading up to her marriage I was drinking but I never drank in the house, and the only drug I was doing was marijuana. Then one day we had a big argument and she threw me out. I wasn't even allowed to go to her wedding.

So Mum got married and went to live with her new husband, taking most of her furniture with her. I was still seeing the woman I used to baby-sit for, and I went and stayed with her. Then one summer evening I got back into Mum's flat with some friends. We were just dossing around, drinking and doing a bit of puff, nothing that serious, and then we all left.

But about nine o'clock I went back in there and I just set fire to the place and then I walked out.

The neighbours called the police and they came round and as they tried to arrest me I got hold of a policewoman by her jacket lapels and this went down as assault. I was held down on the floor by the police and by my neighbour and his two sons, handcuffed behind my back and driven to the police station.

I kicked the cell door for about two hours. I was still trying to calm down, because of how I'd been assaulted. They said I assaulted a policewoman but I had a huge bump on the right side of my head, and four finger-marks on my neck. When they took photos of me they photographed the other side of my head so you couldn't see those marks.

I saw a duty solicitor and my mother was told. But she never came round to the police station. Next day I was taken to the magistrates' court. My mother wasn't there, but my older sister and my aunt came. They didn't know what was going on and I just gave them a dirty look. Then I was remanded to Holloway. I went in a van, handcuffed to the bars on the window and to the seat in front.

• • •

When I got to the Holloway reception block I was really scared. While you're waiting to go on a wing they put you in a holding reception room. There were about 35 or 40 women in there and a lot of them were talking about drugs and all sorts of crimes. I shut myself off completely—I didn't talk to anyone. You get strip-searched and I'd never experienced anything like that. Then I was taken to C1 and the other women told me that was the muppet wing.[1] I was put in a dormitory but there was only one other woman in there—she must have been in her mid-30s. She seemed quiet but after I'd been in there for about four hours she suddenly started screaming and shouting till the officers came and took her away.

---

[1] Prison slang for 'psychiatric wing'

I was on C1 for about six months. I was kept there because my offence was arson. I spent a lot of time banged up because I used to get violent and cocky towards the officers when they used to wind me up. I was still feeling extremely angry. I went to education sometimes and did a bit of pottery and painting but there weren't enough officers to take us over to the education department very often.

After a while I became friends with a few of the women—you either had to get on with each other or be on your own all the time. I had a sexual relationship with a few of them. But I was on a very short fuse and I used to get into fights. I'd never before been anywhere near a woman who had sexually abused kids and there was one woman there who had abused then killed her daughter. She'd been in a child sex ring in Canterbury and she used to talk about it. I just freaked out at that because I was really missing my little niece at the time.

I saw lots of different shrinks but I used to laugh at them and take the piss. The first one stood there with an orange in her hand and told me to peel it. I said I couldn't—I never peel oranges, I cut them up. So I cut it up into eight pieces. I was sent to a clinic in an outside hospital and seen by the doctors there. Then I was sectioned there for about four weeks in the hospital's secure wing. There were three women and 13 men and 11 of the men were sex offenders. They gave me Largactil[2] which knocked me out for six hours.

Before my trial, my lawyer got a psychiatrist and they reckoned it was symbolic that I'd set fire to the bed—my *mother's* bed. Actually there was nothing symbolic about it—it just happened to be the only piece of furniture in the flat that she hadn't taken away! But I went along with all this because they thought it would help my case. I got three years' probation and had to continue seeing a psychiatrist for a year. My mother never came to see me the whole time I was in Holloway. When I'd been in prison about three months I wrote a letter to my mum slagging her off and at the end I put 'PS: By the way, I'm gay!'

She wrote back that she couldn't accept my lifestyle. I didn't see her for ages after I came out of prison, not until my partner suggested I should get back in contact.

• • •

The one person that really made a change to my life was my probation officer, who had a lot of time for me. The staff in the probation hostel I stayed in also talked to me a lot—they just spent a lot of time listening to me.

---

[2] Brand name for Chlorpromazine, a generic anti-psychotic drug

My probation officer having faith in me, and one of my best friends committing suicide—these two things had a real effect on me. I've had a few friends who've died through overdoses and suicide. Sometimes I think they were so depressed and my life's not bad compared with them.

I went to a counsellor, voluntarily, for a year after my release, because I knew I needed help with managing my anger. Now I'm much better at controlling it, though I can still get very angry if people make remarks about my sexuality or my size. And I can still get angry if anyone hurts me or someone I'm close to—specially if somebody should ever hurt my mum.

• • •

After Holloway and the hostel I worked as a volunteer in a women's therapy unit for three years. Then I went to college and did a one-year course to learn plumbing. In 1993 I qualified as a plumber and I now do that off and on. It can be quite well-paid though I won't charge much to people who can't afford it. I can't say I enjoy the work, but I do it to get money.

The work I do enjoy is working as a volunteer for MIND. I'm in their locum pool and I go and fill in for them at one of their day centres, helping people fill in their forms, listening, befriending, being an advocate for people.

My mother stayed married for eight years then she split up. A lot of the fight's gone out of my mum since my brother died in a car crash. He was killed in March on my birthday—that was four years ago. Now I live with my mum and I'm quite close to her, though me and my mum still don't talk about the time I was in prison. She won't talk about it now—she says it's too painful to discuss. I think I felt so angry because I thought she should have supported me and she wasn't there when I needed her.

• • •

What keeps me from going back to offending now? My pets—I've got a dog and a cat, and if I did anything and went back into prison I'd have to leave them—and I just couldn't leave them with anyone else. Then there's my work with MIND. And my mum relies on me now for support. I help her by sharing the expenses with her, and I bring in some money.

The most important things to me today are the people who depend on me, my family, specially my mum, and my pets, my godchildren, my friends. I think the only thing that would make me kick off and offend again would be if someone hurt my family, specially my mum.

One day in the future I'd love to have a family of my own. I'm not in any relationship at the moment but if I was with a girlfriend I'd like her to have a baby, because I really love kids, I always have. I'd also love to get my ideal job, and maybe my poems published in a book. What more could I want?

I'm always moving on. I don't think I was ever a really bad person but now I'm more focused. I've got people I can talk to—I've got a great circle of friends.

I feel things happen for a reason. I wouldn't change a thing. All this has made me the person I am today. It was all a learning experience, even if it was a painful one.

Terry Mortimer

Terry is 45 and is a Pentecostal minister working at the Tramway Christian Centre in Edmonton, North London. By the age of 12 he had a string of criminal convictions and was placed in local authority care till he was 18. He became addicted to drink and drugs, carried out burglaries and muggings, and was remanded in custody several times. He and Bob Turney were at one stage partners in crime, carrying out burglaries together. They drifted apart, but coincidentally both became Christians at about the same time, stopped offending and were reunited recently when Terry saw Bob on a television programme.

In the 1960s my mother was the manageress of a gambling club called the Cresta in Tooting, and my eldest brother Trevor was on the door. Terry Lake the boxer was one of the doormen with Trevor. Mum used to run the bar and bring the money home. But the place got closed when Mad Ron[1] put an axe through the manager's head, and that's how he got his eight years in Broadmoor. I never knew the man but my mum was close to him and my dad knew him. It was a dreadful time.

My earliest memory is of pub gardens. I remember weekends when I was a little kid of about six or seven—Fridays, Saturdays and particularly Sunday lunch—sitting in the gardens of a pub. I'd have a sip of my dad's brown ale and a packet of crisps with a little salt packet in it. My mother's family ran a pub in Devonport and I remember a holiday there once. Again, it was pub life. That's how my mum and dad and brothers lived. As kids we were brought up in that way. We only socialised round pubs and with the criminal fraternity. I'm the youngest of eight, five girls and three boys. There's a big age difference, 16 years, between me—the youngest—and Trevor, the eldest, who was the club doorman.

All my friendships revolved round my dad's mates—barrow boys, plasterers—all sorts of characters. We lived in a council house and it had a staircase with 12 steps up and a little landing. I remember that landing because when I was a little kid, my dad and Trevor had a fight on it. Trevor was six foot three—he was a big fella—and he actually done my dad over the head with a claw hammer and my dad ended up in hospital with a fractured skull.

The house used to get raided by the police because Trevor would fill it with stolen goods. He'd be down at Burton's warehouse one night and I'd get woken up and find my box bedroom was full of fur coats. Then he done a tobacconist's and there were sacks and sacks of lighters and fags in the house.

---

[1] Ronnie Kray

So we lived on this council estate, my brothers had criminal records, and my mum and dad hadn't lived a good life either. My father was a coalman but he wasn't averse to a bit of skulduggery and my mother wasn't innocent either.

I'd seen how my brothers earned money. Trevor was driving a Jag, he had a women's boutique in Battersea, he had a flat, he used to have holidays abroad. My other brother Brian was driving a motor, they were always paying our mum and dad money. At weekends my parents were drinking night and day if they wanted. The message to me was that you could earn a good life at this. The role model was there. Why work? Why go the hard way about things? My brothers were my heroes I always looked up to Trevor because he had quite a reputation. He was a bit handy, he was a villain, a crook.

Really, when you think about it, the scene was set for me to get involved in crime.

• • •

I grew up in that environment, thinking it was quite normal. Then when I started going to school, mixing with ordinary people, I realised it wasn't. I knew jolly well that some kids' parents at school had told their kids not to mix with me because I was one of the Mortimers, a real 'trouble' family.

And so I grew up with a bit of shame, a bit of a chip on my shoulder. I think that created the aggression in me. Because there was a clear distinction between me and our lot, and those toffee-nosed twits down the road. Other kids would get presents and go on holidays and they lived a normal life, with a decent home, mum and dad working.

Looking back, I couldn't have worded it like that but there was a clear social distinction there, and I felt very inferior. I think that made me turn to crime, because I thought 'Well, that's how we do it, that's how we live, that's how we get by. It might be wrong to you but it's right to me'.

I had problems with my reading and I honestly think now, looking back, it was because I was never encouraged at home. My mum and dad weren't too interested in school. It wasn't deliberate neglect, it was just that it wasn't part of their agenda. School was just a place I went. When I was about seven I started smashing people's windows and doing silly things and by the age of nine I was under a child psychologist. By the age of ten I was up before a juvenile court.

I was a terrible truant, absolutely terrible. I used to get half a crown for a week's dinner money, but I'd spend it. I wouldn't go into school but I'd still go out every morning and come home at tea time. I think a lot of the trouble was undisciplined living and lazing, and my attitude towards teachers. Teachers represented nice, ordinary, middle-class, well-behaved society, which I wasn't a part of. I suppose deep down I wanted to be part of it—to be right, normal, accepted. But then I also had this anger towards them, this aggression. It's a cultural thing, it's a sociological thing, you grow up with it and it becomes deep-rooted in you if you're not careful.

I didn't go straight to secondary school, because when I was ten I committed my first juvenile offence for breaking into the school. My sister grassed me up to the caretaker! She thought she was doing me a favour—by grassing me up she was sure he'd let me off. But he went and called the police and I ended up in a juvenile court for breaking and entering into the school and wrecking the headmistress's office and I think we nicked the petty cash as well.

Between the ages of ten and 12, I must have had half a dozen court appearances for breaking and entering, doing gas meters, vandalising houses. By the time I was twelve and a half, my mum and dad had split up, and I went into care till I was 18.

I was first put in custody when I was ten or eleven, when I went to this remand place. As early as that. I hated it, I *absolutely hated it*, because they had taken me from my mum and dad. My father was going to hit the probation officer in juvenile court—he went for him. They had to grab hold of my dad. It was horrible—really quite traumatic. I'm going back about 35 years, and yet I still remember how my father lost his rag in that court, when they took me off into custody. There's nothing your parents can do about it, about your liberty, your freedom. You get put in a cell, then you get put in a vehicle, then you get driven for an hour or two, stopped somewhere then taken elsewhere, through the system, they're shuffling you around.

First I went to a Social Services home in Sutton. I was locked up there an hour or two while they did the paper work and made phone calls. It was a horrible, dread experience, and in actual fact, it just deepened all those feelings that I had in childhood about society: 'I don't fit in. They don't like me. I've got a chip on my shoulder'. I think it actually makes you more aggressive. It just cements all the wrong. It reinforces your misconceptions of society and life and the legal system. Like being told by a constable 'They're taking you to the House of Correction'. I remember a cop said that to me once.

So they locked me up. I was locked in a room at night, and even when we had recreation it was at the Big House.[2] There were just ten yards of open space to get to the recreation hall, and beyond that was a 20 foot high fence. That was the reality of it—if you got caught. So you'd just decide 'Right, well—I ain't gonna get caught!'

---

[2] Main prison

I went to this remand home three times in about a year. They send you there for 28 days to assess you, then they bring you back to court with social worker reports, probation reports. By the time I was about 12 I'd burnt a house down. We'd set fire to a derelict house, ran away over the railway embankment and just thought we'd watch it burn. But unbeknown to us, the roof went off and it was a semi-detached and there were people living in the other half.

So when I was about twelve and a half, I got sent to Malvern House, which was a boys' home in Surrey. At Malvern House it was very much a disciplined regime, but looking back, I actually enjoyed it. If you were naughty, if you played up—and unfortunately I did because I was in that mould—you got 'work sections'. Tree-stumping was one. Four work sections meant one tree stump, that kind of thing. So forever I spent my weekends digging out tree stumps in the grounds. Another job was sweeping the drive, shovelling the coal down the cellar.

They also got us to do a project. We built our own open-air swimming pool. The hillside was chalk, and we built it there over a period of a couple of years. It was all to discipline you, to put the work ethic into you. And believe it or not, before I left that place, I actually enjoyed it. I used to go from the home every day to a secondary modern school. But everyone knew we were the Malvern House boys—so again, there was a stigma.

The only thing I remember being good at was the javelin, maybe because it was a spear, a weapon! But the funny thing is that in my last year, between the ages of 14 and 15, I applied myself, and I actually did quite well. I wanted to be a plumber, so the care people at the home got me an interview with Sutton Water Board.

I had to be released to go to the interview with one of the masters and he took me there in the car. When I got to Sutton Water Board, they looked at my reports in English, maths and technical drawing, and they didn't offer me a vacancy as an apprentice plumber—but believe it or not, they offered me a seven year apprenticeship as a draughtsman! And I said—I said I wanted to be a plumber!

There was no advice or anything from my family because I was still in care and my mother had left and gone off with another man. She'd moved to Germany with a guy called Tom, and I didn't want to know my mum or him. My brothers had grown up and left home, Dad was suffering from prostate cancer though I never knew it at the time. Dad was at home and I loved him. He was a good old stick and I really wanted to be with my dad. Even while I was in care, that last 12 months, every quarter I could go home for a week.

My first job was as a trainee central heating engineer and the only reason I took it was that I wanted to get out of care. It was at a firm in Surrey and I stayed there for ages. But even there I was weighing things up and I was seeing what I could nick. I started going stupid again, breaking into off-licences.

* * *

I was probably 15 or 16 when I started using drugs. Even in care you could get a little bit of smoke[3]—everybody thought it was a bit flash, a bit of a laugh. I carried on using it, I suppose because it made you feel good, you were part of the scene, you were somebody—it was image, ego. I suppose if it's the only life you know, you think it's normal, you just think everyone does it.

Although I drank and I took drugs, I didn't have any problems with them in my teenage years, but it laid a foundation. It was the wrong path to take, and it sure did cause problems later on. At the time I'd never heard of crack and the sort of stuff they have today. Apart from drink, there was what they called 'blueys'—barbiturates, amphetamines, smoke—that's marijuana—grass, hash, Moroccan—there was all different types. And then eventually there was acid—really anything that was available, anything that was going around at the time.

Drugs did play a part in my offending, because eventually with the drugs I could get credit. I wasn't a junkie, but I could get hold of the stuff. Me and a couple of mates, we started meeting guys in a car park on a Friday night, selling, say, £100 worth of stuff—a big packet of bennies or speed, or a big chunk of smoke. I'd sell it to the junkies—then my mates'd mug 'em and get the gear back. So we'd got the money and the gear and we'd go and flog it to someone else! And these things snowballed. I'll be honest, it did get a big scary once or twice because there were too many people getting in touch with me to get the gear. So I thought, 'Hold up—this has got to cool down a bit, it's getting too hairy—you don't wanna get your collar felt'. So even when I was taking drugs and drinking I was a bit shrewd. I didn't want to get nicked because I was on to a good little earner—a couple of hundred a week.

Then I got involved in burglary—this is when I got to know Bob.[4] We used to nick TV sets to order. But soon it developed into mugging. Mugging was easier, because burglary involved setting some place up, getting some wheels, getting someone else to help, and knocking the gear out. All this could take a day or two to sort out. Whereas mugging—they didn't call it mugging then, it was 'rolling 'em', 'turning 'em over'—I discovered that you could roll someone in a few minutes and get

---

[3] Marijuana
[4] Bob Turney, co-author of *Going Straight*

a few bob. Because of my drinking habit and my floating about[5] habit, and my dancing up and down the country habit, I needed cash quicker.

I was 21 when I committed my last burglary. I went out to a party and came home ten days later. I was sent to Feltham[6] and I was on remand there for a few days. I got bail, so I never actually did a prison sentence in that sense. But having said that, from the age of ten up to nearly 18 I was in and out of care and remand centres.

• • •

Then I was in and out of psychiatric hospitals for about two years. I was sectioned, detained under the Mental Health Act, at one point, and I attempted suicide twice. I ended up at a big psychiatric hospital up in the woods in Epsom. It had 2,000 patients, and I remember my family visiting me there. I was sitting there in my pyjamas: the last time they'd seen me was three weeks before in court.

I was given ECT—electro-convulsive therapy treatment—over a period of a couple of years. After I'd had two dozen ECTs—they give you about six at a time, every year or two—I even got to the point where I was saying to the doctors 'Could I have some more?' I somehow had this strange idea that an electrical current passing through my brain might help me. Where on earth had I come from, and where had I finished?

• • •

But then my life changed. One day I was at an outpatients' appointment at the Nelson Hospital in South Wimbledon. I had had ECT treatment, I'd had anti-depressants, I'd had therapy. The hospital had a doctor who worked alongside the consultant psychiatrists, who were a married couple called Dr Joy West and Dr Eric West. The doctor who worked with them was Dr Una Kroll, who—unbeknown to me—was a Church of England deaconess. Not that that would have meant anything to me at the time. She'd also been on television, on these documentaries on BBC2. Anyway, this Dr Kroll said to me 'Terry, the only one that can help you is God.'

At that time I had a feeling of utter hopelessness. I thought 'Well this is it, isn't it? Doctors are telling me now that only the Invisible Man can help me!' It left me in utter despair. There was hopelessness inside me. There was such a vacuum inside of me and I thought 'Now

---

[5] i.e. from one drug to another
[6] Young offender institution

they're telling me to go to God! Where d'you make an appointment to
see Him?'

Dr Kroll gave me a letter to take to the Salvation Army
detoxification unit in Whitechapel in the East End of London. She said,
'Go there, Terry, and these people'll help you'. Because obviously I had
a drink problem and I had a drug problem. What she had said so
astounded me that I went there, and it was that lady and eventually
the people in the Salvation Army who had such a great influence on
me.

I gave my life to the Lord in that detoxification unit in
Whitechapel. I went to bed that night and I woke up the next morning.
And for the first time in my life—and I was 29 by then—I slept in
peace. Then I woke up and I actually felt clean. I'll never forget it as
long as I live, I felt clean. I prayed and some other people prayed for
me, and I knew that I'd experienced the truth of the Lord. And I knew
deep down that all the things I'd ever done were wrong.

I already knew that really, deep down, I knew it. I knew there was
more to life than hurting people and taking things that didn't belong to
me. And I wanted to be clean. I wanted to be pure, I wanted to be whole.
I wanted to be a normal human being. I asked God to heal me, because I
knew otherwise I was going to kill someone, or get killed myself. I had
already stood on the underground station at Whitechapel and I was
going to throw myself under a train.

•　•　•

Slowly, over the next few years, I started studying the Bible and
started to attend church. But it was difficult—I've backslid more times
than I care to remember. One day I walked out of the Salvation Army,
got a bottle of vodka, 20 Embassy, oh brother!

I ended up in Wallington Magistrates' Court again. I thought, 'Here
we go again, now I've done a crime!' But I didn't even remember doing
it. Apparently I was in a pub taking drugs and drink, and I pulled out a
knife on my brother Trevor and apparently had a go at somebody else as
well. I didn't know this till I woke up in the morning in the cells of
Wallington police station. So here I was upstairs in the magistrates'
court. My brother didn't want to press charges; the lads in the pub
didn't either. But of course the Old Bill's nickin' me, isn't he?

But the magistrates decided that if I was prepared to allow the
Salvation Army doctor to help me—if I agreed to go to him for
counselling and therapy and all the rest of it—then they were going to
drop charges. But if I didn't, it'd be the Crown Court for me. There was
no doubt I was going to get a custodial sentence. So obviously I chose the
doctor.

It wasn't a bed of roses. But I knew there was more to it. I knew the Lord was there, I knew it could happen. From being hopeless, I now had hope. I knew that it was possible with God. I didn't have to be wicked and horrible. I didn't have to hurt people. I didn't have to live a life of crime. God was offering me something else.

• • •

Even after I gave my life to the Lord, I did feel bad about how I'd treated my dad, and about other things I'd done. But I've come to accept that the Lord's forgiven me. I truly have repented of it, and by doing that I've done a 180 degree turn. I'm going in a different direction and now I'd love to see the people I hurt so I can apologise. I've tried to bring reconciliation and make restitution, I've tried to say sorry and make peace, but that's not always possible. There were crimes I've done, and I don't even know who to say sorry to.

But I feel now that it's dealt with. The most important thing is that God's forgiven me and I struggle with forgiving myself. That was difficult but I've come to a place now where I can accept myself. It's almost as if I was a different person. But if I meet anyone from my past, or my family, I will beg them to forgive me.

My values, my concept of life, my attitudes, my outlook, they've all changed. I've just done a Cambridge diploma in theology. I've done Bible College, I'm now in the ministry, I'll be ordained this year—it's amazing! I just want to help people, I want to put good into society, but above all, because I'm a minister, I want to give my life to the Lord.

I've got my lovely wife, my three little boys, and I've got the fact that this church I work for has put enough trust in me to allow me the opportunity to be the pastor of a congregation. They've got confidence in me and because of that I want to do well for them. I still find it amazing that people actually trust me and like me. It's incredible!

Working in the church, being a full-time minister, I don't have time for anything else now, apart from the fact that all those desires are gone and I don't want to do anything bad again. I could well do bad things—I daren't say I couldn't—but it would destroy me to think that I'd started doing things like that again. Part of me thinks 'Why on earth did I do all this stuff? Where was I coming from?' It's as if someone opened my head up, took my brain out, then put a new one in.

The important things are these foundational things: who I am, what I am. I'm at peace with myself and that's important. I can live with myself and because of that I can live with others. I can contend with life. I can face issues and I can deal with them now because I know who I am. It's just a wonderful feeling.

I had nothing, I'd come to the end of it. Two attempts at suicide, a couple of years in and out of psychiatric hospitals, electro-convulsive therapy, all that treatment, all the drugs, all the counselling, all the courts, *years* of it, right up till when I was nearly 30.

Now my hope for the future is that I just want to serve the Lord. I want to be the best minister I can be. I want to tell others good news, I want to see lives change, I want to see people set free from living how they live. Even my own family, my brothers, they don't need to be like that. There is a way out, there's hope for the hopeless.

I thought I was a hopeless case. A magistrate once said to me, 'You're a menace to society'. Even a minister of religion called me 'six-month Mortimer'. He said I'd never last. Those people sowed negative thoughts into my poor mind, thoughts that haunted me for years. But God loves me, and if I repent and turn from these things, I'm forgiven.

I'm a real optimist. I'm an enthusiastic person about life. I have an energy and a vitality. If I was 21 again I'd be an entrepreneur by now. I'd be a *billionaire*, to use the words of Del Boy! But I'm not bothered about money. You think of Martin Luther King and Nelson Mandela. They were the visionaries, they had a dream. They had hope. I can see the potential in anything, anyone. There is no such thing as someone beyond hope. There is no such thing.

Peter

Peter, 31, is a technical sales representative for a computer firm. At the age of
18 he was sent to prison for an offence which wrecked his university chances
and ruined a promising career in the Navy.

I decided I wanted to join the Royal Navy while I was still at school.
I'd always wanted to be a Navy pilot. It just seemed right and it had
done for years. My grandfather had been in the Forces. He was an ex-
army captain—a very proud, upstanding man. I think when I was about
11 he was to some extent a role model for me.

As I got towards school-leaving age, I was offered a Naval bursary
cadetship whereby they accept you for entry as a Royal Naval officer
and they will help pay your way through university. So I got all the
gear and started at university under a Royal Navy bursary. I hoped at
the time to become a Fleet Air Arm officer. I had worked towards the
Navy since I was 13. I'd got the bursary, I'd been down to Dartmouth,
I'd learned how to fly—I'd started living the life. But because of what
I did, I had to say goodbye to all that.

There are certain things I still can't watch on the television. When
the Royal Marines band plays *Sunset* each year at the Royal Legion
Festival of Remembrance, it's awful. I force myself to watch it every
year, and I sob my heart out.

●   ●   ●

I came from a very loving, supporting household. Two parents, small
terraced house in a market town, two kids—me and my sister. My dad
was an engineer, and Mum worked as a secretary in between having
children. We had a strong extended family as well: cousins, uncles,
aunts, second cousins, great aunts.

My primary school was very close to where I lived, and I had a
normal, happy time there. I was very quick to pick up on concepts and
ideas and I occasionally did get bored. But I wasn't disruptive because
my upbringing was always—not exactly strict, but I had a very definite
idea of right and wrong, and I was brought up to believe that when you
were in school the teacher was effectively your mother or father and
you did what you were told. My parents were very supportive—things
like testing my spelling, going to parents' evenings, turning up at sports
days.

I went to a fairly standard comprehensive school where I got nine
O-levels and four A-levels—in maths, physics, chemistry and computer
studies, and I went on to university in Manchester, where I studied
physics. My parents were pleased that I went on to university but there

wasn't any pressure. My parents have always said they'd be happy with whatever I wanted to do.

• • •

I can remember liking fruit machines for years. I started playing them when I was about 12, and I became an addict. At what point it became an addiction I don't know—I can't put my finger on it. Obviously before then I'd been with my parents to seaside arcades as a treat with a few pennies I might have for my birthday.

There were very few arcades in the town where I grew up. They were quite a new thing then. At the time Space Invaders were brand new, and fruit machines came out, or became more accessible, round about the same time. Initially I went with mates because they were the big thing—and you went with your mates.

I wasn't aware it was getting a hold of me. It was just enjoyable. I went after school. Then I started playing more on my own, and it started to become secret. It's almost as if it was my private fun. At first it was just 2ps and 5ps, just pocket money. Then I started to spend my bus fare on it and my dinner money. Then when I was about 14 or 15 I started taking a pound, two pounds, three pounds from my mum's purse. I think the most I ever took was about a tenner.

• • •

When I went away to university I went mad—completely mad! I was like a kiddie given the keys to the sweet shop. The university was quite a long way from my home town, and there I was, living in a hall of residence, first time away from home—and I just went absolutely potty with the fruit machines. You couldn't avoid the arcades. I used to walk from the halls of residence to the university, which was a walk of a couple of miles, and there were at least three arcades on my way. The city itself was full of them.

Not only was I getting my grant, I was getting money from my parents and I was getting money from the Navy which nearly doubled my normal grant income. Excluding what my parents gave me I probably brought in about £2,000, which for a student then was a fair amount of money. Yet less than a year later when I actually committed the offence I was £3,500 overdrawn.

I was losing all this money on the fruit machines. The stake was about 10p and the most you could make was £3. If I won any money I spent it, put it back into the machine. That's what's so stupid about fruit machine gambling. The most you can win is about three quid, then you'll almost always put it back in. Literally you put your money in, you hit the button, the wheels spin round and if you get the right combination you win.

Beer had never held much attraction for me, and there wasn't anything else that interested me. Half way through that first year I had friends, including girlfriends, but that was the point at which addiction to gambling really took hold.

Only one of my friends—my closest friend—was aware of what I was doing. I'd known him right from our first year at comprehensive school, and we'd come up to the same university together. But even if my friends had known this was getting out of hand and told me so, it wouldn't have helped. I'd have laughed at them and it wouldn't have stopped me. The problem is, you've got to hit bottom before you'll accept a lift up. Part of the awful thing about this addiction, as with others like alcoholism, is that until you hit your personal low, there isn't anything anyone can do about it. All the care in the world will not help you till you're ready to be helped, though I'd love to be able to say that if you waved a magic wand, it'd all be all right.

I *loved* the university. I didn't do any work: I occasionally turned up to lectures but I spent a lot of time doing nothing because I'd rather be in the arcades. There's a lot more pastoral care in universities now than there was then, but in any case I was hiding what I was doing. I got very good at making sure that I turned up at the right lectures with the right tutors so that I wouldn't be noticed. Because obviously I'd still got to justify to the Navy the fact that they were giving me this money.

By Easter I had a really big overdraft. I was due to go down to Dartmouth with the Navy during the Easter break and I'd got no money. I literally hadn't got any money at all! I went into the bank and the bank manager laughed: 'You're joking, of course!' I was taking cash out for no good reason, writing cheques for everything. So he refused me and that was it.

I was stuck. I was in Manchester at the beginning of the holidays and had to make this quite long journey to Dartmouth, and although most of it was fronted by the Navy with a travel warrant, there were bits of it that weren't, and obviously you'd got to have some money in your pocket. And I *literally* didn't have a penny! My mate had already gone home and anyway we were university students—he didn't have money either. He also knew that I was supposedly a lot richer than every other student. So to go to him would have been very difficult. I couldn't tell my parents either because they'd say 'Well, hang on a minute, what about all this other money we've sent you?'. And I couldn't tell the Navy. They'd say: 'Well, what happened to the money we gave you?' So I sat down and I decided I was going to have to commit a crime.

• • •

I know this sounds awful, but I almost made a list and ticked off the things I could do. I couldn't do a burglary—I didn't know how. If I had done, and had stolen some property, I wouldn't have known where to sell it. I couldn't do a bank robbery, because that had all sorts of nasty connotations. I'm not a violent person, and it wasn't as if I could pop down the shop and buy myself a gun and walk into the nearest bank.

So what I actually ended up doing was this: I got a letter opener in the shape of a knife and I went to the local paper shop and I walked in and said to the woman behind the till that she was to open the money drawer. She opened it and gave me £40. I didn't disguise myself or anything. Absolutely crazy! Even now I can't remember whether I took the letter opener out of my pocket—I don't know. I think I just told her to open the till and I took the money and ran out of the shop.

She ran out after me, shouting. A man in a small white Escort—I remember this, clear as day—followed me down the road, pulled up in front of me and told me to stop. I stopped. I handed over the money and got in the car with him. He drove me back to the newsagents where a passing ambulance had stopped because they'd seen me running off. And they put me in the back of the ambulance along with three old ladies who were just coming back from the hospital! While I was sat in the ambulance, the ambulance man came round and I gave him the knife. I can remember saying 'Here, you'd better have this.' And then I sat there and waited for the police to come. That was it.

• • •

The police took me to the police station and left me for about an hour and a half, locked in a cell. That was the bit that broke me, actually being locked in the cell. I didn't have a solicitor—I didn't want one. I just said 'Well, I've done it'. Initially I didn't try and explain why, but about an hour or so later I did. Because that's when I had the blinding flash of what brought me here and I realised it was the gambling. And at that point I said it for the first time: I said I was *addicted* to fruit machines.

They sat me down and I gave them a statement, told them exactly what I'd done and why. They weren't that interested in the 'why?', but they noted it down and they released me on bail.

I went back to where I was staying in the halls of residence, and at that point the shame of what I'd done hit me. All my friends had gone home. I was all on my own, there was no-one around. And I then thought about killing myself. I went through it, again quite logically, what I could and couldn't face doing. I ended up with planning to do it by drink and drugs—booze and pills. What actually stopped me from killing myself was because I couldn't afford the drink and drugs to do it—I couldn't afford a packet of Smarties!

It was at that point that I rang my mum and asked her to send me some money. I came up with some cock-and-bull story and they sent me some cash and I went down to Dartmouth. I still hadn't told my parents.

I spent a week in Dartmouth with the Navy, learning how to fly. I came back to the university at the end of the holiday, almost as if nothing had happened. I was still way, way in debt, but I got my next term's grant so I knew that I had at least got some money coming in.

By this time I'd started attending Gamblers Anonymous. I think one of the police officers that interviewed me told me about them. The relief! I felt awful the first time I got there but once I'd actually told my story it was such a relief to be amongst people who knew what it was like having the monkey on your back. Because before I'd never found anybody who'd ever had it. I met like-minded people, though it was mostly older people. For most of them it was horses and casinos. And that was it—I stopped gambling. The Navy had to be told about my offence of course and they just said goodbye. Losing the Navy was a major influence in stopping me gambling.

Even to this day I don't really know what the attraction of the fruit machines was. I suppose there might have been something of the 'comfort' element in me seeking out something familiar I had done at home. I don't know if I'd have grown out of it. I don't think so. I could have just graduated on to bigger things. At the time it wasn't really acknowledged just how dangerous this particular addiction can be— even now it's not acknowledged. In America it's actually recognized as a psychological disorder.

I've now read things about this addiction. There are a couple of guys in the States who've done a lot of work on it and they say that the sensation of winning something, even a very small prize, releases chemicals in the brain that make you feel good, and that's why you get addicted. I think it may have been that with me, because there is no rational explanation for why a previously relatively upstanding young man should elect to chuck virtually his entire life down the toilet.

• • •

In that summer term I went to see a solicitor and eventually realised that there was no way round it—I was going to have to tell my parents. So I went home at half term in the summer and finally plucked up courage and told my dad, who then went through and told my mum. My dad was very stoic, as I expected him to be. I think that's the reason I picked him to tell first, because I knew he'd be very stiff upper lip. And then he went to tell my mum.

Even now I can't bear to think about that. I caused my mother a lot more pain than I would ever, ever want to. I heard my mother scream for the first and only time in my life. My sister was about 13, and it was kept from her. I think my parents told her later.

My first magistrates' court appearance was in the June. I pleaded guilty and they remanded me to the Crown Court. My parents attended the committal proceedings and the trial, which was in July, just before my nineteenth birthday. It lasted about half an hour. I had character witness statements—people from the university, my old school teachers, church ministers, people who knew me. So there was all of that, plus the list of all the things I had done: I'd done Duke of Edinburgh, I'd been in the scouts—cub scouts, venture scouts —and I'd got all the badges. My barrister told me that if I was unlucky they'd probably give me a year in jail.

They gave me three years. If I let myself I would still be very, very bitter. People just couldn't believe it. The judge was known to be a very hard judge. He made a comment along the lines that he didn't believe addiction was an excuse and I needed to be really taught a lesson because I'd had all this wonderful upbringing, I came from a good family, I'd had a nice happy life, I was an intelligent guy, I had had every advantage society could offer me, and I'd elected to throw it back at them.

That's the only time in my life I've really known what people mean by the word 'gutted'. I got the chance to say goodbye to my parents. They came down to the cells, then I was taken off in a van to Strangeways prison.

•   •   •

When I was first in prison, I was still in shock. I didn't physically go on hunger strike but my body stopped asking for food and I got very ill because I just stopped eating. When I actually realised what I'd done I was absolutely horrified. One of the awful things I had to come to terms with during my first few days in prison was wondering if I would have done violence with that knife. I wanted to believe that I wouldn't have done, but I really didn't know. I wanted to meet the victim and apologise but I was told I couldn't.

I ended up being very lucky. The prison officer responsible for taking in young people must have looked at the information given to him about me, because I ended up in a cell on my own—it sounds awful but it was the best thing to happen.

You get taken to buy cigarettes and I got a very early taste of prison life, because out on exercise I had them taken off me. A friendly person had pointed out one guy as someone I really didn't want to mess with. He'd got the yellow stripes to show he was an escapee. And he was the guy who came up to me and said 'Give them to me now'. So of course I gave the cigarettes to him.

I was kept to a large extent on my own. During those first two weeks they brought in a wing officer from Thorn Cross, which at the time was an open young offenders' institution, and he interviewed me for a place there. I had been given three years: that is the absolute maximum that an open prison can take and even that was frowned upon. So why he chose me I don't know to this day, but they elected to send me there.

• • •

At Thorn Cross they were very, very good. I've never been fitter in my life, though I was never very good at sport at school. When I asked, they actually started a Gamblers' Anonymous group within the prison, so I was able to continue with GA and they got a few other people to join it as well. I attended education classes, and when I'd been there about a month, they allowed me to go back to university two days a week—the same university I'd been in. I effectively continued my course. Because I'd failed my first year exams I wasn't officially allowed to attend classes, but the university were very good and they allowed it. They turned a blind eye to the fact that there was this guy sat at the back of lectures who shouldn't be there.

I used to get up at 7 a.m. and I had to be back at the prison to get to bed at 9 p.m. Because it was an open prison you had your own key to your room. In fact it was like a hall of residence with bars on—though if you wanted to you could literally walk out.

The other prisoners thought what I'd done was the most hilarious thing they'd ever heard! Because I was so amateur, I was an object of ridicule: there'd been a report in the local paper about me nicking 40 quid. I think the only sympathy I got was for who the judge was. I was not attacked or anything at Strangeways but at Thorn Cross there was one guy who started to bully me. A little later on he was called in by the staff, and he never came anywhere near me again.

Eventually I ended up being quite useful to people—I helped them with their education and I also helped people to answer official questions. A lot of them had got worries about gas bills, social security money and so on—and because I was quite used to reading forms and because I could understand them I could help everybody else. And that's how I made my way through my sentence. I did a year and got out on my first parole. I served from July one year to July the next year.

• • •

I stayed on in Manchester. My friends were still at university—most of them had stood by me while I was in prison. But I didn't finish my degree. I just couldn't do it, though the university were very supportive. I was trying to work nights, doing bar work and working at a petrol station to pay off my overdraft, and I was trying to work days at the university. It took about five years but I eventually paid off the debt.

I decided that I wasn't going to continue with my degree for a variety of reasons, one of which was that I didn't enjoy it any more. There wasn't a real goal to aim for any longer, because I'd left the Navy and I'd worked for that since I was 13. Everything that I'd worked for had gone.

While I was working in the pub I met my wife—we started seeing each other seriously when I was about 22. I told her about my background straight away. Whether she really understood or not, she accepted it. I tried to explain to her about the gambling: how much success I had I don't know.

Then I sat myself down and decided what I wanted to do. I decided that as I quite liked computers I'd take the first job I could get that was closely related to them—which turned out to be selling computer supplies—disks, ribbons, ink cartridges, that sort of thing.

For that very first job I didn't mention being in prison—nobody asked. I stayed in that job a year, then I moved on, and each time I was moving on it was to better my prospects. I was quite successful at selling. It was easy because technically I knew what I was talking about. So I started selling more technical things and moved on through four or five different jobs, and nobody ever asked if I had a criminal record. I did quite well, got a company car and so on.

• • •

Gambling doesn't hold any attraction for me any more. I have become serene—any other gambler will recognise that expression. I am aware of a lifestyle choice I made, not to choose that particular lifestyle. I gave up attending GA meetings about a year into my serious relationship with my wife, because that was the point at which my lifestyle changed. Gambling is addictive, full stop. But there are different things that kick it in. I have a lifestyle now that precludes gambling, though having said that, I know that GA is there. But to some extent gambling makes me feel sick, even now.

I'm happy with my life in many ways. I've got a wife, lovely kids, a relatively comfortable lifestyle. But I also see myself as a talent wasted. My wife could tell you about those things I still can't watch on television.

I don't recoil in horror when I go in to a pub with fruit machines. The only time I recoil in horror is when I see a 12 or 13 year old playing on them. But I don't have any missionary zeal about this, because I'm quite aware of the fact that I'm part of a very small minority and just because I can't cope doesn't mean that others can't. The only thing that I would perhaps change is the availability of gambling to very young children. In theory only people over 16 are supposed to play fruit machines but nobody stops the younger ones.

My family and my career—those are the important things to me now. I need to carve a life out for myself. My official designation is as a salesman but what I actually do is design and propose systems for companies to achieve certain goals—such as secure systems for the Internet, for banks and building societies. I've been in this job three years. The guy who gave me the job is one of those friends from university who stuck by me. So he's aware of my background.

Now I've applied for a job I really want, moving away from sales. I've had two interviews, and two days ago I had a letter offering me this job. In the offering letter it tells you to fill in all the forms. You have to give references; fill in the corporate credit card application; fill in the corporate car leasing application and so on. Oh, and by the way, they tell you, fill in the Rehabilitation of Offenders Act form. On this form, on which you have to declare any previous convictions, there are some covering notes that say something like 'Please note that we do check with the police and if you lie we will withdraw the job offer instantly'. I've got to answer it by tomorrow at the latest.

My own personal code by which I now live my life wouldn't allow me to lie anyway, but the Apex Trust, an organization that helps ex-offenders get work, has given me advice. They've told me that the best way to present my previous conviction is to write a letter to attach to the form, giving a brief background, explaining what happened and saying it was a long time ago—13 years ago.

If I get this job then that's a particular dream realised and I'll move forward from there. If I don't—I don't know what I'll do, and at the moment I don't particularly want to think about it.

Postscript: A week after we interviewed Peter, he rang to tell us he had got the job '. . . and they didn't even mention my offence'.

Frank Cook

Frank, 45, has spent 27 years—more than half his life—in top security prisons, mainly for violent firearms offences. At one of his trials he was described as "a Chicago-style gangster", and possibly a dangerous psychotic. He became notorious as one of the most violent men in the prison system, who fought, rioted and took hostages. His life was transformed by the time he spent in two therapeutic regimes: Grendon (then called Grendon Underwood) and the Special Unit at HMP Hull, where he discovered his talent as a sculptor. He was released in December 1996, and a few months later he took part in a Channel 4 TV documentary, "Hard Cell", with the criminologist Dr David Wilson, about the value of therapeutic prisons. Frank is now a sculptor, artist, journalist, lecturer on crime prevention and the co-author of a new autobiography.[1]

The weirdest thing happened to me one day. I'd been in solitary for about six months—I hadn't seen a human being apart from the screws who came to the cell door. They kept on coming in and fucking me about, chucking water on me and all this bollocks, but I wouldn't even call them names, I wouldn't even say 'You bastards!' because by saying that you're giving them life. You're saying 'You've affected me that much that I've spoken to you'. So I didn't speak to them at all. I actually wrote 'Yes' and 'No' on my hands so I wouldn't have to speak to them. They used to try and trick me, but I wasn't entering the game—I wasn't jumping on the roundabout. I wouldn't even question anybody because if you questioned somebody you'd be vulnerable. I used to isolate myself to such a degree that I stopped drinking hot fluids—I weaned myself onto cold water. I conditioned myself not to have warm tea so if it didn't come I wouldn't care.

When some people go into solitary confinement they whistle, that's their way of saying they're not bothered. Other people go quiet and cry. I had a discipline to such a degree I wouldn't let anything go. No matter what they threw at me I wouldn't budge. They could torture me and break me but I would not display any emotion whatsoever. I also knew that if I'd turned round I'd kill the lot of them—I'd waste them— they'd be on the landing, dead.

Then one day I allowed my soul to show emotion. Like I said, I'd been six months in solitary, without a stick of proper furniture, no window or anything, with the screws throwing hot water at me and hitting me over the head and fucking about with my food. I had one of those cardboard tables and a chair, and one day I suddenly smashed them on the floor and I screamed at the screws.

---

[1] *Hard Cell,* Frank Cook and Mathew Wilkinson, The Bluecoat Press, 1998

The Governor came in and he said to me 'Welcome to the human race'.

• • •

I was born in Doncaster into a gypsy culture. I believe on reflection that had I been allowed to stay in my own culture, and if there hadn't been so much conflict between my mum and my dad, I'd have been a better person than I am now, a happier person. Despite the fact that there was criminality in the family, I don't believe I would have had the problems I've had. The reality is I couldn't get on in prison for trying. I didn't go into prisons all those 27 years meaning to cause trouble—I just had problems getting on with it. I couldn't go with the flow. I felt trapped, cornered. As a young child I was free.

A gypsy is a person by birth nomadic, of no nationality, no sense of belonging, known to travel around. It's in our blood, our heritage. I have come across maybe two gypsies in prison and they are similar to the Aborigine: you actually feel that they're dying in prison, particularly the older ones. If you lock them away they'll die on you—you'll kill them, spiritually, within themselves. A true gypsy will become disturbed within himself and try and kill himself.

I was travelling till I was about eight years of age. My mother couldn't cope with the gypsy culture because she was a non-gypsy from a South Yorkshire mining family. It was made quite clear to her that she was a non-gypsy and she felt alienated. I was never close to my mother, never have been, and her loss was no great loss to me. I had no great feelings of her presence or of her going. My father was very difficult. He was sent to prison on many occasions.

Our lifestyle was very hard for my mum and her answer to all her problems were 'If I get a house, he'll settle down and the kids can go to school'. Then she could live the lifestyle she was previously accustomed to. But the struggle proved too much for her and she had a nervous breakdown. My father had disappeared by this time and I was sent to a children's home.

I had two brothers younger than me, but I certainly wasn't close to them. If I fought with them, in sibling rivalry, I had to fight both of them. They were very close—all the family were close but me. They were close to each other, and close to my mum, but I was totally different from the rest of the family. That's just the way it was. I didn't feel part of my family, never did, never have done and to this day I never will. I felt totally alienated. I saw myself as an outsider, a one-man-band, and I kept myself to myself and made my way, forged my way through life.

I didn't have any need for friends. I didn't need human beings. I used to look at people and I didn't feel for them as people. I had associates but it wasn't until the very senior years as an adult, in prisons and such like, that I felt the need for people. So I was quite a bit of a loner when I was a kid. I could play with the other kids—I'd play with them and do all the rest but I didn't need people, I didn't need them at all. The need for people has been conditioned and smashed into me by prison, by isolating me and juggling around with me.

Persecution certainly came into my life very early. My father would say 'Now listen, go up there to that house with this watering can and request some water'. So I'd stick this big watering can on a trolley and off I'd go. My father was a very, very strong man, and he was very obsessive about the fact that if it was a lady who opened the door I was to call her Madam and say 'Thank you' and 'Please' and show respect. I wasn't to go into the building, I was to get the water and say I was grateful, then close the gates after me.

I can recall occasions when I've gone to very nice houses and they've said 'What do you want?' and I'd say 'Excuse me, I'm a gypsy from up the camp. My father's asked me if I could ask for some water. Can you spare some water?' Then I'd get water thrown all over me.

Once I went to a house—I was about seven years old at the time—and the lady smiled and said 'You want some water, do you?' and I said 'Yes I do, please'. She seemed so nice, then she went and got a pan of water and she chucked it all over me! Another time I went to a house—I was only little and it was night-time—and they were having dinner in the kitchen. The kitchen door was open and I knocked and said 'Excuse me, I'm sorry to bother you but could I have some water, please?' The man sent his two teenage sons to come out the kitchen in the middle of their dinner and they kicked me all over the lawn and beat me.

As gypsies you're called names all the time, and you've got the police constantly coming to the camp accusing people of anti-social acts and crimes.

•   •   •

Being a traveller up to the age of eight, when we moved into a house, I only went to school on infrequent occasions, but these weren't significant enough to get me into the mould of it. I'd do something like two months of primary school—that's if my mother got her way and persuaded my father to let me go. My parents only sent me to school because they were plagued to do it. And it also depended whether I wanted to go—because I met with a lot of hostility there. Gypsies! Children are not very tolerant now but they certainly weren't in those days. And I was alienated from my own community as well because of my mixed parentage.

So going to primary school for the first time I was excited but also anxious. If you're a gypsy and you go to school, they talk to you as if you're on a different planet. I was immediately chucked into the role of being a second-rate type person. I didn't take umbrage at that—I just automatically assumed that role. But I did feel different and alienated and this resulted in me being a bit robust. I was either too robust for them, or sullen. So I didn't get on too well at primary school. I used to play games with the other kids but I was different. I always wanted to be an Indian, whereas the average boy wants to be a cowboy. I wanted to be the crook and not the cop.

I got chucked in at the deep end in the second year of the secondary school. That was very short lived, and my time there was pure havoc. I was put in the dunces' class for starters. It was totally alien to me and I'd nod when everybody else nodded, but it was all rubbish to me.

I was illiterate into my late teens. I was eventually considered too violent for the children's home and so I went to borstal and places like that, and it wasn't until I was in solitary confinement in a young offenders' institution that a nun taught me to read and write a bit, showing me pictures in children's reading books. It was only when I got into my second prison sentence that I could really read and write and that's when I started gathering momentum.

I was sent away to approved school after my very short stint in secondary school. I could relate to that even though I didn't like it and it was painful and did my head in. The funny thing was, I thought to myself, 'I'm here because I've done wrong'. That somehow made it logical. Whereas going to school was totally alien to me.

• • •

I was 12 years old when I was sent to an approved school—for receiving a stolen pushbike wheel. When I was first sent there I was bewildered, I was intrigued, I was fantasising and being macho about it. But I was frightened as well, because I knew this was something serious. That was my first offence. They said it was because I was a gypsy. They actually said that. They stated it like this: 'We're going to send you to an approved school where you will learn to become a decent citizen and settle down and come back to Doncaster with skills and contribute to your community and be a good person'.

They did a lot of that kind of thing at the time. They used to round up gypsy children like chickens and put us in homes and send us to approved schools, or put us with foster parents. Oh yes, they used to do that. They used to grab you and lob you in there and say it would be good for you. I have a distinct remembrance of the child person[1] coming round to the camp. Like the police they used to wear a uniform and they used to drive a blue van. That van had a cage in the back, similar to a

---

[1] Social worker

dog handler's cage, and I was put in that cage on three occasions when I was rounded up.

They used to round up girls in particular, and tell them their parents weren't fit to have them. They'd give the family a load of papers and move them on—and the girl would find herself living in some middle-class family and saying 'Yes, Mam', and being called a different name and told to forget where she came from and all that. I've bumped into people like that years later, and I've said 'What happened to you?' And they've said 'They carted me off!'. They made sure they weren't allowed to get in touch with their families. Plus the families were moved on, they couldn't read and write, and plus they were very paranoid and feared the system. The system's based on bureaucracy which is about reading and writing and they couldn't do that. We were moved from place to place by the police, and all it did was reinforce our paranoia and hostility to conventional lifestyles and to the authorities that prevailed.

When I left approved school I went straight into professional crime. I decided I wanted to be a villain. My father would encourage me to steal. All my family were thieves, and I've always been a thief but for years I never got caught. I was stealing every day all the time, quite naturally. But most of my offences were crimes of violence, and violence is a much more serious thing. So I was always in and out of approved school, detention, borstal, borstal recall, and then young offenders' institutions and prisons—for 27 years of my life. All of my sentences— seven years, five years, another five years—they were all the same, firearms offences, where I shot at people, and sometimes, unfortunately, I've actually shot people too.

Within the prison system there was a lot of support on offer, but I rejected most of it. I was all right if a screw was decent with me and he talked my language and understood me. There are some screws that'll talk straight to you. People with a bit of nous—they're men among men in the silly world of prison. Then there are some other nice ones but they're not allowed to be what they really want: the system won't permit it. But 90 per cent of officers won't connect with you, and I haven't got much time for them even now. They're just pieces of machinery.

•   •   •

Grendon Underwood was the first place that began to change me, and then the Special Unit at Hull Prison. Grendon kind of opened me up and modified me, though I was far from an angel. A guy called Joe Chapman was an officer on the YP wing and he gave me a lot of help. But all Grendon really did to me was take a truly dangerous young man out of the conventional prison system which wasn't doing him any good: in fact it was making him worse.

Before I got to Grendon I'd been in solitary confinement for eleven months throwing shit about, stabbing people and such like. They took me to Grendon where the staff made it perfectly clear at their meeting that I wasn't welcome, wasn't wanted. But the governor insisted I should stay.

For him to meet the staff half way, I had to stay in the hospital wing and I was dealt with on an individual level.

Grendon modified me from being someone who would kill for fun. Even after Grendon I was still capable of behaving recklessly and dangerously.

I've done some bad things since Grendon, but in comparison to what I was capable of doing previously they were nothing. Before Grendon, what I used to do was very clinical. I'd pride myself on not becoming emotionally involved with my acts of violence. I perpetrated them without even thinking—no regret, no hostility towards the victim, no feelings of guilt, no feeling at all. Nothing personal. I used to pride myself on being a professional going round robbing banks and that sort of thing. And that's the way I was. For me guns had a trigger and you could pull it this way or you could pull it that way. Pull it this way—you live; pull it that way—you die. On, off; on, off. You live, you die; you live, you die. That's all it was to me.

•   •   •

Then on my last sentence I went on to the Special Unit at Hull Prison. Like all the other inmates there I arrived from solitary confinement. I'd been sentenced to seven years for what I now regard as an absurd, ridiculous and reckless offence, and at the time I arrived in the Special Unit I had literally given up. It was my last chance to change my ways, but I was at a very low ebb on my arrival. The Unit was experimental. It was geared to behaviour modification of men considered to be the most dangerous and disruptive in the prison system. I was allowed to wear my own clothes and forge my own identity. But it was only after a massive amount of counselling from my personal officer and two teachers that I was able to start working from a stable base. In that Special Unit, I started developing a conscience. It was a slow process, and they only started to kick it off. The Unit did change me dramatically, but making me fit for society and life was a slow process. Age, as well as the input from unit staff, helped to change me.

I started clay modelling, and it became apparent to the teacher, Steve Dove, and to myself that I had a talent for it. My first clay model was of a man in prison. I called it *Deflated not Defeated*. Then I started working with wood. One day I looked at a piece of waste timber and saw a prehistoric fish in there, and I went on to carve a fish from the wood.

Humberside County Council bought this sculpture, *Prehistoric Fish*, for £600, for exhibition in the Hull Maritime Museum, and part of the money went towards education for young offenders. Then I exhibited a t a winter exhibition in a local gallery, and I got an immense amount of recognition for another two sculptures. One was called *Fertility*, the other was called *Supportive not Oppressive*—a life-size wood sculpture of a man supporting a pregnant woman. This piece was donated to a local maternity hospital for exhibition in the foyer of their new wing. Through my sculpture I made a lot of friends, and they've continued to support and encourage me.

This was how I started having feelings of self-worth. I don't want to sound all namby-pamby about it, but I think that when you start feeling something for yourself, you start feeling for others. Input by probation officers and prison officers in that Unit encouraged me to feel good and to tell myself I was good. When you start doing that you start thinking good, *being* good, and you start mixing with good people—it's a knock-on effect and then you continue and continue.

Jane Manning, a local journalist, helped me write my autobiography, then I started working on criminology and penology with students at Humberside Polytechnic. I decided to concentrate more on academic areas and on developing my personal and social skills. I spent much more time studying psychology and sociology, which were a great help to me. For the first time I began to be able to stand back from potentially confrontational situations.

I also had lot of help from my wife Tina and my two little girls. Tina is a very strong woman and she gave me her unflinching support. I also believed my two little girls deserved better than a father who was in prison. I used to try and compensate by spending hours in the craft room making them wooden toys, rabbit hutches and bird cages.

As my confidence developed, and I became determined never to be involved in any sort of crime again, I decided it was time to begin bridge-building with the police—I'd been at loggerheads with them for years. With the help of the Hull A wing team, police officers who had dealt with me in the past were invited into the prison to meet me. Two top detectives visited me on the Unit. They agreed there was no comparison between the new Frank Cook and the one they'd known before. Part of the meeting was taken up with discussing how I could help the police, and we decided that the most positive step would be for me to actively discourage any local youngsters who might look up to me from vandalising their community. The meeting ended with handshakes all round.

I took up this work immediately, and I've continued it through contacts I've made in the media. Also, with the help of a local broadcaster, I narrated a crime prevention audio cassette aimed at young offenders. It's now used by various police forces and alternatives to custody groups. Because of this work, and after a visit to the Hull Unit by Jimmy Boyle, I was invited to a two-day conference on power sharing. Over those two days I was placed completely on trust, and I was later told that my behaviour was 'beyond reproach' and my contribution to the conference was excellent.

●   ●   ●

It's very hard now for me to comprehend what I did. I have profound difficulty with it. There's guilt, fear—fear of what I've done. I can't begin to explain what I've done, I can't even grasp it. I am only just coming to terms with it even now. I say to myself 'I spent 27 years in prison. That's a long time!' I'm saying that now, trying to get my head round it. And I resent saying it, but I think the system's been very, very tolerant of me indeed, when you take into account what I've done.

If we were in a public house now and there was anything hostile I'd move away from it as quick as possible. There's a 'fight or flight' syndrome: I used to be the fighter, but now I'm the flighter—I'm off!

Now I'm just trying to make my way through life, doing my journalism and art and TV work and books. Lectures are very important to me, because I'm putting back something that I took out. I don't pull any punches. My lectures are very painful, very, very emotionally draining and heart-wrenching but I do it and I do a very good job. I know I do, I'm not bragging. I perceive myself as trying to make things a bit better and to prevent more Frank Cooks being created and being allowed to do what they want to. So I've come a long way.

●   ●   ●

Now I have the support of certain organizations—the New Bridge in particular, which befriends prisoners during their sentence and after release. I've been with New Bridge now for nine years—and I phone almost every day, though sometimes I'm working and I forget—I'm only human. I've also got a lot of support from my wife and children. And I've got the support of positive individuals. I work very hard at mixing with people of a healthy mentality, good people who are valuable to society, themselves and myself.

All my relatives are still thieves—I have relatives in the gypsy culture who don't even know me, living a different lifestyle altogether. I see them going about but I don't speak to them. It's just that they're in a different world. On the occasions that I do go to a certain pub in our town that's full of travellers, I can slot in, and everything seems all right.

But I've been conditioned totally differently and my aims and insight are now totally different from theirs. I know that within two or three hours the gambling will be so heavy - they don't just gamble like ordinary people gamble. They bang and shout and throw money and gesticulate and want to fight. It's all geared round macho stuff and power. And that's when I bail out because now I've been taught differently.

Total poverty might make me go back to crime—if there was no food on the table I'd go out and steal to put food in the kids' mouths. Or situational violence—if we'd been burgled and somebody threatened my wife and children.

What's important to me now are my health, my family, the ability to work and a degree of success. I'm hoping for the success of my book, continuing to do the work I'm doing, and there's films to be made, and more books to be written. Mainly I want happiness and quality of life. Even the most difficult thing out here is better than being locked up like the living dead. It's nice even to get rained on. If it's raining I thank God I'm alive—I love rain!

Mary

Mary, 40, was sent to prison in her mid-20s for defrauding her employer. On release she spent 14 years working as a legal secretary before taking her law degree. She is now in the process of qualifying as a solicitor and hopes to practice, specialising in criminal and matrimonial work. She married a life-sentenced prisoner, and does not wish to disclose her own or her husband's identity – so pseudonyms are used here for both.

I'd been working as a secretary at a firm of solicitors for about 18 months, and my boss and I went out on a social occasion with some colleagues. One of them kept saying that all prisoners should be hanged and flogged. I said all prisoners weren't like that—I'd been a prisoner myself. That was the first time my boss found out my background. He was brilliant. I think he was fascinated to know in what ways being in prison had changed me. I went on working at that firm as a legal secretary for the next 14 years, until my boss retired.

• • •

I was adopted and I have found that this often plays quite a large part in criminal behaviour. Having said that I was always aware that I was adopted—my parents handled it very well indeed, and they were a loving family. But when I was about five my sister was born and I think I regarded her as an intrusion. I just couldn't see the point—my parents had me—why did they want her? She used to take up so much of my parents' time at home. I was never close to my sister.

I later met up with my blood sister who actually was the same age as my adoptive sister—also five years younger than me—and she said I was lucky to have been adopted as she'd had an awful childhood with our real parents.

I did well at primary school and passed the eleven plus for the grammar school. I got six O-levels but I was a bit iffy about staying on at school and doing my A-levels. I thought I'd rather leave and earn some money. My father was keen on me staying on to do my A-levels but I couldn't care less. One part of me wanted to leave school. The teachers said if I stayed on and worked really hard I could get A-levels, but I also wanted to get out and see a bit of the world. My mother probably thought she was doing the right thing by writing to all the big firms in London that did training courses for secretaries.

I went on a Unilever training course, passed all the exams and after that I was a very well qualified secretary. I stayed in that job with Unilever for five years, though I was bored out my skull.

Then I got a job with Allied Dunbar which was completely different. It was really fun: the work was difficult, but it was a really nice atmosphere—very open working conditions which I had not experienced before, and quite young staff. I stayed on in that job for four years. Then they decided to move offices out to Swindon. They wanted me to move with them but I didn't want to so I was made redundant and I got a very good redundancy package. I was about 25 by this time. That's when the disaster happened.

• • •

I went to work for a physiotherapist in private practice. She was self-employed and I carried out a very complicated fraud whereby the money her clients paid her didn't go through the books. I just drifted into this: I hadn't started to do it with criminal intent, more as a challenge really, but once I'd started it was very difficult to stop. In the end I had defrauded her of about £4,000 which was a lot of money in those days, the early 1980s. I spent the money on more and more expensive clothes, things like that. I knew perfectly well it wasn't legal. I did think I ought to stop, but the more money I took, the more I became trapped. I think I was addicted—addicted to spending money at that time.

I got found out because one of the customers happened to ring up on a Saturday and my boss picked up the phone and she found out immediately what was happening. She must have been so horrified. She rang the police and I was arrested.

To be honest I was really relieved when I was caught because there was so much stress when I was committing fraud. I was always looking over my shoulder and now and then I would tot up all the money I'd taken and I'd be horrified. The police came round to my house and I was taken to Holborn police station and charged.

I was let out on bail. My mother had to come up from Dorset and put up bail and of course she was horrified. Then I had to wait eight months before the trial. I vaguely knew I could go to prison. These days I'd be sure to go to prison and I'd find out all I could about it. But you just hope it won't happen and you carry on. I went on temping, doing boring jobs. Then in 1983 the case came to court and I got two years and was sent to Holloway prison.

• • •

I just couldn't believe what was happening—it all felt so peculiar. I was there because I deserved to be, but there were women there who had never had a chance. There was no hope for them and they seemed bound to end up in prison. There were loads of women there as well educated as me and we all gelled together. Then this other girl and I got sent to Drake Hall, an open prison in Staffordshire. She had been doing frauds all her life and was always in and out of prison, but nobody had ever stopped to ask her if she needed help.

I couldn't get over how much nicer the officers were there than the Holloway officers. I didn't find prison too bad as I'd always gone to work and was used to a structured life. A lot of the rules were silly but you got used to it. But some people came there from Holloway and they just couldn't take it and they asked to go back to closed prisons.

I didn't look for trouble but if things were ludicrously wrong I would say so. For instance in Drake Hall the food was always cold and I asked them why. They had perfectly adequate hotplates. I said to the kitchen man, 'Why can't you get your act together so we can have hot food?' He went crazy and complained to the Governor. The Governor went to the kitchens and he agreed that the food was cold. So after that they went to the other extreme and the food was always very hot. Much later in my sentence the food went bad again and the women went on a hunger strike but because of that they were stopped from having visits.

I had a friend called Jean who wasn't very strong physically. One of the officers really disliked Jean and gave her jobs that wore her out. I worked in the laundry which suited me fine, but Jean was put to work on the farm, which was work she just couldn't do. One day I asked the officer why she gave Jean work she wasn't capable of. The officer got really angry and said 'You'll go where we tell you to go!' But three days later Jean was moved from the farm. There were dreadful things happening to the women in the prison. I saw so many women in prison who'd never had a chance—there were young gypsy girls for instance, put in prison for very minor offences.

After two or three months in prison I saw how pointless this kind of life was. I spent most of my sentence working in the laundry. All my friends came up to Staffordshire to see me in prison and whenever I saw them I realised how much I was missing.

I think being in prison did change me, seeing what happened to other women. I now think it's disgraceful that I should have been involved in fraud the way I was. But as I said, I do think fraud is addictive and in a way it helped me to go to prison and see the way prison was destroying so many people and I decided this was not for me. That fraud was my one and only crime.

I came out of prison on my first parole in 1984 and I had to be careful because I was still on licence. It was just so nice to be out, to be able to walk about and do what you wanted and eat a meal when you wanted without looking at your watch and knowing there were two hours to wait. But I did miss some of the friends I'd made in prison and when they came later to Holloway on accumulated visits[1] I went back there to see them.

* * *

At first I had to live with my mother in Dorset because the authorities didn't like the idea of me living in London—they try to stop you going back to the same circumstances. But after three months I was very fed up and I wanted to get back to London and get a decent job. My probation officer didn't seem to mind, so I went back to London and I answered an advert in the *Evening Standard* for a secretarial job. I didn't realise till I got there that it was a solicitors' firm. The subject of my having a conviction never cropped up and I certainly didn't mention it. As I said, it was 18 months before my boss found out. He was very sympathetic and said most people didn't see prison the way it really is.

About four and a half years ago, while I was still working at that firm, I started thinking about doing a law degree course. I think being in prison did have a lot to do with that decision, and it was also partly to do with developing a social conscience.

I heard that Thames Valley University ran a course on criminal justice—much wider than just criminal law—and you could do it two evenings a week. There was an enormous reading list and it took me four years, but I did get my BA.

* * *

I met my husband indirectly though going to visit one of the firm's clients in prison. This client, a lifer, was asking for an appeal and after I had visited him a few times he told me that another lifer, Jim, wanted me to visit him too. At first I thought he wanted me to visit him as a professional. Then when he explained that this was not what Jim had in mind, I said 'I didn't realise this prison was a dating agency!' Then I got a very stilted note from Jim, saying 'Would you come and see me?'

Over the next six or seven months I visited Jim a lot and we got really fond of each other.

We got married in 1998. The prison Governor was brilliant. Jim is very quiet and reserved and he has always protested his innocence, and he sometimes comes over as very stubborn because he refuses to take part in any of the offending behaviour programmes. But the Governor said we could get married and it was quite astounding that he allowed Jim two hours outside to get married in a registry office. There was no

---

[1] Temporary transfer to a prison nearer home to see family and friends

obvious security. Jim came to the wedding in a taxi and the officers took the handcuffs off for the ceremony. One of my cousins had travelled down in the train from London with the registrar who knew everything that was going on, and was very good to us.

We have often wondered whether we would have liked each other if I hadn't been to prison myself. I certainly understand what's going through his head, but it shook me rigid to find out how insecure he is, and how cruel a long-term prison sentence is. Last September Jim's 12 year tariff was completed but because he would not admit to having committed the murder he was convicted of, he wasn't been granted parole. His next chance is coming up this year.

The only problem I now have is in not telling people about Jim. I can't say I'm not married, but I am now temping as well as studying to become a solicitor and I can't go telling people I work for that I'm married to a lifer.

My priorities now are my marriage and my husband—to get Jim out of prison so we can live a normal life—though I know we'll have problems with him readjusting.

And my law studies are important of course. I don't think I'll have any problem becoming a solicitor. I contacted the Law Society and apparently it will be all right as my conviction is spent. The Law Society have clamped down on who can become a solicitor. When I first applied to join the law degree course at the university I had a very gruelling interview. They deliberately make it very demanding as they don't like people dropping out. The woman who interviewed me was a judge's wife and she said my past conviction would be no problem. It does strike me as very strange that if you use your brain to do something wrong, like fraud, you are more likely to be accepted as a solicitor than someone who might physically damage somebody else in a one-off offence. We are the laughing stock of Europe because of our penal system. I really would like to change things.

Sadly, Mary's hopes of a normal married life with Jim were not to be fulfilled. Just before this book went to press she contacted us to say that the marriage had broken up:

> I attribute this in part to the inevitable lack of contact between us. But the largest part of the blame must go to Jim's own fragile state of mind, which I am sure has been caused by the number of years he has spent in prison with no hope of release. I am very angry about all this, not particularly for myself, since I am not a natural victim and will survive—and am surviving. But I want people to know what really happens to lifers, and how very cruel our lifer system is.

Chris Sheridan

Chris, 46, is now a probation officer. But he was born in prison to a
shoplifter mother and spent most of his childhood in care, his teenage years
in approved schools, and his early twenties in prison.

I was born in prison. I don't think my mum would ever have told me this
and I would probably never have known had a social worker not done
so. He was one of the social workers who later abused me. The police
checked and there was a child born around that time in Aylesbury
prison, which was a woman's prison then, though it's a young offenders'
institution now. I haven't been inside there yet, though I've stood
outside the gates. I don't like this thought of being born in prison—it
doesn't seem fair to do that to any child. It seems that I'd got to be part
of the system all my life.

● ● ●

I don't know if being born in prison pre-empted how people treated me. I
think my mother's record and her name had a lot to do it. I stayed with
my mum in the prison till the age of 18 months, then I went into care in a
home in Bristol. I don't know why—I suppose I had no-one to look after
me. So for the four years from 18 months until I was about five and a
half I was at this care home. That I think plays a significant part in
who I am today, those four years and the care I got there. The home is
now under investigation for child sexual abuse in the late 1960s and
1970s. It was a terrible shock to find that out about the place where I'd
always believed that I was safe, the one place in the world where I
had good memories—though not many memories because I was too
young. In the children's home there was a nun called Sister Muriel who
was my carer. She's the person I remember as being the closest to me. I
know I was closer to her than I was to my mother.

When I went back home at just over the age of five, my mum was
living with a man who was to become my stepfather. There was a
younger half-sister already there, aged two, and she was the apple of
his eye, even though she wasn't his own daughter. He'd been with her
since she was a baby, and I was the new boy in the household. My
stepfather was an electrician, and I just wasn't the kind of practical boy
that he wanted round the house. My sister was more practical than me
and she understood about his electrical tools—she knew the different
names for them even at that age, and I just couldn't remember them, so
there was this immediate kind of tension between me and her. We
never really got on as brother and sister at all. I was always being
compared to her and always being put down in her eyes so we never

played together. When my mum and step-dad used to go out, often they'd take her with them and I'd be left at home on my own, locked in my room. I never see my half-sister now. I haven't seen her in 16 years. There was a big incident when I was about 17 when I was living at home. I was sleeping on the couch and my sister came in with a boyfriend and there was a big argument. The police were called and my mother was asked who they should remove from the house. I lost out, and that's when I ended up being homeless.

The family home I moved back to at the age of five was on a typical council estate in Horfield in Bristol. But I only stayed there for about two years.

My mum used to take me shoplifting. She'd nick the stuff, give it to me and then walk out the shop, and if we got caught I'd get a clip round the ear and be told not to steal. I always remember getting caught with an umbrella that she'd given me. We got caught and I got a smack round the ear and she said 'Don't steal!' I remember when I was training to be a probation officer I did a report on somebody who'd done exactly the same thing and I remember saying to her 'Why use your kids? Why put them through that?'

I was seven when I was taken back into care. I remember hearing my step-dad telling my mother 'It's either him or me—either he goes or I go'. I think they lied to get me into a children's home and that's one thing I still find hard. I resent the fact that my step-dad clearly didn't want me in the house. My stepfather just didn't like me—full stop. He used to call me a 'ninny' or a 'nincompoop' or a 'nitwit'—those were his three expressions for me. 'What're you doing, nincompoop?' he'd say. When we went out I remember being embarrassed at this. During the school holidays, when I was about six or seven, I was locked out of the house. The door was locked at nine in the morning and I'd come back in the evening. If I was late I'd get a good hiding. My dad used to beat me quite a lot. I think my mother used to beat me too. Occasionally I suppose I deserved it. One time I nicked ten shillings out of her purse. It was the first time I'd ever stolen anything, and I went down to the local shop and I bought 40 Players cigarettes and some matches and went up to the local station, waited for the steam train and got on this train down to Severn Beach. I remember going into the café and buying a doughnut, a cup of tea, and putting sixpence in the juke box. *My Old Man's a Dustman*—that's the record I put on. Then I went out on to the beach and tried lighting these cigarettes, gave up, threw them away and went home. That was a day out for me. That incident, taking that ten shillings, was part of the reason I was deemed out of control.

So I was put back in care because I was deemed to be an 'uncontrollable child'. At the age of just seven I was 'uncontrollable'.

I resent my step-dad but I don't really resent my mum because in the 1950s women were seen and treated differently. For instance, I was openly called a 'bastard' by my primary school teachers because my mum wasn't married. This got around, and I know she was called a lot of names in the street, though not often to her face. But at school I was quite openly called a bastard. Kids are kids and will say such things, but this was the teachers as well. I think all this is why I was a timid little boy. I never really made close friends because I wasn't living at home with my family. I sometimes used to go back home in the holidays from various boarding schools, and then after I left care I went back to live at home a couple of times but not for any length of time.

One of the regrets I have now is that I have nothing from my childhood, no friends—that's a big regret. I can't change it but it's something I miss. Other people have friends they've known from childhood and I just don't have that. I have this photo of me with a school class at my first primary school in Bristol and the only two people I remember from the picture are myself and the teacher.

I don't remember the transition to secondary school because of being in care. If you were in care, you just went from school to school, different classroom to different classroom. I couldn't read till I was 13 or 14. I never really learned to read and write properly till after I left school, when I actually started reading books and taught myself to read. I left my last approved school aged 17. I did do two CSEs at the approved school, English and maths. I think I got a G and an F! I couldn't spell to save my life until 1989. I would have to have a dictionary with me all the time. I finally learned to spell on a computer.

• • •

I remember the day when I was taken back into care and I think an incident that happened on that day probably shaped the way I felt for the rest of my life. I never felt I escaped that incident.

My social worker turned up at the house. I'd been to the county court where I was made a ward of court and I was going to be taken into care. I didn't understand all this, but one summer's day this guy turned up and he asked me if I wanted to go on holiday and of course, like any 7-year-old kid being offered a couple of weeks' holiday, I said yes.

I didn't go back home again. I never really went home again after that. This social worker took me to a children's home on the outskirts of Bristol. It was pretty grim. I don't remember actually arriving but I remember being upstairs in the bathroom. I was told to take all my clothes off and I had a bath, then they combed through my hair with a nit comb. They got me into my pyjamas and took me downstairs and into this big room where all the children and all the staff were assembled.

The headmistress had my underpants and they were soiled and stained, and I remember she held them up and she told everyone what my name was. She said I was called Martin Teale—I was christened

Christopher but because they already had a Christopher in the children's home, they decided to call me Martin, my second name. So I was known as Martin until I left care, though I hated the name. Anyway the headmistress said 'This is Martin Teale' and she dangled my dirty underpants in front of everybody and said 'This is the type of boy we've got'. That was my first day back in care, and I don't think I've ever lived that incident down.

I used to go back to that home on holidays from different schools and I never felt part of anything there. I always felt I was at a disadvantage because there were staff there that knew me and I always thought that people remembered that incident on my first day. They might not have remembered, but to me it was very real. I don't know how anybody could do that to a child but that was how the care system seemed to operate. It seemed to operate by humiliation—they would humiliate the child. There were some kind people there too of course, but I hated going back there.

I think when you're scripted as a disruptive, out-of-control child, you're treated like that. I knew what I wanted: I wanted love, and someone to hold me and give me a cuddle, but you didn't get that. You got stuck in a corner. I would say that a lot of the things that happened to me were torture. They were not only physical torture, they were psychological torture. Like making me sit behind a chair while the television was on so I couldn't see the television, though I could hear it. Or making me sit with my head stuck in a corner. I know that happened to a lot of kids but that doesn't mean it was right. Beating with a slipper wasn't right either.

●　●　●

The first time I was sexually abused was when I was seven. It happened in a boarding school in Somerset where these two guys came in to me and another kid, and they paid us to let them fiddle around with us. I don't know if it had any real impact. I don't know if I thought about it. But the real abuse started with this housemaster when I was at another residential school. It started quite simply. I was in a dormitory and he used to read stories to us at night, and then he'd go round and give every boy a kiss on the forehead. That's how it started: then it got to a kiss on the cheeks, and his hands would always be doing something as well, with your chest or your tummy, and it just went from there. Over a period of time he just went a bit further and a bit further and the kiss was on your lips, and the hand was on your private parts. I don't remember resisting because I didn't really think anything about it at the time. Besides, he gave me things which nobody else had given me. He gave me hugs and kisses and was kind and bought me presents, kept me out of trouble.

What he did to me was horrendous. The way he abused me was all for his own gratification. He took my childhood away and he turned me into an extremely disturbed child. I might have been disturbed before but I became even more disturbed and that was never picked up by anybody.

I've still got images in my mind and sometimes I wish I'd made it all up, that the images weren't so real. I wish it would go away but it doesn't. It's not just about the abuse, it's about the tastes and the smells and about a certain atmosphere. Something will happen, somebody will say something, and that will trigger off all the memories.

This carried on for about three years. Continually. Even when I was on holiday in different children's homes he'd come down and see me. Then I remember later when I was 14 I was at this home in Gloucestershire and I hated the place—it was just like the workhouse. I was supposed to be on holiday but it was run like a workhouse. One day I was in one of the dormitories because I was ill, and this other boy and I set a fire in another dormitory. It got put out but we were taken into the head's study and asked to own up. Of course neither of us said anything, so they separated us and the guy who ran the place got a cricket stump and he beat me until I admitted that I'd started this fire. At 14 I didn't admit to anything so it took a long time to beat out of me that I'd done it. I've still got the injuries now.

When he'd left I did a bunk and went off to the police. But all they did was ship me straight back to the home in a van. So I ran away from this place, got on a train to Paddington and got picked up by British Transport police. I told them an out-and-out lie. I mentioned the name of that housemaster who had abused me. I said he had paid for my ticket and I'd just made a mistake and I'd got on the wrong train. I said if they phoned him, he would confirm what I was saying. And he did. I was given first class travel straight back to him, with sandwiches and tea and goodness knows what else. The irony is, I was trying to get away from this guy abusing me, and the only place I could go was back to the place where he was. That happened a few times: whenever I was in trouble I just had to call him. It's hard to describe abuse. The only reason I think I could ever reoffend if somebody abused my son in that way. He's nearly seven and I have quite unreal fears of abuse being perpetrated on him.

That abuse I've described was only the first part. He wasn't the only man who abused me. My social worker abused me when I told him. He tried to pass me round to other paedophiles. This went on for years. When I was 17, I had a paedophile put a gun to me and threaten to shoot me. I watched him load the shotgun, and he actually put it into my chest and said 'If I pull the trigger nobody's going to care'.

It wasn't long after that incident with the gun that I tried to commit suicide. Normally I tried to avoid drink and drugs because of things that had happened with my mother. I'd discovered she was an alcoholic and I'd seen her trying to commit suicide a few times. I'd also found out that my real father was an alcoholic. He was in the American Forces and I believe he'd killed somebody. But on this occasion when I was 17 I just went down to the pub, drank as much brandy as I could and took as many paracetamol as I could. I spent four days in intensive care in hospital. When I came to I was extremely angry and violent.

• • •

I've used a lot of violence, and I've had a lot of violence used against me. I'm lucky I've only got one conviction for violence. I whacked someone over the head and gave him a serious beating. I put another guy's teeth through his jaw. You don't know the strength you've got. It could take four people to control me, though I was very thin and not very big. Violence would have been my most repetitive crime if I'd been convicted of it, but I very rarely was. If I committed the same offences today as I did then I would have had a long record of serious violence.

The first crime I was convicted of was the theft of an orange, some cigarettes and a few coppers from an old boy's cottage. I used to go there and chat to him and one day I just put my hand through his window and took the stuff from the windowsill. I suppose you could say I was a burglar.

I never had any legal representation when I was convicted of that first offence. I was just told to go into court and plead guilty. When they said 'You're going to approved school for three years' I remember I just cried and cried and cried. The police were gutted as well, that I was getting three years for an orange and a couple of coppers.

Then when I was about 13 I got caught shoplifting. I got a caution and I had to take the stuff back. I've never shoplifted since because I just felt embarrassed about this guy giving me a lecture about shoplifting.

Isolation and boredom led me to shoplift. I was ostracised. I was just a mixed-up kid and I used to commit petty offences. I used to go round taking the odd cigarette from a packet. One of the worst things I did was taking some money from Sister Muriel when I went to stay with her.

• • •

I was devastated when I was first sent to the approved school, though I don't know why, because I was used to being sent to remand homes on holiday from boarding school. At the approved school I was different from the others. My accent didn't fit in, and I was an oddball, I wasn't part of the crowd. I was isolated. I was always fairly much on my own.

I got bullied but I was also one of those people that people were sometimes afraid to turn their back on. People were worried what I'd do: they thought I was a bit of a nutter. Somebody once stuck a palette knife in me and I just waited for them—so they were always looking over their shoulder. People don't like that sort of bloke around. I served over two years of that three-year sentence.

Some of my later offences I don't think I would have necessarily even have been taken to court for, except for my name. But I was who I was and the police always treated me like that. Mention my name and that was it, you were nicked. I've got seven or eight convictions, but I can hardly count the number of times I've been in a police cell assisting them with their enquiries. Sometimes I'd be picked up three or four times a week. Now that I'm a probation officer, lads come along and say to me that the police keep hassling them, and I can believe it—they *do* keep hassling you. So I say to them 'The longer you go without committing an offence, the less likely you are to be hassled': though in my case, it was only after I changed my name back to the name I was christened with that a lot of the hassle stopped.

The only other time I was in prison was for fine default. I'd been convicted of other crimes as well, and I decided I couldn't be bothered with people coming to my house all the time: bailiffs and the police. So one Sunday night I thought I'd hand myself in, get it out of the way and start afresh.

Which is what I did. I got 90 days in prison and I served 45. I managed to con a gay bloke out of some money in the nick and paid off my fines. Here I was, I'd been abused by other people, but at that particular time I hated gay men. In fact I had a phobia about men in general. There were very few men I could actually get close to. So being in prison in a cell with four other blokes was a nightmare. I don't know how I coped really. I was petrified. You hear all sorts of things about adult prisons and I was petrified there was going to be some sort of raping going on. Even though I was in my 20s by this time I was absolutely petrified.

●   ●   ●

What made me change my life? The only person to influence my offending behaviour was *me*—because I never ever felt comfortable committing crimes. I never thought that this was the way my life should be. I thought I had more in me than just that.

I've been offered to get back into crime—people have offered me things. I still know criminals and I've been asked to get involved in various frauds, things that would be easy. There's been lots of opportunities—but that's not me. I've never believed that's me, because I don't think I'm a criminal.

One of the things that helped change me was this: I remember when I was growing up people would say to me, 'You'll be no good, you'll always be the same'. That was repeated to me again and again throughout my life: 'You're just a waste of space, you're a waste of time'. Lots of people have said that. I remember somebody sitting down and saying to me 'You're at approved school now, you'll be in borstal next year, then you'll be in prison. You'll be in prison continually and you'll keep going back there because that's the sort of person you are. That's where you've come from, and that's the way your life is going to be'. And I suddenly thought 'Why should they dominate and run my life? Why should they tell me how my life is going to turn out and what I'm going to do?' I thought the only way I could beat them was by not allowing myself to be what they'd scripted me to be—just another con.

So I've tried to learn from my mistakes. I'm always trying to push myself a bit more forward, trying to take opportunities. When I left care and moved into a different circle, I changed my whole life. I reinvented my whole life, so I didn't have this horror of the life I'd had.

At first, with all the people that I introduced myself to, I made up a lot of things. I pretended my father had worked for a big company, that my mother lived in Hampshire, that I went to a private school, that I had holidays abroad. But of course there was no foundation to it, and people remember lies. One day, when I was in my mid-30s, one of my friends took me to one side and he said 'You're a really nice bloke but you're full of shit!' After that I decided I wasn't going to be ashamed of my past. It all happened to me, so I decided to put it in context.

That was back in 1987. I'd decided by then I wanted to be a probation officer. I'd done some voluntary work but it was a question of getting my confidence. People said to me 'You've got the ability, your life deserves better'.

I see myself as an under-achiever, because of what the state and the system did to me as a child. After approved school I did so many different jobs it was unbelievable. I was just drifting from job to job. Had I been given the opportunities and the chances that everyday people get, I know that I'd have been a lot further on today—not just materialistically but also spiritually. And I think I would not have done a lot of the things that I have done. There are things that I bitterly regret.

I have extreme difficulty with personal relationships, particularly with women. Although I say I trust people, I don't think I really do. I don't have the ability to take someone at face value, and to accept something that's given for nothing without waiting for the catch. Because always in the past there *was* a catch. It's dreadful how you tend to script your own future as it's coming. Most of my relationships have ended in chaos and I think if I'd been given the right type of care, the right type of education and upbringing, I wouldn't have had the deep-seated problems that I have today, that I'm still trying to work out, that still make me feel bad, still make me feel guilty, still make me feel I have to keep apologising. From being born in prison up to what I am today, I think I've been a success. But inside I'm still telling myself I'm a failure. There are so many things unresolved.

I still feel bad that I've got a lot of criminal convictions. I can't duck it, it's there. Some of the offences were petty offences but I know they were offences that had an impact on the people they affected. You're not born a criminal. You're not born a bad person. You're not born delinquent. It's the way society treats you—that's how you grow up.

I've had to be tough and I look quite hard. I've got tattoos. The first one I had done five or six days after I got to approved school. The word it spells is 'LOVE'.

Hugh Collins

Hugh is 47 and is now a writer, the author of a critically acclaimed autobiography. He lives in Edinburgh with his wife, the painter Caroline McNairn. Brought up in the Glasgow gangs, he served his first custodial sentence at the age of 16 and spent only one year outside prison in the next ten years. In 1977 he was sentenced to life for murder, and was given an additional seven years for three attempted murders of prison staff. He was released in 1993 after serving 16 years.

My dad was a hero figure to me, a real Robin Hood. I was born in Stoke Hill hospital in Glasgow and I was an only child, and in 1952, when I was about 18 months old, my father was sentenced to ten years' imprisonment. At the time he got the ten years my mother had disappeared as well—it turned out she'd been imprisoned for prostitution.

I grew up with the knowledge that my father had got ten years, and that it was for bank robbery. But in fact it was for slashing the manager of a dance hall. Apparently at that time the idea of the ten-year sentence was to act as a deterrent against the razor slashings in Glasgow. Before that you'd get an average of 18 months or two years. So my father kind of walked into overnight notoriety. I don't think there was anything special about him, but he'd got caught up in this notoriety and became a gangster figure in Glasgow.

My dad's friend Ginger McBride gave me a dagger, my very first knife. Ginger and the others filled my head with stories about my father being a bank robber, this villain with a big heart who stole from rich people to look after the poor.

I can remember being taken to see my father in Peterhead prison. At this stage I was told that he was in the RAF, so I used to think the screws were pilots. I can remember seeing him, he must have been about 22 I think, this really handsome-looking man, and this reinforced my hero image of him. Then I'd be told stories by guys coming from the jail, bringing me wee presents. They'd tell me a lot of nonsense—'Your dad runs the jails, he's a big shot'—all this kind of stuff. So I grew up with that, and it had an effect on me in primary school.

At first I was proud of it. I stood up in the classroom and said my dad was a bank robber. It was one of those situations where you get asked, 'What does your dad do?'—and I stood up and I said, 'My dad's a bank robber'—and of course, everyone was in hysterics.

• • •

It was my mother who really suffered from the anger I had as a child because of my old man getting ten years. I felt if he'd been next in the queue, or a week earlier or something like that, it might have made a difference. I felt my family'd been ripped apart by some judge deciding to use my father as a deterrent. It wiped out my life, wiped out my mother's life.

I really hated my mother. One of my most disturbing early memories that had a big impact on me was seeing my mother having sex with some guy. It was the noises I heard first. They'd given me a toy yacht to play with, but I went in and actually saw them, and at first I thought he was hurting her. I hated her after that. It took me years and years just to accept that she was a woman and my dad was in jail, but as I was growing up I felt that she'd abandoned him, and I felt this kind of prejudice towards her. I'd had all these things drummed into me about my dad being a really good guy who robbed rich people and gave to the poor, and in my eyes she'd betrayed him.

After a while I went to live with my granny—my father's mother. I'd been taken up to visit her before and I always loved going up there. There was a big, big family and I was the youngest, so everybody looked after me. There were three aunts and four uncles, but the uncles were more like brothers to me, and I grew up with them. I lost contact with my mother—she re-married and had another son.

My gran couldn't do much to help me in my education—she'd too big a family to look after. She was just a wee Irish woman, an Irish immigrant—the area that we lived in was all Irish immigrants, all Catholics. But all the same, I quite enjoyed school at first. My grandad from my mother's side was a lecturer for the Socialist Party, and he taught me how to read and write and do arithmetic even before I went to school. He'd give me half a crown if I did well. But when I got to school that went against me. They said I was too young to be doing sums at that kind of level, and I got accused of cheating at mental arithmetic. That certainly had a bad effect on me. Then I think I became embarrassed about my father's imprisonment being common knowledge.

So as I got older, I felt different. I remember feeling rebellious but never really knowing why at first. Then I knew I was different because of my old man. I started wearing army belts and I had a lot of fights when anyone said anything about my dad. If somebody slagged him, I'd be up the back of the school with them. Then I started to take pride in the fact that I felt different. I started hanging round with the fighters in the yard. My father was a hard man so I felt it was expected of me to follow in his footsteps.

I began dogging school for weeks on end. My dogging period was filled with adventures: I stripped lead from derelict houses and broke into a van and stole boxes of tea. Around this time I had my first experience of the police when I was caught breaking into a baker's shop.

● ● ●

I can well remember the day of my father's release from prison. I was out in the front close when all the cars arrived. He was totally fucked up when he finished that sentence. At that time there wasn't things like rehabilitation. I don't believe in rehabilitation—I don't think it happens in prisons anyway, though they might be trying to do it now. But at that stage in the prison game, people were just fired out the doorway with 20 quid and told to get on with it. They were totally institutionalised by the conditions at that time. They weren't allowed to talk to each other and they had really basic conditions. So he must have been fucked right up. And losing his wife as well.

By the time my father had finished the ten years, I'd already joined gangs and all this kind of stuff. Yet at the same time I was an altar boy, and I was being primed to be a priest, of all things! Or else I was supposed to join the army, or some other kind of job with a uniform. All the Irish families had a son that was either a priest or a copper. One day I went in the chapel and found my granny in tears because she couldn't pay the rent. That night I went out with another boy to steal and get money for the rent.

About this time—I must have been about 12—I stabbed my older brother, the one above me, Alex—he was really one of my uncles of course. He was always beating me up: it was the time of Cassius Clay, everybody was wanting to be boxers, and I was Alex's personal punchbag, though he didn't mean any real viciousness by it. One day we were fixing a bike and he hit me with a steel ruler. I turned on him and stabbed him with a screwdriver. It punctured his lung, and everybody in the family was a bit shocked so I got left alone after that. It kind of changed things.

By the time I got to St Roch's senior secondary, I was very involved in the Glasgow gangs. At the junior school I was only involved in petty stuff, breaking into shops, stuff like that, and getting caught by the police and taken home to my gran. But once you got into senior secondary, you started thinking about your ticket, army belts and all this kind of stuff. By this time I was on my way—I had the studded army belt, the long hair, the sky-blue denims.

It was a kind of wild area. St Roch's was a Catholic school and there was a Protestant school, and we used to go up and fight with them. I was steeped in sectarian stuff at the time. It seems unbelievable now, but teachers used to say, 'Go on, smash the windows'—they'd give you the nod for it.

I was obsessed with football throughout school, and played for the school team in both my primary and secondary schools. It was part of life, playing football, playing behind school or in the streets. I had trials for Glasgow Juniors, but I was embarrassed because I had my brother's boots on, so I started to shy away from it. I was good at swimming as well. I went to a couple of galas and I won a few medals.

But all this ended when I was expelled from school at the age of 13 for having long hair. We'd started to listen to the Beatles, and everybody was growing their hair, but mine was just a wee fringe. St Roch's was just a scabby school and you didn't even wear a uniform, but the headmaster wanted everybody to get their hair cut. I refused and he put me in the lassies' class. I was quite happy in there, passing notes all over the place. Then I had my hair cropped very short. The headmaster took me out and ridiculed me and then he ridiculed my granny in front of the whole school. So I rammed the nut on him and then did a runner. I broke his nose. The school took it to court, and that was me expelled. I was delighted with it to be honest. But that was the end of my education.

• • •

About this time—I must have been 14 by then—I met up with Albert Faulds. This guy Albert came from the same background as me, a big family, quite a poor family. Actually I was terrified of him. He was a really vicious guy who liked to go out and fight with people. He'd just got out of approved school and like me he was hanging around with nothing to do. Both of us kind of looked up to the Kray twins and John McVicar, and later, as a young offender, I had posters of them up in my cell.

About this age I had my first experience with drugs. I started off with bombers.[1] My old man gave me and Albert a big bag of them. He gave us purple hearts as well. I think we nearly ODd[2] at one time. Our skin was going all black, and we weren't eating anything—we were a bit of a mess. We were drinking cider and wine as well, taking a couple of slugs, and kidding on we were drunk. A couple of times I got steaming with the cider, but I hated the taste of drink. So I'd kid on I was drinking it. But the bombers—we were really off our heads with those things, just yapping and yapping for days at a time.

At the age of 15 I started a trade[3] as a painter and decorator, and bringing home a wage meant everything. I couldn't wait to go to work,

---

[1] Amphetamines, speed

[2] Overdosed

[3] Apprenticeship

just to wear the boiler suit and have a wage packet. But that only lasted about six weeks, because before I finished the trade I was sent to borstal for breach of the peace and having an offensive weapon. It was a meat cleaver that Albert gave me, and I was in a gang fight. We called our gang The Shamrock and eventually it had about 50 in it. I honestly don't think I was conscious of breaking the law—it was just a way of life. Getting a custodial sentence, being put into jail, brought it home to me, but you weren't really conscious of things like the law. You knew there was coppers and you kept out of their road, but your way of life was just criminal all the time.

But when I was first sent into borstal just after I turned 16 I was greeting.[4] I felt everything had been taken away from me. It was the terror of what my granny would say—things like that, things that men don't talk about.

My first experience of custody was in a boys' remand home called Larch Grove. I felt lost and afraid. Everything I'd known was outside. I think this is the immediate gut reaction you feel on every arrest. As the years went by I learned to adjust and camouflage my immediate losses very quickly but that fear was always there. I experienced the same thing years later in the jail, going into solitary confinement. All my pals were up the stairs. I think it was just the loss of everything. The familiarity had been taken away from you again.

But at the same time I do remember making a decision to become seriously dangerous to make my father proud of his boy.

So my first time in custody was for breach of the peace, weapons and violence, and after that it was a gradual escalation. But the bigger the sentence you got, the more you got used to it. You became kind of fearless in a way. You'd just go into the jail, and you knew that it wasn't going to do anything to you. Jail was just about being beaten up by the screws.

I had a tantrum in Larch Grove remand home, so I was sent to Barlinnie jail's borstal wing. I stayed there two weeks before I was transferred to Friarton detention centre. It was miles from anywhere and it was a really brutal regime. Then I was sent to a borstal called Polmont. When I'd been in the borstal nine months, my granny died, and after that I kind of lost contact with most of my family. They all went off and got married and things. This was where the gangs really became your family. It was my mates from the gang that were waiting at the borstal gate for me.

When I got out, everything had changed. In borstal we'd all been running about trying to emulate the Kray twins with the suits and the mod style. But when I came out everybody had long hair, all talking

---

[4] Crying

like Americans. But Albert had stayed the same. When I came out of borstal I drifted from job to job but eventually I found stealing much easier than working.

I hadn't touched any drugs in borstal, but the first day I was out somebody spiked me with two tabs of black microdot.[5] I had 16 hours of just pure hallucinations. It was terrifying—I didn't enjoy it at all. Then I got into hash, I loved hash.

The drugs were always there. At that time you didn't need money to get drugs. You just went to somebody and said, 'Can you get this?' and they'd get you it. It's different these days where you've got junkies breaking into houses, or shoplifting, to try and feed a habit. At that time you didn't need to pay for this stuff, people gave you it.

I first mainlined heroin in Perth Prison in 1975 when I was serving a two year sentence. I used to sit in a cell with a guy and he'd mainline it. And I asked him 'What kind of stone do you get off it?' And he's an Edinburgh guy and he says 'It's barry, Hughie'. *Barry* means good. So I said, 'Fuck it, do us one up'. Ever since that first time I've had problems with heroin all through my life. I loved the feeling of heroin. I'd rather be on heroin than be straight. I loved it because it cushioned me from everything. Heroin obliterated all the pain and I loved that drug more than anything or anyone. I left prison with a heroin habit, and within a matter of months I was back in prison charged with three attempted murders.

But I don't think the drugs contributed to the violence. I got caught up in violence. I enjoyed the danger. I really got enjoyment out of fear, and the release you get out of the violence. That was a much bigger problem than the drugs.

I recall the alteration in attitudes towards me the more violent I became. Violence was acceptable and respected. The Glasgow gangs appeared to disintegrate for a time as a result of deterrent sentencing, but prison brought together the most violent of them. I got hooked on jumping counters, snatches and extortion, all with guys from gangs I had met in prison.

• • •

After my father came out of jail I'd gradually become more and more involved with him. He got stabbed in the neck one time, and I got the guy that done him. My father was quite proud of this kind of thing. I stabbed this guy—I stabbed him a couple of times. My father was there, and he never questioned me in any way, or challenged any kind of behaviour. In fact he was proud of me and he used to introduce me to

---

[5] Tablet form of LSD

his mates as the leader of The Shamrock Gang. His attitude was that if you get caught, don't start greeting[6] if the police come up to the door. So the violence was kind of let loose in me, and this went on happening for roughly ten years. Albert and I were always up and down to Manchester shoplifting, all that kind of stuff. And then we came back to Glasgow and got into extortion, just marching into shops demanding money. An ex-copper put us onto brewery pubs, so we hit all them as well. We were taking a lot of money, and we were giving a lot away, trying to impress people, buying big drinks—all the usual showing-off stuff. Albert was the most vicious guy I'd ever come across, and we had a fall out in Manchester, so I took a bit of a back seat to give him a chance to cool down. We'd been chased by coppers, and I'd dived into a canal and nearly drowned. My bottle went after that, and I said I couldn't go out thieving any more. Albert took it the wrong way, and we ended up falling out.

After that first borstal sentence I was soon caught shoplifting again and given six months in Barlinnie Young Offenders' unit. In fact between the ages of 16 and 26 I only spent about a year outside. Between 1967 to 1977 I was in Barlinnie, Saughton, Perth—mostly for petty crimes. I remember there was one occasion when I came out after serving a month's sentence. I got released that morning, and I had to go to the High Court—it was a gang thing, perjury—and I had to go straight back to prison in the van. So I'd only been out for about three hours! Other times, I'd maybe have two or three cases to go up for.

•　•　•

In 1977 at the age of 26 I got sent to prison for life for murder. The guy I killed was in a gang called The Peg. He was quite a big guy, he could handle himself. I'd got into a flash with him in Barlinnie young offenders'[7] which was a really fucking brutal place. Somebody had said something when we were watching TV, and he turned round and dug me up.

So I said, 'I'll see you in the hall then', and I went over to the screws and said I wanted a square go[8] with this guy. They told me to fuck off—though they'd usually leave the two of you in a room and only got involved if the fighting got out of hand.

In the mornings, your door usually got opened about six o'clock. But that next morning my door's opened at quarter to six, this guy's in with

---

[6] Crying

[7] Institution

[8] Fight

an iron bar and he's done all my joints. He really took me down—I couldn't walk properly for about six months,

He got liberated that day, so I couldn't make a comeback. Then I never came across him for about six years. The day I met him again, that was the day I killed him in a fight in a pub.

I've never really come to terms with what I did, although it's really no different to any of the other violence I've done. The others were just lucky to survive. But something changed. When I knew he'd died, something in me changed and I felt like a monster. It's never been the same since.

My Catholic upbringing plays a part. I try to be realistic and say he had a blade and I had a blade, but when I'm on my own it's the Catholic thing that comes up, so it's fear. I don't know if it's remorse.

After the murder it went all bizarre. I just walked away. I went into a chip shop, wringing with blood, there was steam coming off me. Everybody just went 'Jesus Christ!' and I went 'I'll have a fish supper'. I got my fish supper, put the blade in the dustbin and walked up the street. I just walked up the road, jumped on the bus and sat across from the driver. It was a Saturday night, the bus was jam-packed and it was noisy, but it just went totally silent. One guy was looking at me, and I said 'What are you's all fucking looking at?' and everybody just put their heads down the whole journey.

I went over to my house, and I'd a double-barrelled shotgun in there. I pulled my shirt off, and jammed the gun in the door. I think what was going through my head was 'I'm done—I know I'm going to get done here, but I'm not doing a fucking life sentence'. I think if somebody had knocked on the door, I'd probably have shot them. In my head I was going: 'If I shoot a copper, they'll shoot me—and that'll be that over with'. I know that sounds like real cowboy stuff, but we were all crazy on acid and heroin.

We were recklessly dangerous. Ordinary people could walk into you, and end up stabbed, and then your interpretation was: 'They done me up'. You justified it like that. You were butchering people, and you thought 'They fucking bumped into me!'

When I got the life sentence, I really went right ahead with these screws—I think I was trying to get them to kill me. I stabbed three screws. Just convicted of murder, I stabbed three screws!

When I was first in Perth prison they tried to put me in the state mental hospital. They stuck me in front of two psychiatrists, but I never got committed. I told the governor that I was going to try and kill a screw if I got let out of the cell. They had me in a dungeon in Perth for just over a year. They use cells that the public don't see, cells they say are not in use. So my mother's come to Perth prison, and she's banging on the gates, wanting to see the governor. She's worried—there's been rumours that I've had my legs broken, been killed.

They brought her in to see me. I was covered in blood, and when you're like that they just come in and hose you down. There were no stitches, i t was just all cuts, and my head was bleeding. It was a horrible image, but she was the only person I had on the outside that could help me, and I clung on to her then. That's when I started to build a relationship with her. She visited me for the whole 16 years, every visit she was allowed.

The same year I got the lifer I was given a further seven years for the three attempted murders of prison staff. I did 16 years on that sentence—I went inside in 1977 and came out in 1993.

• • •

In 1978 I was transferred to the Special Unit[9] at Barlinnie. In the unit, they sort of latched on to the idea of 'deprivation'. In the seventies that was the kind of 'in' term and it was used as an excuse for everything.

There was one time when my mother came into the Barlinnie special unit. I remember I was eating a packet of crisps, and you could hear it all over the cell, and she just broke down for some reason. I tried to put my arm round her, but I physically couldn't—it just felt alien. She's lying in hospital just now with a brain haemorrhage, and I don't know how to deal with it. Recently, when I was looking at her in the hospital, I just thought, what a waste of all these years. I've lost out, and so's she. It's her that's really the victim of it all. It was a difficult life for her. I look at her now and I feel ashamed of myself. I regret everything. The things I have done to her. Called her a whore, just really abused her. It was blatant that any time I went to see her, it was just to get money off her, and then I'd be off again.

My dad appeared at the Unit to see me too. He was in shock. He said to my mother at one point, 'I think we've produced a monster'. I thought, 'What a fucking cheek he's got—I chipped people for him!' I felt he was trying to use my situation to get back together with her, and I saw it as a weakness. And it shows you how far I had come as a criminal, when I could look at my father and think 'that weak bastard'. I felt no sympathy nor any kind of emotion, no upset. Just, 'That fucking arsehole should be backing me up now'.

It's ironic—I've not spoken to my father, and he's not spoken to me since 1980, because of the Barlinnie unit. He just couldn't handle the place—first name terms with staff, staff coming out on your visits, staff talking away to him. But I'd formed real strong relationships with one or two guys in there.

---

[9] A therapeutic unit: see the discussion of such units in the *Introduction*

Jimmy Boyle was in there and he took an interest in me and pointed me in another direction which involved tough discipline, and learning the harsh facts of life. To get me off the drugs, Jimmy and this other guy, a prison officer called Malcolm Mackenzie, would challenge me into the yard with gloves, and you couldn't back down. So I was getting doings every day but I came off the drugs.

At this time my dad was still coming to see me, and I think he was angry that he'd never had a chance like that himself. One day he came up to see me, and he sat with me in my cell. You could have a visit from nine in the morning until nine at night. Now that may sound great, but if you sit with your mother or your father all day, you're going, 'Jesus Christ—when are they going to leave?'

In the unit it was as if you got an overdose of everything, and I think that's what the idea was. It was like an adult nursery. Let them act out their fantasies, with the sex, the sculpture, the art therapy side of it, let it burn them right out. Art therapy provided an avenue to pour out all the anger, but being handed a paintbrush didn't change my life. Only people have the ability to invite change in someone else's circumstances. I was neurotic when I was in there, paranoid about everybody, but I thought I was normal. When I look back on it, I was certainly in a real state, but I thought it was everybody else that was in a state, and it was me that was normal.

Jimmy Boyle had been in the unit about four years at that point. He'd gone right ahead in Barlinnie jail, and I always respected him. He was another kind of hero figure to me. In Scotland, everybody liked Jimmy Boyle—he was really well respected. So I wouldn't fuck the place up, in case it damaged his chances of getting out. He was trying to straighten himself out too. I was fortunate I landed there at that time because Jimmy Boyle was the person who had the most influence over me. I hate to admit it, but he was. He was into sculpture, getting on with staff. My dad was forever coming up and saying 'Jimmy's just working his ticket. Don't you start getting caught up in this'. I was still thinking 'What the fuck's going on here?' I was still saying to myself, 'It's just a con'. But I actually thought Jimmy'd read my files because he was telling me things about myself that nobody else knew about. In fact it was just common sense. In a lot of ways Jimmy became a father figure to me.

You found you got lured into defending the place, and defending relationships with screws and things like that. The times I used to sit and say to myself 'What the fuck am I doing here, forming relationships with people that wouldn't spit on me out in the street?' You'd a lot of the middle classes coming in, because we were like the pet lions—it was a trendy thing at that time to come and visit us.

One time I broke into the governor's desk and read my own files— and they had me down as a sociopath. Soon after this, we were all sitting in a cell and—this shows you how stupid I was—I said to Jimmy, 'I'm not too bad—they've got me down as a sociopath'. Everybody looks at me and wee Malky, one of the screws, he says, 'Do you know what that means?' and I says 'Yes, kind of friendly'—which is what I thought it meant because of the word *social*. So Malky says 'Jesus Christ, you'd better fucking wise up!'

It was like an education to read these files, and after I read them I understood a lot about fear. Part of the reports said things like 'If he's dishevelled-looking, just give him space'. So any time I felt like just messing about, I wouldn't shave, and just roughed the hair up a bit, and started looking like a zombie, and they would just all clear out of the road!

I had a right blow-up one day. Suddenly I just couldn't handle the place. Sitting with my family, all I wanted to talk about was stabbing the screws, what the screws had done to me, and if it went off that subject, then I'd just go silent. Everybody was getting nervous. It was really strenuous coming to visits with me because I was very disturbed— I'd become disturbed by the violence. This one day I took cocaine and smack, and I was playing snooker, looking for trouble. I said 'I hate this fucking place. Get me out!' The unit seemed to be taking everything away from me. Screws were getting familiar—I mean, before that I'd never spoken to a screw in my life. Any sentence I had done, I'd always had this image of my dad in my mind, this Robin Hood character, and his attitude was you just don't speak to these people, even if they're smiling at you or trying to help you. Then to find myself with these young guys, these screws trying to be familiar! I just wasn't handling it. So I had a big mad tantrum, I was going to kill everybody.

I got up next morning, and there was no punishment. But Jimmy took me out for a walk, and he says 'You need to get this out of you. You're totally fucked up. I know you think you're normal and we're bonkers, but it's you that's off your head. But you can recover from it. I'm not working my ticket here, I'm for real'. So he gave me a—not exactly a lecture, but an insight into what he was about, and as he started to talk, I saw just how fucked up I was.

Then I started to copy everything he did. He would get up at six in the morning and go out for a jog. I would be waiting, and I'd go jogging behind him. He must have been demented with me. And then when he was doing his sculpture, I'd be saying 'What are you doing now, Jimmy?'—and he'd give me sculpture tools. And then I'd get up at six next morning again to go jogging with him. In the end he just cracked up—he just went 'Fuck off!' Then I started to hate him, I felt rejected by him.

After the Barlinnie unit I was sent to an ordinary prison, Saughton in Edinburgh. I'd stayed in the unit more than seven years. There'd been a lot of publicity, and psycho headlines all the time, and you start to think it's for real. Then I went back into the traditional system for the remaining eight years of my sentence and I got a right rough ride with the screws. The warders there tried to put my back to the wall. The Scottish Office civil servants described the provocation as testing, part of rehabilitation.

Saughton was just a first offenders' jail but you had to kind of weave your way through the place, because there was always somebody who was going to fire into you to prove something. There was a couple of confrontations and I had to go in with an iron bar and a knife tied on to my hands, just to call a guy's bluff, though I knew he would back down. There were just daft things like that but I managed to get through it.

• • •

Being released from prison proved more difficult for me than going in. Everything I'd lived for over the past 30 years had been taken away in what seemed like a flash. One minute I'm being tested, and the next thing I'm passing through the prison gates for the last time. Through those 16 years I thought I wanted to be out. But I soon began to realise that prison was all that I knew and wanted to keep. In prison I knew where I stood. I had power in there. I had a reputation, I was a somebody. And then . . . wham! I'm on the street being treated like some arsehole.

When I first got out, back on the street I didn't have a fucking clue what was going on. I'd been used to walking into jail dining halls, and guys getting out your road, just because it's you. But suddenly you're in a bar and someone's got their elbow in your face. I hated bouncers in bars, and if they even looked at me I would go straight into them. So there was a side of me wanted back into prison.

That first day outside I was full of heroin before nightfall, desperately trying to figure out a way to get myself back into jail. When I was first out, if I was leaving the flat, I had to have a destination to go to. I couldn't just go out for a walk or something. I'd go faster and faster, and it would get like a kind of hysteria. I was bonkers when I came out. It was just a flood of emotions came out of me. I was amongst artists, living in a gallery, and I thought there was cardboard people outside. I smashed up a couple of times, and then I said, 'What the fuck have I done?'

Caroline, my wife, took the brunt of the frustration for those first two years. We have a good solid relationship now but back then I could easily have killed again. I wanted to kill somebody—anybody. I could easily have slid into a scenario, justifying my actions. Fortunately I had people, friends who knew that problems would surface, friends who protected me—and I made it.

People have allowed me to move on. Caroline, her family, friends, neighbours, local shopkeepers. They let me live my life without having to be dangerous. I grew up with heroes—John McVicar, Reggie Kray, Jimmy Boyle. These people have also let me move on to other, more important things in life. The most important things in my life are Caroline and my family, having friends, having freedom. I have found my self-respect through these things, although I've never claimed to have changed—it's a word I very rarely use.

Caroline's been great, sorted me out, gave me space and things like that. And I've been surrounded by good people. I don't mean good people in that they are all nice, but they are people with patience.

In February 1997 I published my autobiography.[10] The day before publication the drugs squad dragged me off the street and terrorized my wife. I was thrown back into jail for a week and charged with dealing. That was enough to have my parole licence revoked. The drugs squad dropped the charge the day before the trial and I was fined £150 for one joint and some pain killers.

I'm 47 now and I'm skint. I don't have much money but I enjoy being out. It's been nearly five years now—the longest I've ever been out of jail since I was 16. I really want to experience my life without drugs, without that power kick. I've been in a couple of situations where I've been put on the spot, but I've talked my way out of it. I'm a firm believer in counting to ten. Those first couple of seconds, your legs start shaking, but you know you're not going to go down with anybody. If I take a doing, I take a doing. I recognise danger now—I don't go near places where there's a bouncer—whereas before I'd be saying, 'I'll go where I fucking like!'

Work and relationships are really the most important things in my life now. Caroline's middle-class, and her family went through a nightmare: it nearly ruined her career.

I've got a wee nephew, Caroline's sister's wee boy. I saw him born. Wee Fraser's had a big impact on me, watching him growing up. I've never had a relationship with a wean[11] before, but now I've watched a wean growing up. I do feel responsible to him. So really family is important, and also I can work. I've burst the ego bubble. I've done that in the jail. I've gone through the sculpture, gone through wanting to be Jimmy Boyle Mark II.

I've drifted away from my own family. It's not that I don't like them, but they're still living in the same kind of world that I left. They say to me that some guy's changed, but he still goes onto building

---

[10] *Autobiography of a Murderer,* Macmillan 1997, Pan Books 1998
[11] Child

sites and demands ten fucking grand or they won't be working there. Just because he's not out chipping people, they're saying, 'What a good guy'! Their interpretation of change is totally different from mine.

What would make me return to crime? I'd want to kill anyone who caused harm to my family. I'd want revenge.

What about the future? I look upon each day as a bonus. I shouldn't be here. This in itself is the future. That's all I want, to continue. I'd love to wake up not remembering, but I think that'll take another five or ten years, if I live that long—just to get rid of 16 years' experience, just to get rid of it. I don't think I'll ever forget what I've done, it's just I want to move away from it. And I'd just like to wake up one morning not remembering.

John Bowers

John is 52. He used to be a professional burglar, and served a total of 15 years in prison. He is now the editor of *Inside Time*, a national newspaper for prisoners, and lectures to schools, colleges and foreign students on crime and punishment.

The catalyst in making me change my attitude to crime was the governor of Dartmoor. He fined me a week's wages for self-mutilation. Now I'm a stubborn person, and when I got back to my cell it was if I thought 'Right, what this bastard's done is the last straw and it's broken the camel's back'. And I determined there and then that I wasn't going to let these people continue doing this to me any more. It may have been my own fault and I was going to have to do something about it—but I wasn't letting them have any more of my life.

• • •

How did I get involved in offending? After I left school it was just a slow process into crime. I left home because of problems there, and I didn't want to go back, so I started to drift around. I had a couple of months of working legally for people, and I used that money for food. I didn't bother to sleep in a bed because I was sleeping rough. Soon that became my pattern of life—doing a bit of work for people, odd jobs here and there, getting three quid in my pocket.

I first broke the law when I was about 16 and I climbed into somebody's house for food. There were no thoughts of crime at first. I was just climbing in somebody's kitchen window nicking food. It was a necessity because I was starving. It really was as simple as that. It was simply just for food, and I didn't think of it as a crime. But I found it so easy that I started doing it regularly, knocking on people's doors to see if they were there, then going in and stealing food.

There wasn't any great explosion, I wasn't being led into crime by other people. I've never in my life been influenced by anybody to commit crime—I've always been my own person. All my problems arose through me working on my own, though there was a period later in London where I did work with a couple of other guys. But that wasn't being influenced by them, that was just simply me joining up with them. As soon as it got a bit heavy and I saw guns produced one day I was gone—I didn't fancy a sentence of 15 to 20 years. As time went on I became a professional burglar, specialising in jewellery, cash and silverware.

• • •

I was born in America at the end of the last war, the son of an American serviceman. Then my father vanished so my mother and I came back to this country when I was about eight months old. I've got three half-brothers—one older and two younger—and I found out about four years ago that I also have a half-sister. We're a very disjointed lot. I don't have any contact with any of my family now. My stepfather's dead, my relationship with my mother is terrible—always has been—and I've lost touch with my brothers. I feel very distanced from them all. I think mine was the typical dysfunctional family—was and still is.

I can't remember anything much before the age of seven—it's all very hazy. I can vaguely first remember my stepfather when I was about six or seven years old. My mother and stepfather conducted their relationship as if it was a battle zone. That taught me a very good lesson in life about the sort of relationship I never want with a woman.

I think my stepfather's view was that if you feed somebody, clothe them and give them a bed, then you're looking after them. That was his basic view of life. The nuts and bolts. That's the sort of guy he was, and that's the sort of relationship those two had, my mother and my stepfather. I don't think I ever saw them put their arms around each other in all the years that I lived with them.

I must have started my junior school when I was about five or six and stayed there till I was eleven, but that period is all extremely hazy. I can't remember having any friends that I used to enjoy playing with. I used to kick a ball around with a couple of boys, but I wouldn't say I had friends. I was a bit of a stranger, a bit of a loner. I think all that was to do with the fact that things weren't right at home. Even as a youngster I was aware of this, and because of it I felt different from other kids—I was always feeling I was a bit of an oddbod, a bit of an outcast.

Right throughout my education, the feeling persisted that I was from this dysfunctional family, though of course I didn't even know what the word *dysfunctional* meant then. It was just that I felt odd—I was from an odd family. I was always a bit of an outsider, a bit of a loner which was to manifest itself later on in life when I started to commit crime—because I did most of my crimes on my own.

At school I was quite a naturally bright kid. I remember always being very good at spelling, English, arithmetic and that sort of thing. I went on to pass the eleven plus to grammar school and I settled down pretty well there. I was in the middle stream: I wasn't one of the ultra-bright, top grade ones, but I wasn't lagging behind either. I always loved sport—running, football, anything that was going. In fact a few years later I was offered trials for Southampton, but by then I was too much involved in crime.

Then slowly but surely I started to struggle because of things at home. I started pretending to go to school when I wasn't going. I used to make up my own little notes and just play truant—not for lengthy periods of time, but I found I just couldn't concentrate at school with all the rubbish that was going on at home.

I left school at 14 without passing any exams. One day I thought, 'I've had enough of this place!' and I just vanished. It was another 30 years before I passed my GCSEs —in Channings Wood prison.

• • •

I remember the first time going into Winchester prison as a youngster. That was in the days when you were given old tin knives to cut your food with. Actually they weren't even knives, they were just old pieces of tin. We had to wear really shitty, smelly clothes, and the whole thing was repulsive.

I was very young, and obviously your attitude to going into prison changes over the years. It depends on the way that you've been living— you may be on a bit of an adrenaline rush, or you've forgotten what prison's like, you've forgotten what a police cell's like. And then suddenly, you're nicked! You're fingerprinted, you're back in that cold cell again. And all you want to do at that point is to say sorry and be let out. And then realism catches up on you: you realise that unless you're very lucky you're going down, and usually with me I was wanted by the police, or I'd done so much that I knew I *was* going down. So then it's 'get real' time.

Once you'd done your sentence you'd be full of good intentions. You'd say 'I'm not coming back, I'm never coming back to prison'. I've shaken the hands of hundreds of men, and I don't think there's many that wanted to come back to prison, only the die-hard recidivists and the institutionalised people. No-one in their right mind wants to come back. But then after a few months all your good intentions vanish and you go back to the old haunts.

Now I'm older and wiser I can see youngsters entering crime just the same way as I did. They need an alternative, just as what I needed was an alternative. When I first came out of Winchester Prison, what I needed was to come out to an alternative to crime. But because I didn't have one, I just blundered on in crime. Crime had now become the focal point of my life.

I've always likened crime to an addiction and when people say to me 'You're an intelligent man, why didn't you just stop?' my answer to them is 'Go and ask any smoker or drinker or drug addict or gambler why they don't just stop!' We all know very intelligent people who smoke. They're slowly killing themselves but you just try stopping them! You try stopping the alcoholic! They can't just stop, and with criminals it's the same—just like with any other addiction—you can't *just stop* committing crime. Sadly the only way to stop the alcoholic may be to tell him that if he takes one more drink he's dead. And if you're lucky he'll stop. But like the criminal, he needs an alternative.

You get a status with crime, you get your shiny bits of tin and your gold watches and you get your birds. But what have you *actually* got? It's only when you're older that you can look back and think, 'Well, what *did* I achieve? What *did* I get out of all those years in prison?'

I served 15 years all told in detention centres and borstals and prisons. My longest sentence was seven years for a series of burglaries. That was also my last sentence. I came out in 1991.

●   ●   ●

I suppose you could say that incident with the governor of Dartmoor was the start of a change in me. After that, a whole stream of people came into my life. Before that I didn't even know these sorts of people existed. There was a woman counsellor in Channings Wood prison; there was a lady teacher that I met when I came out of prison; there was Eric McGraw, the Director of the New Bridge organization—all these people started to come into my life and act as support roles.

Of course, these people were around before, but I wasn't receptive to anyone helping me then. For years and years I was a bit like a horse with blinkers that can just see where it's going and nothing else—it misses the crowd, it misses everything. Perhaps I didn't want to see all these people before. Perhaps they were there right in front of my face offering me support.

That brings me back to the addiction, back to the guy with an alcohol problem. All these people are offering their hands to him and saying 'Listen, we want to help, we so much want to help'. But that bottle, that vodka bottle, becomes—*is*—his god. On a good day he knows that he should give up drink and that he's killing himself, he's wrecking his relationship, he's wrecking his business. But he can't.

You've got to have an alternative. Until you give somebody an alternative—an acceptable alternative—to the life that they're leading, sadly they'll blunder on, still leading that life.

Maybe the answer lies in being ready to accept the alternative at a certain point in your life. And the frightening thing is so many youngsters at the moment aren't ready for that alternative. So they have to go to prison, and then to another prison and another, then, maybe when they're 35 to 40, suddenly the alternative becomes attractive. It's like the guy who's smoked for 30 years and has always known the alternative is to give up smoking and feel better for it. It's not until he gets lung cancer that he suddenly gives up smoking. He finds the alternative life, but what a price he's had to pay for it.

When I stopped committing crime it was because I was ready to stop. What the Dartmoor governor did to me may have been a catalyst, but at Dartmoor I was ready to stop crime because I'd had a gut-full of it. I was getting older and for the first time in my life I was developing a conscience about what I'd been doing—not only to other people but to myself as well. Everything was being screwed up.

This is where the stubborn nature in me came out and I said 'I've got to stop'. I'd got to stop for a variety of reasons: the conscience, the age— I was about 44—and the fact that if I got another sentence, I could see I was looking at it being a long one. I was looking at spending my fifty-fifth birthday in prison. And then my life's gone! So I thought 'Right, that's it. I either stop now or I'll probably end up dying in prison'.

But the alternative way of life didn't really kick in until I'd been out for a couple of years. Now people say to me 'What keeps you out of prison? You must be terrified of going back to prison'. Actually I couldn't give a toss about going back to prison. In fact I don't think that *physically* prison is difficult at all—it's comparatively easy. What keeps me out of crime now isn't going back to prison. The deterrent for me is what I would lose if I went back inside. That is my deterrent: it isn't prison itself, it's all the things I have got now in my life—a job, a relationship—things I don't want to lose. So now crime is not on the agenda in any shape or form.

After I'd been out for about two-and-a-half years, the phone rang and it was a guy I used to know. He said, 'D'you want to meet me?' And like a fool I did meet him, but only out of curiosity. He offered me a couple of thousand to get involved with him in the usual rubbish: 'ten minutes' work'. I was so annoyed at even listening to this bloody prat, even contemplating it. I thought to myself 'What are you doing, listening to this shit?' So I just shook his hand and got up and said, 'Look I've got to go. I don't know if I'll ever see you again in a crime capacity. I'll have a drink with you if I see you. That's fine and we'll talk about your wife and your kids and football, whatever you want to talk about, but just leave me alone, don't ever ring me up again'.

It's all about the penny dropping, it really is. You suddenly realise what you've lost in the past and what you want now. You suddenly start being receptive to help. You realise that people genuinely want to help. I was very cynical about the people inside that I called 'professional helpers'—because they were being paid to help me. I know now that's being disrespectful to a lot of people in prison who do a damn good job. But that was the jaundiced view I had. Psychiatrists, psychologists, they just became a standing joke—ten minutes of their time and a report written about you. So in the end I just gave up on the professional help in prison.

But when I came out of prison and started to meet the non-professionals—the people that would sit with me and support me, then I started to get a different view altogether. And I've had a lot of help. A lot of people have sat with me for long periods of time: they're not paid to do it but they really want to help. There's no 'do-gooder' element about it. Some of them were people that I'd argue with very, very fiercely on all sorts of points but they still sat and persevered and showed they wanted to help.

• • •

My whole life now is so different from what it was. There's the jobs that I've got—editing *Inside Time*, lecturing, which I really enjoy, going round meeting people. And there's my relationships, and the fact that I've still got a brain and I'm still very fit—it's all interwoven now. I suppose now I'm almost desperate—I don't like sitting still for long periods because I think I'm missing something. I like to get out and about, I go to London, see friends, ring people up.

I think possibly a lot of ex-offenders feel that they can never really take their place fully in society because of the person that they once were. I've found it very difficult to laugh properly in company because I didn't think I had the right to be there. Quite often now I'll be in company where some of the people know me, some don't. Suddenly the topic of crime will come up—they might start talking about burglary. And I stand there and feel guilty, because I'm the person that actually used to do the burgling! Even now I still drive past houses, nice houses, or I walk past, when I'm out on a stroll, and I think 'Christ, I actually used to be looking at these places to do them!' There'll be a guy out doing his front garden and he'll nod and smile and I'll think 'Christ, there was a time when I would have burgled that guy and I wouldn't have known him from Adam!' There wouldn't have been anything personal in it. It would have been deeply personal to him of course—but not to me. He was just another anonymous victim! These days I go and talk to the police and Neighbourhood Watch co-ordinators, trying to impress on them safety measures, anti-burglary precautions! I feel like knocking on people's doors saying 'There's a bloody great ladder out there in your garden, lock it up, will you!' Or 'I can see your shed open from the road!'

I think criminals are probably stuck with a guilty conscience for the rest of their lives. It doesn't matter how much you move on, you're always thinking of the strokes that you pulled, and the guy or the woman that you pulled them on. I'm not saying that it's a bad thing to keep thinking of that: what I do for a living now is like paying a little bit back to society. You'll never make full restitution—but you are doing something in your own way.

There are other dangers you have to look out for. I like a bit of attention and I like a bit of recognition but I can also see how people get carried away with their own self-importance. You do need somebody to say to you 'Come on, you're just an ordinary guy, even if you've been on the telly and everything'.

When I first started to give talks in big public schools like Eton I could come away and think 'I must be really special now'. I've thought, 'I'm on the telly, mate! Look at me!' And then in one of the schools I spoke at this teacher brought me down to earth. She said to me 'John, don't get carried away'. It was a leveller. She wasn't saying 'Don't ever forget your past'. If people hit me with that I get very, very angry, because you can't retaliate against that. That's taking unfair advantage. If somebody says to me 'You're an ex-criminal, and don't you ever forget it', there's nothing I can say to that. I've got no defence at all. But I think what this teacher was trying to say to me was 'Listen, it's OK, the talks are going well, you're doing little bits of media work. It's good that you're doing something as you are now, it's a nice feeling. But don't get carried away. Because in the great scheme of things you are just another little cog in the wheel'.

That's the feeling I get now when I come away from talks. If they applaud I think 'That's nice, they enjoyed it'. But the main thing is that I come away feeling 'Good, they've at least recognised what I was wanting to say'. You get a lot of feedback from the students. They come up and shake my hand and say 'It's been really interesting what you've said today. You've given us a totally different perspective on crime. We've often wondered why people begin crime; we've often wondered why they steal in the first place; we've often wondered why they keep going back to prison. You've just opened up our eyes'.

I've thought a lot about why I began criminal offending. I don't know whether it was just the need for food when I was in my teens. A frightening thought did occur to me after hearing someone give a talk about genetics. I thought 'Maybe there's something in me that meant I was always going to be a bit of a criminal?' In other words, if I'd had the perfect childhood, if I'd had a really good family, would I still be the person that I was?

The genetic theory is that some people have got a predisposition towards crime. I'll dispute that till the day I die—I can't possibly accept that theory. When I was born, I can't believe I was born to go to prison, born to commit crime. It's circumstances that lead you, perhaps from the day you are born. Let's not put the blame on parents, let's not even use the word *blame*. Something comes along in the life of every criminal—and it doesn't matter what criminal you care to name. I often look at people like Rosemary West or Dennis Nilsen or Myra Hindley and I picture them as little kids when they're one, two, three years of age, and I think 'These people surely can't then have been aimed, geared at crime. How did they become criminals?' You're certainly born with characteristics: you look like your mum, your dad, perhaps you've got the mood swings of one of your parents—but I don't think you inherit crime. I think that comes with all the different contributory factors—parents, environment and so on.

Does prison work? Some people have said to me over the last five or six years, 'John, prison did work for you because being in prison stopped you offending'. I say that no, prison didn't really work for me, though I spent 15 years inside. In the end I sorted my own problems out—prison didn't do it for me. Prison didn't cure me. When Michael Howard said a few years ago, 'Prison works', I understand why he said it because of course a prison will stop you committing offences when you are trapped inside it. But as a rider to that he should have added 'temporarily'. Prison just stops you for a period of time. And then you come out and you carry on again.

Some people are a danger to society and have got to be locked up, no doubt about that. Prison is an expensive way of keeping criminals like me out of the way but it's an easy solution. There's a terrific number of people who keep coming in and out of prison. You know you are going to be sent to prison for six months, two years, whatever. The judges know it, you know it. The screws get the cell ready because they know you are coming back and the whole prison machinery rolls on.

• • •

I left prison seven years ago and I've managed to straighten out a lot of areas of my life—attitudes to people, relationships, the paranoia that you get as a criminal in a prison. But there's one area that I don't think anyone can help me with. That's the relationship with my mother. It's 38 years since I left home, so all she really knows of me is what she saw of me as a young boy, and all I know of her is the woman that I grew to really despise because of the kind of woman she was. I dare say both my mother and my stepfather had their respective stories to tell, but I'll never know them, because my stepfather's dead and I don't talk to my mother.

It's up to me to do all the forgiving and the mending of bridges and I still can't bring myself to do it. And until I feel that I really, genuinely want to, I'm certainly not going to make some sort of half-hearted attempt. Some people say 'Why don't you just go round there and see your mum? She's an old lady now. Clint Eastwood said "Make my day!" Why don't you just make her day? Why don't you just say everything's all right?'

Well, I'm not going to take that to my grave, that I went round and told a pack of lies. I just can't bring myself to have any sort of relationship with my mother. Maybe it's scars from the past, maybe now it's my own guilt, because I used my mother for so many years as the person who was responsible for all my problems. Well, she might have made me leave home when I was young, she was responsible for that.

But after that, no, she wasn't to blame. I realise now that I was to blame for whatever went on in my life. But it took many years for me to come to terms with that.

Who knows what it would be like if I walked round to my mother's house now and sat down with her? Maybe we could get some sort of bond together, maybe I'd just want to dash out after five minutes. But I don't believe blood is thicker than water, I don't believe just because she's my mother that I've got any great need to love her and protect her and cherish her—just because she brought me into the world. It's the same with my brothers, and if my father walked through that door now — my real father I mean—God only knows what I'd say to him.

About four years ago my half-sister got in contact with me through a remarkable coincidence. She had been searching out her mother, her real mother, because she'd been adopted. She finally managed to track down our mother and while she was chatting to her she saw a photo of me. Then a few days later she happened to see me on television and she tracked me down too. We met again a couple of times, but since then we've drifted apart. I'm afraid there's no closeness between me and any members of my family. I don't think blood is thicker than water at all.

• • •

I've been happy to contribute to this book, but I wish it wasn't necessary to write a book like this. All those lives wasted, all those regrets. But if any book on the subject can do a *scrap* of good, then it's got to be written. I think perhaps it's only ex-offenders who can really put their finger on the pulse of what needs to be done.

The important things in my life today are health, work, relationships. I need money to pay the rent but that's just for peace of mind really. I don't aspire to any great things. I don't want a grand house or the latest car.

Nothing would make me return to crime now. I can't possibly see anything that would make me return to offending—even if I lost my job, my health, every relationship I've got. Whatever happened in life, I cannot possibly envisage ever returning to crime. I don't think anything or anybody could ever make me offend again. I'd like just to carry on as I am now with my health and my job and my relationships and to sleep easy in my bed at night. I'm living now as I think deep down I always wanted to live, and I have peace of mind. I sleep all right now.

Milos 'Mish' Biberovic

Mish is 44. In his twenties he became involved in the London drugs scene and was given a ten year sentence for importation of cocaine. He was released six years ago and became a video producer and director. He now works independently.

One particular incident completely changed my attitude to offending. It happened right at the end of my ten year sentence, when I was finishing it off at Blantyre House, a prison in Kent for long-termers who will soon be released. The ten years was for importing a large quantity of cocaine into the country—I was nicked in Dover and sentenced a t Maidstone Crown Court. I'd been told that because it was a first offence, I would probably get five or maybe a seven maximum. And so when I got the ten, it was an initial shock. Immediately you start working out when you'll be released, and the first thing that came into my mind was my three-year-old daughter—how old she would be the next time I saw her in freedom.

But then immediately that was taken over by a defiant attitude. I just got very, very angry and aggressive towards the judge. At the end of the trial he said to me 'You should apologise. Have you got anything to say?' I said 'No, bollocks, nothing!'

And that's how I was towards the screws, towards everybody that I had to deal with during the whole of my sentence till near the end. Just kicking against authority. When I was sent to prison I felt defiant and I *was* defiant. My thinking was 'There's nothing you can do to break me.'

When I got to the last two years of my sentence I was interviewed in Maidstone jail, and the PO[1] told me the kind of things Blantyre did, and asked me what I'd like to do when I got there. I said I'd like to concentrate on education, because in all the other prisons I'd been to there'd been very little in the way of education. So he said 'OK, we'll get you put down for education'.

When I arrived at Blantyre I found that, just like everywhere else, I had to do the shit work first. You go in the kitchen or you mop the floors or work on the hotplate, that kind of thing. I stayed in that kitchen for two or three months. I was there far longer than I should have been and nobody told me why.

One day the governor came into the kitchen. His name was Jim Semple. As he sat down to taste the food, which was part of his duty, I walked over to him and I said 'Governor, I've been in this kitchen far too long. I want to get to the education department. What's happening?'

---

[1] Principal officer

He said 'Oh, get away from me, go and speak to the PO about it, I don't want to know, I'm not interested!' In my hand I had a pan that I was washing up at the time and I threw it across the kitchen and it hit the wall and bounced off. I tore my apron off and I walked out. I thought that's it, now they're going to ship me out. So I went back to my cell, put my PE kit on and went off towards the gym to start getting rid of some of my aggression.

And then I heard somebody call my name. I turned round and it was the Governor, about 50 feet away from me along the corridor. I said 'What do you want?'

He said 'Can I talk to you?' and I said 'Yeah'. But I stood where I was so he had to come to me.

He put his hand out and he said 'I want to apologise for my behaviour earlier today. I'd had a bad day, I'd got some things on my mind, and I shouldn't have lost my temper'.

And that was it for me. For the Governor to have the courage to admit he'd made a mistake and to shake my hand and then to arrange for me to come out of the kitchen—which he did after a couple of days—and get me into the education department, that just *transformed* my attitude towards authority and prison. I could talk to the man on an equal basis and from then on I just looked in a totally different way at prison and at where I was and at my life. It made a radical change. I still keep in touch with that governor now. He sends me Christmas cards, I write to him occasionally and let him know what I'm doing. Now we're friends, he calls me a friend.

● ● ●

I suppose my resentment of authority started in childhood. My dad was very strict as a parent and so was my mum—in fact she was the more physical one when it came to punishment. But I remember us children being very frightened of my dad. If we sat round the dinner table, one look from him was enough to keep us in check.

I never felt like I could do the right thing for my dad. I felt that I never pleased him. He was never happy about the way I behaved. There were things he wanted me to do and become which I didn't want to be. I didn't want to be a lawyer, I didn't want to be a doctor—the usual things that your parents want you to become. In fact I didn't have any clear-cut idea of what I wanted to be.

I was one of three children: I have a twin sister and a younger brother.

You'd imagine that I'd be quite close to my twin but I wasn't. We're quite different in a lot of ways and I didn't feel that I wanted to be close to her. As for my brother, who's four years younger, there was nothing but conflict between us. I just didn't like him. He seemed to be a sort of daddy's boy, and I was always vying for my father's attention. He was the apple of my dad's eye. I could never get that sort of love and affection from my dad that my brother got. So we were always fighting, and whenever we did fight it was always me that got punished, because my dad always said 'You're the older one, you should have known better'. And I thought that was unfair. Sometimes, if my brother wanted to get me punished by my dad, he would kick up a storm over nothing. So I used to give him a larruping every now and again, to even things up. I thought, 'If I'm going to get punished, I'll get punished for something'.

I don't consider that I really had a happy childhood, and the more I've spoken to other people about their childhoods, the more I believe that. For a start there was the peculiar circumstance that my parents came to this country at the end of the last war from Yugoslavia and couldn't speak English. So they had lots of problems. We didn't have any money so we always felt like we were second-class citizens in a lot of ways.

I was actually born in this country, but I didn't learn to speak English until I began to go to school, and that made me feel a bit isolated from rest of the kids. Eastern Europeans were looked upon as being 'those bloody foreigners'. My dad used to suffer from that when he went to work, and it sort of rubbed off on us.

The first day in primary school, me and my sister walked into the classroom. We held hands—I know this because my friend, who I still see now, says he can remember us walking in and introducing ourselves and everybody laughing when we told them what our name was and where we came from. So we straight away felt isolated and we responded in a negative way. We became sort of aggressive because of it —I certainly did anyway. I became defensive, and this feeling went right through my schooldays. I remember in primary school kids saying to me 'What's your name?' and I'd tell them what my name was and they'd think 'Well, you're strange'. So that made me feel like an outsider from an early age. I used to feel that if I was different I'd really make something of it, and let everyone know that I was.

I still get mail coming into the office with my name completely misspelt, and that still compounds the feeling of being an outsider. When I was younger I had a habit of going into a shell because of it, and I still do it to some extent.

When we started to go to school and my dad started to go to work, we began learning English. But it was always a second language in those days. Obviously if you're at home with your parents who are only just beginning to pick up English themselves, they're going to speak the language they're comfortable with—so Serbo-Croat was what we spoke at home. Even to this day my mum can't speak English very well, because she didn't have to interact with English people. Because my dad went to work and we went to school we did learn it. But we were certainly made to feel that we were different.

My parents couldn't be very supportive to us at school because of their own trouble with the language. But the real problem for me was my dad setting these high standards that I just couldn't achieve. He kept comparing his own education to mine, saying 'I was very good a t this, why can't you be?' I had a lot of trouble with maths, learning my times tables and all that stuff. I've got an artistic trait—I still paint now, and that's what I wanted to do. So again this made me feel different from everybody else. But in any case, I wanted to do things differently from my father.

This feeling of difference was compounded—though in a more positive way—when my sister and I were two of the very few kids in our school who passed our eleven plus, and we both went to grammar school. So we were unusual in that way too.

I didn't feel happy moving on to the grammar school, chiefly because I didn't know anyone else there. None of the friends I'd picked up in primary school had passed the eleven plus, and I didn't like the idea of that school at all. It was another new thing, having to start all over again, perhaps having to go through all the 'feeling different' again.

I did very well in art. There were O-levels in those days so I got art O-level. I also passed English language and English literature—that was because I got an appetite for books quite young and just kept reading and reading. History was the other subject I passed and I still love it this day. But I left school as soon as I could. My father wanted me to stay on and take A-levels but I didn't want to. I just found education an unpleasant experience.

My father and I were still having confrontations, but by then it had got to the point where I was too old to be slapped. I'd told him when I was 15 'If you hit me again physically I'm going to attack you. I'm not getting hit any more'. Because he was stubborn I became stubborn so he couldn't break my spirit.

There was certainly no pressure on me to leave school and bring money into the home. On the contrary, my dad was the archetypal breadwinner and he wanted to support us: if I'd wanted to go to university he would have carried on supporting me. But I wanted the opposite—I don't know whether that was to annoy my dad. When us children actually did go out to work and my mum said we ought to be paying housekeeping money, my father refused. It was a point of pride for him to support his whole family until he felt he'd done his job.

When I was 16 I applied to join the Royal Marine Commandos. There's a strong tradition of military involvement in our family, and until it came to me, every male in the family had joined the armed services. I got the papers through and they said I could come along for an interview.

My mother wanted me to go, but you had to get permission from both your parents, and when my dad had to sign the form he just tore it into bits. He said 'I'm not having you join the army of a country you don't even belong to. You might go to Northern Ireland and somebody'll shoot you in the back of the head'. I said 'It's something I want to do!' But he refused and tore that form up into little bits. And that's something I've regretted ever since. There was my dad again, trying to steer me the way he wanted.

So then I got into commercial art. I started as an apprentice in a company which went bust and then I went into another one which went bankrupt as well. I was only earning £5 a week, and a friend in the building trade told me he was earning ten times that amount. So I joined him as a builder and I stayed in that trade about 15 years.

• • •

I started using drugs after I left school—I think I smoked my first joint when I was 15. I used to go drinking in pubs then as well. Nothing serious, lager and lime with friends, just to look grown up. Then we came across people that were selling puff[2] and powder[3] in pubs. And we'd buy it off them and you'd think, well, if your pal wants to buy it off you, you might as well buy a bigger lump—and it just escalated from there. I used to smoke hash and I was taking amphetamine sulphate—the tablets and the powder. In those days there were loads of amphetamine tablets about and we would buy those and then we got into buying bigger quantities and selling it to other people, which of course is illegal.

Offending was just something I sort of slipped into. The drugs scene was a lifestyle, and in West London, the area I come from—the Portobello Road, Ladbroke Grove area—it was rife. Everyone in the area would do it, and it became like it was acceptable. If you didn't use drugs you'd be considered strange. You'd again feel like an outsider. It was just the culture that I entered into and so did all the people that I knew. I never felt 'My life's going downhill, better take some sulphate!' I just did it and it got a grip on me.

It did cause problems in later life, definitely. Not the puff so much but definitely the speed I was selling. It was because of drugs that I got my ten years.

---

[2] Marijuana

[3] Amphetamines

That happened the year my father died. A lot of things happened all very quickly in one year. My dad died, the woman I was living with, the mother of my three year old daughter, left me, and I lost my job.

I always wanted to be somebody my father was proud of, but I hadn't achieved it by the time he died. I knew he was dying, and we had a private talk in the back garden. He asked me 'Are you happy in your life?' And I wasn't, but I said I was, just to make him feel good, so that he could die happy, knowing that he'd achieved what he'd set out to do—to get his kids happily married off with their own homes and jobs.

Soon after he died I got nicked. I'd always known that using drugs was a misdemeanour but I sort of rationalised it. When I was selling stuff in large amounts to people, there was the risk of going to prison and I knew full well that if I was nicked doing that I'd get a long time. But all the same it was a shock when I got ten years.

● ● ●

I was sent straight to Canterbury jail, which is a local nick. The longest sentence there is something like two or three years, for small offences. So when a guy comes in with a ten, people are sort of in awe of him—I noticed that immediately after the sentence. I remember walking across the exercise yard that night coming back from court and everyone looked out of the windows and shouted to me and my co-defendant, 'What you got?' My co-defendant got a seven, and I got a ten. That was like a life sentence. Ten years!

I was transferred to Albany prison on the Isle of Wight. There my sentence was at the other end of the scale—the lower end. The guys in there were doing 20s, 18s, 14s and all the rest of it. They made me feel better, I was amongst my peers, a bit of camaraderie. And I embraced it too. It rubs off. In prison, lifers have all the status and all the privileges. They think they're special because they're doing such a long time. Like the IRA terrorists. Certainly we had loads of them in Albany, and they were in another league entirely from everybody else. Like the guys I met last year when I was filming in the special unit in HMP Shotts up in Lanarkshire. There were nine guys in there— hostage-takers and murderers and violent men, the most violent in Scotland. Other people look at them in awe.

When I got to Albany, two screws started going through my property and one of them took my chess set that had belonged to my dad. I said 'What d'you think you're doing?' and he said 'There's a weight at the bottom of this, what's inside?' I said it was just a lead weight to keep the figure on the board, and he got annoyed and started scraping about in the box and I said 'Don't fucking do that!' He said 'I can do what I want. We've had loads of people like you and we've broke them'. I said 'Shut up, you wanker, you fucking watch too many jail movies!'

And that's how I carried on throughout my sentence. It was just conflict all the time. Initially I lost a lot of time. I got nicked three times for fighting—two of the nickings were for fighting other cons. I went on using drugs in prison, smoking puff.

I never got parole. At the time Margaret Thatcher was prime minister and she was on the crest of a wave of anti-drug policy. She went to Heathrow Airport and said 'Any drug smugglers that come into this country we're going to punish in a severe way'. The home secretary at that time was Leon Brittan and he said there would be no parole for violent offenders, bank robbers and drug offenders. That's what they said to me and I never got parole.

• • •

If that incident with the governor of Blantyre hadn't happened I would have come out of prison as bitter and twisted as I was when I first got to Albany. You just think all the screws are shits, and that's how you behave towards all of them.

Up until that incident with the governor, I didn't really know what I was going to do when I came out, and I would certainly have considered going back to crime to earn a living—not so much because I wanted to take my anger out on society, but because it was a practical move to make. If I didn't have any money, if I was given some silly amount for my discharge grant and just slung out on the street, which is what happens to most people, that's what I would have done.

Like I said, I got some kudos from having done a ten. Once you remove that status from a person in prison—once he's addressed his offending behaviour—what are you going to replace it with? He's got to have something to get some respect from other people. If he's been robbing all his life and then he doesn't do that any longer, you've got to put something else instead of it. You've got to have some sort of aim in your life.

If you've lost that reputation with your mates, if you're not doing crime any longer, if you say 'Look, I don't want to be a robber or a dealer any more', what are you going to be? A nobody, signing on.

• • •

When my brother came to visit me in prison soon after I was sentenced he said to me 'Listen, this is the best thing that ever happened to you'. I took that very badly. But there was truth in that because I was plucked out of a lifestyle which was destructive, where I was on a downward slide, and put into prison and made to have a rethink about everything. So it was positive in that way. And I used it for that reason.

Obviously in prison I had lots of time to rethink my life, to think about some traumatic things that happened very quickly—when my father died, when my child and the woman I lived with disappeared. So it was a complete change—everything had to change. And I just thought, I'm not going to carry on the way I was before. I'm going to do something different, get my life back on the rails. I used my time in prison really in a very positive way because I did re-educate myself. I had a good education at school, there's no doubt about it, and that's where I got the taste for it. I wanted to continue that in prison. I wanted to make sure that I kept my body and mind in a physical and mental state that was capable of going outside and dealing with the sort of pressures I was bound to find there.

When I was at school I didn't want to know about education. It was this anti-authority thing again. If my dad said 'I want you to read a book' I wouldn't read it. I would have done before if he'd left me alone. That's the authority thing again, if someone's standing behind you. But given the freedom, the choice, it's different.

I'm a self-motivator—in my work, in everything. I've got a nervous energy and if I've made my mind up to do something, I'll do it and carry it through. I've got a stubbornness in me—you could say it's a personality trait. On the positive side you could call it resilience which you can apply in your work. A lot of people in prison try to go to education and they'll apply for a course. Then the education department will say, 'We haven't got this course', and people will give up quite easily. I didn't—I was determined. I wanted it and I got it.

One thing that compounded all this for me was when I spoke to a guy in Albany and he said to me 'If there was a drug available that I could take that would knock me out for my entire sentence and I could be woken up at the end of it I'd take it'. And I thought that was the stupidest thing I'd ever heard anyone say about prisons. That person's life was going down the drain, whereas he could have done something to change it. But he didn't. And I thought, 'I'm going to do something while I'm here'.

For me prison was a positive experience. I know—I'm thoroughly convinced —that if I hadn't gone to jail at that time there would have been some sort of disaster waiting for me. Because I was up to my eyeballs in gear, I was taking sulphate, everything to try and blot out my father's death, my job loss, my daughter going, everything. And I didn't care—I became reckless because of it. The crime thing didn't matter to me, it was something that gave me a buzz, this getting involved in crime.

•   •   •

I've been out of prison nearly six years now. I was left to my own devices in a lot of ways but that's how I like it. I wanted to take the reins and I stopped using drugs. I was very fortunate to get a job with *Prisons Video Magazine,* which is a production company which makes documentaries about prisons that are shown to the prisoners themselves. I'd made a video diary with Jack Murton, with whom I shared a cell, about his life in prison. Then I was contacted by Richard Astor who headed the magazine's Trust at that time and told there was an opportunity for me at the company.

I enjoyed my work. I enjoyed the bit of recognition I got from my job with *Prisons Video Magazine.* I liked the challenge of going into prisons with a film crew. I interviewed Jimmy Boyle for the magazine, and the first question I asked him was: 'If you hadn't been the notorious Jimmy Boyle the criminal, do you think you would have become a successful sculptor?' And he said 'No'—he wouldn't. And I wouldn't have got a job as a producer/director if I hadn't been to prison.

Now my relationship with my girlfriend helps me as well. She's what you call straight, very straight, the way she's been brought up, she's never got involved in any criminality. She's often said to me, 'Do you know anyone who isn't a criminal?' Because a lot of people I see even now are bent in one way or another. Or former-bent or prospective-bent! So she says 'Don't you know anyone who's straight?' She and her family are the only straight people I know.

My elder daughter is 16 now. Her mum took her away from me and brought her up on her own, but she found it a very tough task and over the last couple of years it got to the point where my daughter was beginning to manifest the type of behaviour that I did with my dad, that defiance.

So she came to see me one summer holiday and her mum phoned up and said she didn't want her back, which was a trauma for her—though not unexpected as far as I was concerned. So she now lives with me. And now my girlfriend and I have just had a new baby daughter as well.

One of the things that kept going through my mind when I was in prison was that I wanted to try and be a good dad, to try and make up for all I'd done. I felt really guilty about having got nicked and not being there to support my daughter and her mum. But that quickly disappears when you come out, and you try and compensate by buying them more toys and stuff like that, which is not a good thing because you're appeasing your own guilt really, you're not making life any easier for them.

How have I kept away from crime in the last six years? I've done it myself. I'm not legging myself up but that's how I've done it, and it's only because *I* want to take the reins. I read somewhere that if you don't get a grip on your own life, somebody else will. I was in conflict with my

father for most of my life, then eventually he died. I had a great deal
of respect for him, but his death freed me up to make decisions for
myself and I've grabbed that with both hands.

The most important thing to me now is my family, without a doubt.
I know this is probably clichéd and corny but it's true. That's what
keeps me together. I've often thought about what would make me go
back to crime and do what I did before. If I lost all that, I suppose, if I
lost my family, I can't say with my hand on my heart, 100 per cent, no, I
would never commit another crime.

If I'm on my own, as I was just before I was nicked, I'm aimless, I
don't care about myself so much, I'm prepared to take risks. But when
you've got people in your life, you've got a second chance to really be
yourself—and that's what I have done.

Michael Fraser

Michael, 36, is a self-made millionaire with his own company manufacturing door frames and partitions. He lived in children's homes for most of his childhood from the age of five, and has never learned to read and write properly. He began committing petty crimes from the age of 10, then got involved in burglary and car theft. He was remanded into custody, narrowly avoided a prison sentence by getting a job, and managed to turn his life around. He is now on the board of The Apex Trust, a charity which helps ex-offenders, and employs former prisoners in his own factories.

I drive a Ferrari worth £130,000 and I ride around in a chauffeur-driven Bentley. People resent me and hate me for it. They'll shout 'You black bastard! Nigger!' This happens often, *very* often. They're thinking, 'He's black, he's got to be a drug dealer'.

I don't mind. I can get over it. I *am* a black bastard! My parents never were married, so it's true!

I go into prisons now and talk to people who are due for release or who have only got a year left to serve. The first thing I say to them is this: 'I can't read and write, I can hardly spell, I've got no idea of maths or anything like that but I'm successful because I've fought to be successful. I've done what *I* wanted to do. The reason why I think I'm successful is because as a child I channelled all my efforts into going against everything that was right. And then I changed what I was fighting for, for something I believed in'.

• • •

I was one of six children: I had three brothers older than me and two sisters younger. My earliest memory was that my mother didn't get on with my father and he used to beat her up—I didn't understand why. My father drank heavily but he was a very hard worker. He was actually doing two jobs by this time. He was working in the day in a factory and working at night as a driver. He was very strict with me, but he was still my hero.

My mum left my dad when I was four. When she ran away the family totally split up. We didn't know where our mum was, and my dad found it very hard to keep us together as a family. He used to beat us—I think because he was frustrated, trying to hold the family unit together and not being able to deal with it. We were all put into care when I was five and I stayed there till I was 18. So I grew up separately from my brothers and sisters and I wasn't close to them until much later on in life.

When we were put in care I found I could get away with a hell of a lot more, because no-one would beat me like my dad used to. As far as I was concerned, there was nobody in authority there who could do anything to hurt me.

I think being disruptive was just a cry for my father's attention. I think I craved attention and the only way I could get it was by being bad. I think I had a relationship with my father where I felt that every time I copied anything he did, he sort of praised me for it, whether it was good or bad. As a youngster I think I was probably like my father. That was important to me. I felt I was a mirror image of him when he was younger. My father got killed in a car crash when I was about 16. I didn't find out for a year, and I had no relationship with my mother till years later, when I was in my twenties.

It's quite strange because I've always been into this family thing. There was an Irish family I was friendly with, who lived near the children's home. I so much wanted to be in a family atmosphere though it never happened. But they were really good to me, this family. I *love* family life. I would *love* to have been brought up by a family. My two sisters were—they were fostered, and my older brother was adopted. I always wanted that.

• • •

Education was never part of what my parents were about. At school I had learning difficulties, and if it was noticeable, as far as I was concerned it was a weakness—so I wouldn't show it. Rather than trying to learn, I'd cause trouble in the class, because I knew I'd get thrown out, and then I wouldn't have a problem trying to explain.

I felt different from other children at school because everybody seemed normal and I was the one who would be in trouble. As far as I was concerned the others were all very good, whereas I would always argue or disagree with what was happening. Whether it was right or wrong I'd still fight for what I believed in. And I stood out because of that.

Physically I was quite strong and as I went on through school I used to be more or less the cock of the walk. I felt I'd got to get out there and be somebody and fight for what I wanted. I was very disruptive, causing a lot of trouble. I used to attack teachers and generally be disruptive in the class. I was a bully too. I used to take money off people: I used to go and say to other kids, 'Give me your dinner money!' and if they didn't I'd knock them over and take it. The Indian lads used to hide their dinner money in their turbans, and I used to make them jump up and down so I could hear where the money was rattling, and I'd take it off them. And I can still remember to this day what I was like with members of staff in the children's home.

I didn't feel happy going on to secondary school. I couldn't manage to keep friendships from school because I was in children's homes and I really didn't have any social contact with anybody else. To me going to secondary school just meant I was getting older and realising school wasn't for me. I didn't want school, I didn't enjoy it, it wasn't part of what I wanted to do. So I became even more disruptive. I got worse as I went into secondary school. I actually got a kick out of saying no to people and going against what they believed was right—the teachers, anybody in authority.

• • •

I was probably about ten years old when I first broke the law, pinching petty cash from the children's home. I was actually influenced by another kid in there. Even though I was bad, I wasn't *really* bad. At that age I still used to play with little matchbox cars, which I loved. But this kid told me I was childish playing with cars. He became my best friend. He taught me to smoke, later he taught me to have sex with girls, he opened my eyes to a lot to things I didn't know about. And he became very influential even though he was younger, because the things he was doing I found exciting.

When I was about 12, I was actually arrested. At this stage I used to be allowed to go home for the weekends to stay with my dad, and my dad had left his car up the road. My brother was allowed home as well, and me and my brother went and fetched this car and smashed it up, and the police arrested us and locked us up.

I thought my dad would kill me for it. But surprisingly he laughed about it. He seemed to think it was funny that I should do it. The police asked my name and I said 'Charlie Drake' as a joke. My father laughed because he couldn't believe that anyone that young could have that sort of cocky attitude. I'm not proud of it now but at the time I thought it was good.

So my father laughed about me smashing up his car and I felt good. But still, when they put me in that police cell, even at that young age I thought, is this it? Is this what my life's going to be? As a child probably you can go one way or another, and I sort of realised even then that I didn't want to end up going to prison.

So I decided to do something with my life. Even as a kid I was always a 'car person': if I saw a large car I used to go up to the bloke who owned it and say 'I like your car', and offer to watch it for him. I used to sit outside a gambling place and guard cars for people. One guy had a Daimler and I said to him 'I like your car, it's a lovely car', and he used to pay me to watch his car because he was scared I'd damage it otherwise. But I used to love to sit there guarding his car.

I left school at 16. I didn't have any qualifications, I just came out and that was it. There was very much the feeling that I had to get out and get on with it. I still had a care order on me so I was actually still living in children's homes. But at the age of 16 you got moved on to what used to be called a 'working boys' hostel', which is geared up to try and prepare you for life outside. You have your own room and you go out to work to pay rent and get on with your life.

I started work as a trainee bench hand in a very small factory, and to this day I don't know what a trainee bench hand is! I ended up cleaning machinery, doing odd jobs around the factory. There was a foreman and about eight employees.

Everybody was scared of the foreman and so for a while I played along. He told me to clean the machines and eventually I began to ask him when he was going to let me do this trainee bench hand work. He kept saying I could start in a couple of months but it never happened.

One day—I picked the day, I picked the time—I waited till he was in front of everybody and he told me to clean a machine. And I said, 'Clean it yourself!'. I did it on purpose—I wanted to belittle him. I was upset because he hadn't done what he was supposed to do. He hadn't started me on training to be a benchman.

So I walked out of that job and I left the working boys' hostel and went to live with some friends. These friends were into burglaries and thieving and eventually I used to go out with them. I'd keep watch while they broke into houses and pinched cars, and I found it exciting. I'd found it difficult struggling for money—and they could pinch all this fantastic stuff. But we were always scared to death that the police were going to get us.

One day we went to sell some stuff in a jewellery shop, and while we were in there I lifted a ring, gave it to this girl, got caught and got done for it.

I was remanded into a youth custody place for assessment by social workers. That place had a great influence on me because it taught me more than I ever knew about crime before. The people you lived with, you were all the same, in the same situation. You're in an atmosphere with everybody else—why should you be any different? We were all in there for the same sort of reasons, and we were all similar people anyway. The influence is there for you to be just like everybody else. You see offending as part of your way of life.

The social workers told me I'd be going to prison for receiving stolen goods. I decided I was going to have to get a job because I thought it might keep me out of prison. I thought 'If I have a job, then I can at least tell the judge I'm working'. I didn't think they would lock me up if I was working—I thought I'd get a fine or probation or something like that.

So I ran away from the assessment centre and set about trying to get a job. I went for this interview and the guy interviewing me was from up North and he'd never had any dealings with black people like me. I can still remember him saying 'Yeah, we'll let you know'. I walked out and then I went back half an hour later and I said, 'You said you'd let me know!' He said 'Yeah, I'll contact you. Don't come back'.

But I kept going back. I was going back every hour, on the hour! He must have thought I was a nutcase. And eventually he said, 'You've got the job, because of your persistence'.

So I went to work as a labourer and a forklift truck driver. I think I must have seen a nice side to that guy when I kept going back to him, because he became like a father figure for me.

I really enjoyed the job. I wasn't doing anything special—I was just in a warehouse atmosphere, working loading and off-loading things. I got on well with the guy's wife, who was the secretary, and we had a great time there.

When the court case came up I found it really did help that I had a job. I got a fine and I was put on probation instead of going to prison.

• • •

Once I got out of trouble I'd planned to pack the job in, but I found I enjoyed what I was doing. I also enjoyed the sense of being able to have money and not look over my shoulder because I'd got it by wrongdoing. I felt, I've got the money because I'm working. It's hard to explain but I think I also enjoyed the fact I was doing something that was 'normal'. Whenever I'd been in trouble there was always a doubt in my mind. I was always thinking, 'If I'm in trouble, if I've done something wrong, something's going to happen to me. I'm eventually going to be caught up in it'.

The people I was hanging around with at the time we were doing the burglaries went on to do armed robberies and bank jobs with shotguns and everything. They're still doing it now. I see them occasionally when they come out of prison. When I meet them they say, 'Oh God, Mike, look at your Ferrari, look at your Bentley'. I try and say to them, 'You could do it as well'. I say the same thing to people when I go into the prisons. I say 'You can do it if you want to do it'.

The foreman at that job eventually became a very good friend of mine and we're still friends. But when I first got there I caused him as much trouble as I could and he said he'd have to resign from the company or they'd have to get rid of me.

Instead the guy who ran the company said he'd put me in a small workshop, working at a machine on my own. And even though it was monotonous and boring, I loved it. I loved working that machine, which was used to cut locks out in door frames. I had control over that machine: it was a fantastic thing to work and I loved it.

I did that job for about two years. I used to daydream, set myself targets. To do 100 frames in a week was fantastic, but I was setting myself targets to do 100 frames in a day! And I used to do it—I actually did do it! My boss thought it was brilliant that I was setting these targets for myself. I was making him a fortune and we had a good relationship. I had my own keys to get into the unit. He trusted me totally, and I used to work seven days a week.

• • •

At about this time I got married. My wife was a nurse and she had her own car. I was impressed that a professional like her could think anything of somebody like me. I was working seven days a week and it was good—it was really good. Then suddenly the firm's work started drying up.

So I set up my own business making these door frames and I went into big debt—by this time we had two children and we'd bought our first house. But I'd actually given up on the marriage because to me the goal was making money—and that's all I did do. I worked on my own every day, every night. I used to wake up in the night and think, 'I'll go to work, I can do some more frames'. I would promise people I'd deliver their order in a week, then instead I'd do it in two days. And of course they were over the moon.

It was great to be praised. It was great because people were actually saying 'You're brilliant, you've done it, well done!' This is something I think comes from my childhood when I never got any praise at all.

I knew nothing about accounts, I just worked, and I worked my butt off. We'd moved from our first small house into a four-bedroomed detached house—then we moved from there to an even bigger house. It was worth quarter of a million back in 1989. My wife had her own life and I was working unbelievable hours, making a hell of a lot of money.

Then I decided I'd missed out on playing around. So that's what I started doing. My wife knew, and we split up. I gave her everything, everything I had—except for the business. I said to her 'You can have everything else, but please don't go for the business'.

I fell in love with somebody who I think only loved me because I was wealthy, and we got married. Then about three years ago she had an affair which destroyed me, and this second marriage split up too.

I actually gave up on work and I went through a stage when I was drinking a lot. I never did drugs—I like to feel I'm in control, and you become dependent on drugs. I don't like the idea of becoming dependent on anybody or anything at all. I hate the fact that I smoke, because it means I'm dependent on cigarettes. But drugs have never been a part of my life. I was absolutely scared of them. Absolutely. My drinking was just a stage, and I knew I'd end up killing myself if I carried on.

All this time my business was expanding. It had reached a stage where the turnover was £6 million a year and it was growing. By that time I was employing 40 or 50 people. Luckily one of the guys who worked for me could see what I was going through with my marriage. He runs the company for me now, as managing director, and he's very successful. I listened to him and I slowed down.

• • •

Today I'm more enthusiastic about people than about my business. I work for the Apex Trust, which is about employment for ex-offenders, and now I'm on the Board. I enjoy that sort of lifestyle now. I do still go into work and I admit I love all the trappings I get from it. But I'm not that enthusiastic about actually doing it any more. I get enthusiastic about Apex and things like that. We're doing a big project now where we're getting government ministers to come and learn about prisons and I'm involved in that in a big way. I sponsored it and I'm really into it big time. I believe they brought me in because I can provide a link between Apex and the community and the ex-offenders.

I started doing my charity work in prisons. It pays to go into prisons. It does work. When prisoners see someone like me who came from nothing being successful it inspires them. And if I can inspire one person, fantastic. Every time I go into a prison, if just one person is inspired— fantastic. The more they know about people who come from nothing and create something, the more people will get out there and do things themselves.

I love success coming from nothing—I get a kick out of that. But I think we are a very resentful society in the UK: we don't like people being successful too long. We don't like to see them up there—we'd rather them drop.

Nobody believed in me. I wanted to prove to myself and to everybody else that I was capable of doing something—though I didn't know what. At that stage I didn't know I was going to be, or how successful I was going to be. I didn't have a clue. I just wanted to do something that was positive. I wasn't motivated by money—I was motivated by the fact that I'd achieved something. Luckily I was in a market that needed something and I found the niche in that market. And I was motivated by that.

I employ quite a number of ex-prisoners in my own company. I'd say that 95 per cent of the ex-offenders who come and work for me will get on and be successful in not returning to a life of crime. Five per cent will probably go back to crime. I've got people working for me now who've been in prison for all sorts of reasons: car crimes, battering, assault, burglaries. You name it, they've done it—everything. That's no problem to me, as long as they're going to come in and channel all their efforts into doing something with their lives. That's fantastic.

I am not a do-gooder—that's the last thing I ever want to be. If somebody wants to get on in my company, they'll get on. If they don't, they can go. I have no problem with it. I'm there to say 'If you want to do something I'll guide you and help you. If you don't want to do it—get out'. End of story.

Sometimes when I go into prisons, the prisoners tell me I'm lucky, but I say, 'No, I worked for it'. You'll often have 12 blokes round you and there's always somebody in the group who'll have a little dig at you and say, 'Well yeah, it's OK for you, you've got there'. And I say, 'You can get there too. But if you don't want do it, don't do it. Carry on doing your crimes'.

• • •

I've kept in touch with my brothers and sisters though we were brought up apart. My two sisters are dead now. They died in 1986 and 1987. Both of my sisters had been in and out of prison all their lives. One became a prostitute. She used to work in Birmingham and I'd race around trying to catch her and stop her doing it. But she ended up killing herself with a drug overdose. My other sister died just 12 months later from stomach cancer, caused by her being kicked in the stomach in prison.

I'm still in contact with my brothers. My oldest brother went into prison as well—we've got similar personalities but I think I'm a lot stronger than him. He's been out of trouble for about ten years now.

Back in 1984, when I was 22, I made contact with my mother. I put an advert in a Halifax paper because I knew that's where she came from. I hadn't seen her since I was five. And she replied to this advert.

I got so excited when I went to see her. It was a strange feeling, thinking 'This is my mum'. The first thing she wanted to know was where my dad was. When I said he was dead, she was relieved because she was totally scared to death of him. But as quickly as I could, I tried to get over to her my memories of him, because I had loved him. She said he was a bad man, he used to beat her up, and I said, 'I know he did, but why did he beat you up?' And she said, 'Because he couldn't express himself in any other way'. I was beginning to form a relationship with her, but I couldn't call her Mum. I don't know why—I just couldn't. And in the end things just didn't work out between us.

It's affected the way I look at things now. If I have a relationship, or if I meet somebody and I get close to them, I always wonder what's going to happen. I believe I build up the feeling inside me that if something is going well, something bad's going to happen. I don't like pain, I mean pain inside. I hate pain inside. I don't want to be hurt and I probably build up a barrier to stop that happening.

I think other problems of my childhood are still with me now. I haven't got the patience to learn anything. My writing's terrible and I can't spell to save my life. And I'm terrible at maths or anything like that. If I want something done these days I can just phone up my secretary. I don't have a problem writing a cheque, though if there's an alternative then I'll use it. But I'm not ashamed of all this any more.

People have always said to me 'You went through a rough time— losing parents, losing sisters and all that'. But I only went through what a lot of people go through. If you feel sorry for me, you make it worse for me. Life really can be hard—but you've got to be able to pull yourself out of that. Success isn't the big house, the big cars. Success is getting on with life, being happy in what you do, just getting on with it. That's what success is.

I don't know what will happen in the future. I really don't know. I've still got the bad parts of me where I'm frightened of commitment. But I just take things as they go along. I'm happy enough, I just get on with it, life goes on.

Today I'm proud of my success: I'm more successful than I could ever have wished for. But I'm still searching I think, searching for that ultimate—something. And I haven't found it. I've created what I want but I'm still hungry. Part of me is over the moon. I love the cars— Bentley, Ferrari, chauffeur—this is lovely, it's brilliant. But I'd give it all up tomorrow if that could make me really happy.

Marie

Marie, 43, is now training for ordination as a Methodist minister and hopes to serve as a prison chaplain. When she was in her thirties, she was jailed for five years for robbing two post offices armed with a replica gun. Many of Marie's problems stem from the fact that she was born male, and grew up as a boy. She suffered in the 'wrong' body until the age of 20 when, after the latest in a series of suicide attempts, she underwent an operation and established her true identity as a woman.

This young girl and I robbed two post offices dressed up as men. In the first post office I remember getting out the gun—it was a replica gun the girl and I used in our magic act going round the clubs. I took about £3,000. I remember telling the cashier she could keep the small change and just give me the notes. What struck me—and I've never forgotten it—was that there was a woman in the post office with her small boy and they seemed quite unaware of what was going on—they were choosing sweets or something. Then we went on to the next post office and got some more money using the gun. But when we left we met a police car on its way to the first post office and they chased us and stopped us. The officer who arrested me was amazed when he discovered I was a woman. We were very amateur—for instance we used my own car which had a distinctive roof rack and all sorts of dents and bumps.

I now feel I was very stupid to have committed those crimes. I could have had to do 16 years for those post office raids. I also feel very regretful because I know that the lady who ran that first post office had to give up the business because of what I did.

• • •

I suppose it's quite ironic that I did the post office raid dressed as a man —because I started life as a boy although medically I was a girl. I was the youngest but one of ten children—the youngest boy in this very large family. I had five brothers and three sisters, all older than me, and one sister three years younger. I think my mother was ashamed of having so many children. Later when we were at school, if we were asked how many children were in the family we had to say there were four.

I always felt different from my brothers and sisters, and I never felt I was loved or wanted. When I was three I recall my sister being born. I regarded her as yet another hindrance in my life: I hated her from the start.

I was treated much worse than all my brothers and sisters. I never got what the other kids got. I remember for Christmas one year my younger sister got a bone-china child's dinner service, my older sister got a Singer sewing machine worth £100 and I got a 7/6d compendium box of games. I believe this was because I was the son of a neighbour. Years later when my mother got blind drunk one Christmas Day, she told more or less told me so.

As soon as I could start dressing myself I was always dressing in my older sisters' clothes. I always wanted to wear their dresses.

I was five when my older brother started sexually abusing me. He must have been about 14 and he used to threaten me and say that if I told my parents they'd get rid of me. He'd say 'They don't want you anyway'. He did start doing it to my younger sister as well, and actually I got very jealous of her because what he did to me was the only physical affection I ever got. My parents never hugged or cuddled me. Later this brother who abused me always used to say about me, 'There's something wrong with him': he must have known I was not like normal boys.

The abuse went on for five or six years and when I was 11 my brother got me and my younger sister up in the loft when Mum and Dad were out shopping. But they came back and caught him doing it. My father beat my brother with the buckle end of his belt and after that the abuse stopped.

My father regularly beat us all on the bare bottom with his belt. He was a Derbyshire miner and I think he beat us partly because he was dominated by our mother. He had to hand over his pay packet to her and she'd give him his pocket money back. She used to say to us, 'Wait till your father gets home' then she'd save up all our misdemeanours and embellish them and then he would beat us. My mother was a very hard woman. Her father—my grandfather—was very strict as well. He would keep a cane handy at the table in case we behaved badly. He was a typical miner, a small man with a cloth cap.

There were two secret hiding places in our house where I used to go and I felt safe. Monday was washing day and my mother used to dry the clothes on a clothes horse in front of the fire. I used to hide behind it because I loved the smell of the damp clothes. The other place was in the airing cupboard where I used to climb up on top of the washing. It was safe and warm and nothing could hurt me there.

●　●　●

From the moment I started at primary school I always wanted to play with the girls. I didn't like the boys' rough games. From the start I was called names like 'poof' or 'sissy'. Luckily I made a very good friend called Ann. We started infant school together. After the first term we had to move to a new class and I got told off because instead of moving on I stayed playing with a rocking horse. I wet myself—I was only five years old—and the teacher told me to go home and get changed then come back. But I was so afraid of what my mother would do to me that I went off to the toilets and hid for what seemed like hours. In fact it was only a few minutes. The teacher knew I hadn't gone home so she sent Ann home with me. My mother stood me on the kitchen table and stripped off my underclothes in front of Ann. She said, 'Just look at him! I'm sure Ann wouldn't wet herself at school', then she sent Ann away. I thought that was it—Ann would never want to speak to me again. But she never said a word about the incident to anybody. She was a true friend to me and we stayed friends right through primary and into secondary school.

I could never show pain—I always had to smile. The problem was that I always felt so different from the boys. I would only play with boys if some girls were there too. I wouldn't play war games and soldiers unless I could be the doctor or nurse. I avoided the showers and I used to keep covering myself up when we had to get changed for games. I used to hide in the toilet because I always used to sit down instead of standing up like the other boys. Even from the age of five I hated my penis. One night when I was just five I tied it to the headboard of my bed to try and pull it off!

Nobody at home ever picked me up or cuddled me or encouraged me in anything I did at school. I could read the newspaper at home before I even went to school. But for the first couple of years at primary school they thought I was illiterate because for some reason I wouldn't read to the teacher. They called my parents in to the school. My mother was very angry she had to come in—she said it was so embarrassing and I was bringing trouble on the family.

I failed the eleven plus. I panicked in the exam. I could never do exams—I'd just go to pieces. But I was quite happy about going to the secondary modern because I'd made some really good friends at primary school—mostly girls—and we all went up to the secondary modern together. I stayed friendly with Ann and some other girls. I was tiny—I didn't start growing till I left school at 15. Once I got to the secondary school I was always being called 'queer' and 'sissy' and 'poof', even by my own brothers and sisters.

●   ●   ●

I was made to leave school at 15 by my parents. My older brother had just left home and they needed another wage packet. My dad took me down the pit and told me I could either work down there with him or in a Nottingham tailoring firm called Daks and Simpsons where my sister worked. I couldn't stand the idea of getting myself dirty down the pit so I went to Daks and worked on a sewing machine sewing sleeve linings. I had to hand over my whole wage packet to my mother, just as my dad and the rest of the family had to.

After seven months at Daks and Simpsons I signed up for the army. I think I really believed the army would 'make a man of me'. I had to pretend to my dad he was signing a form to do with work, to get him to sign the army forms. I went into the Royal Army Medical Corps because I liked the idea of nursing. As it turned out I only spent six months in the army. By this time my mother and father had gone to run a restaurant in Skegness and they conned me into leaving the army. They had three of us children working for them in the restaurant and we were on call 24 hours a day, seven days a week. I got very depressed and I made a number of suicide attempts.

Eventually I got away from working in the restaurant and after various jobs and a disastrous few months in the RAF I returned to my home town and went to work in Burton the Tailors there. I was 18 years old.

• • •

I'd always loved acting, because then I could be someone else. I loved the theatre and when I went on holiday to Skegness Miners' Camp with the family I loved all the shows. As a young child I remember standing up and taking all the bows from my seat in the audience as if I was in the show myself. When we got our first TV set this was the opening of another world to me. I must have been quite small—five or six—but I used to love watching the variety shows and films. I could just lose myself in them.

In my first year at the secondary school they put on a pantomime. It was *The Pied Piper* and I was King Rat. There was this older girl in it and I got a kind of crush on her. I followed her around and I very much wanted to be like her. Funnily enough, at secondary school I had quite a fan club of girls who fancied me and I hated that.

When I was 18 and working at Burtons, something happened that changed my life. I still loved acting and I joined a drama group. We did a play where I had the part of a man who has to dress up as a woman. I had a tight dress with a cleavage and when I put it on during the dress rehearsal I suddenly knew that this felt right. Although I'd put on my sisters' dresses when I was a kid, I hadn't done it since and now at the age of 18 it had much more impact on me.

When I was about 20 I went to a party and got involved with a girl. She started kissing me and I was repelled. I felt physically sick and I had to make the excuse that I'd drunk too much so I could get away. I decided I must be gay so I contacted a gay club in Nottingham. But that didn't feel right either.

I was still in the drama group and the lady who ran it was impressed with how I looked in women's clothes and said I ought to dress up professionally. So I started going round the clubs all over

Derbyshire doing charity shows as a female impersonator. I had very glamorous dresses and I used to do impersonations of Shirley Bassey and Petula Clark. Sometimes I would do hen parties and stag nights, getting paid £40 for a 20 minute act.

I felt real as soon as I put on those clothes. I realised that this was actually me. Amazingly while this was going on my body changed and my hips rounded and my breasts were filling out. Later the doctors couldn't believe I hadn't taken drugs but I had not. I wrote to my own doctor and he suggested I should come and talk to him, and he sent me to a specialist.

The first psychiatrist I was sent to in Nottingham was sure I'd taken medication. Then I was sent to a doctor in London. He made me feel very humiliated—he was sure I was dressing up in women's clothes to fulfil my sexual fantasies.

This is when I attempted suicide by taking 64 pills of an anti-depressant drug. I was about 21 by then. I was hospitalised in the Derbyshire Royal Infirmary and I missed two whole weeks of my life. Then I spent nearly six months in a psychiatric hospital.

There they did a lot of physical tests and discovered that genetically I was a female. I thought it would be a simple physical matter to have an operation to make me into a woman but the operation was left incomplete—it was the first time the gynaecologist had done this kind of operation.

It took another two years, but eventually I had the final operation to make me physically into a woman. I had a wonderful plastic surgeon who did everything properly. The only reason I was kept in the psychiatric hospital for six months was so that when I finally left, I could go out as Marie.

While I was in there I would get dressed in the usual masculine casual wear of jeans and a sweatshirt. I had shortish blonde hair and already people were thinking I was a woman. I would have people giving up their seats and opening doors for me as if I were a lady. Mind you, I had no counselling at all either while I was in the psychiatric hospital nor once I got out, to help me cope with the changes.

● ● ●

I was never involved in crime as a child, apart from nicking sweets from a local shop at age of five or six. It was my own stupidity that led me to commit my first crime, which was fraud and deception. It was because of a relationship I had.

I was married briefly but it didn't work out. The breakup of my marriage was one of the influences that led me towards offending. I was married for three years and my husband stuck by me through all my many operations. Then he went back to his mum. After he left I really lost it because he was my first love, though at this point I could not have a full physical relationship.

It was all about rejection again. I tried all sorts of ways to kill myself—electrocuting myself in the bath, slashing my wrists. Once I tried to hang myself with my tights, tying them round my throat and to the door handle. But even that went wrong: the tights stretched and I woke up on the floor.

After my husband left me, I had a relationship with another man. I really loved him and would do anything to please him. But he left me for another girl. I wanted him back, so at his request I bought him all the equipment he needed for his carpentry business and I gave him £600 for a car. He told me he was going to give me back the £4,000 I had loaned him. Then I saw him packing all his stuff into this car with the girl he'd left me for in the first place. I was done for fraud and deception but I was only given two years' conditional discharge.

So the first influence on me to commit crime was that man. The second was a girl I'll call Jane that I met because I was friendly with her parents. I was in my thirties by this time and living in a flat in Staffordshire. Jane was only 19 and she had a little girl. She asked if she could move in with me with her daughter. We were just friends— there was no sexual relationship between us.

By this time I was doing a magic act round the night-clubs and eventually Jane became my assistant. One evening Jane and I had had quite a lot of wine, and she said 'What if we robbed a post office?' We had a replica gun we used in our magic act and she said we could use that. I didn't take her seriously at first, but she said we could practise disguising ourselves as men. So we did that just for fun. Next morning Jane took her daughter to the nursery, then she said 'Let's do it!' I thought she was joking but she said 'If you don't do it with me I'll do it by myself'. I was sure she'd be caught if she did it alone so I agreed to do it with her. As I said, we were very amateur and when we were chased by the police we were bound to get caught.

We were both petrified when we were arrested. Jane tried to go QE[1] on me, saying I had forced her into it at gunpoint—whereas in fact as we were driving round together, looking at all the post offices before choosing one, I kept saying to her 'We don't have to do this, you know' and she was saying she'd do it alone if I wouldn't join in.

As I listened to the judge passing sentence I was working out that I was going to serve 16 years because I heard him say five years for each post office—that would have been ten years—plus another three years for having a gun in each raid—that's another six years, which makes

---

[1] Turn Queen's evidence

16. But the officer with me told me it was to run concurrent, making it five years.

So I was given five years and Jane and I were sent to the same prison, New Hall in Yorkshire, then I was moved to Cookham Wood in Rochester.

• • •

Going to prison had the most significant impact in stopping me offending. It meant I could stop and think about my life. When I got caught after that car chase, I was relieved because I realised by then that—though I didn't come from a criminal family—I was in danger of being trapped in a downward spiral of crime.

I went into the education department in prison. Then I took part in a 'Beyond the Gate' project to prepare people for release. I only served 20 months in prison because I got out on my first parole.

But three years ago, in 1995, I was at risk of returning to prison. I still had my parole to finish when I was busted for drugs. I wasn't personally involved, but the girl I was living with was into drugs. The police who arrested me could have had me sent straight back to the prison but instead they strung out the proceedings for me. Otherwise I might have still had a parole to finish. I dreaded being sent back to prison.

• • •

The church is what keeps me away from reoffending now. I love my church, and the thought of people praying for me gives me a buzz. There is nothing now that would make me return to crime. These days I am happy, especially with my sexuality. I like to think of the Shirley Bassey song *I am what I am*. I live on my own and I admit I do get lonely. I do get easily led and, as I've said, I've been in relationships in the past where I have been led astray.

But now I have got my church. I always believed in God but now I see a purpose to my life, which has led me to where I am now. I go round speaking to women's groups and I always tell them there is a better path, even if you have suffered abuse, than to have had a violent husband and have attempted suicide many times as I have done.

I want to get into the ministry, to be a prison chaplain if possible. If I manage to work in prisons I'll be able to tell the prisoners 'I've been there'. I've already been to Rochester prison helping with the services and I have been back to Cookham Wood as a prison visitor. I went back into the prison a week after I was let out—I was given a gate pass just a week after my release.

I love making people laugh at social events and in church. I love entertaining people. Most people in the church know that I was in prison but not the full details about my background. But now I have decided to write a book about my life and then I will tell the whole truth about everything.

I have been invited to give a testimony talk soon at the men's prison in Rochester. It means a lot to me because I can show prisoners that they can turn their lives around just as I did. There is a better life waiting for them out here.

Life itself is important to me now. I love life—now I love waking up in the morning.

Tommy

Tommy is a pseudonym: this interviewee has chosen to remain anonymous. He is 30, and was brought up during The Troubles in Northern Ireland, joining a Protestant paramilitary organization at the age of 16. Between the ages of 14 and 23 he served six sentences in borstals, young offender institutions and prisons for violent offences, fighting and sectarian rioting. He is now a youth worker on the mainland, and visits schools and youth clubs telling people how his life has changed.

31 January 1987, Sunday night: I was 18 years old and I was on the floor in the back of an estate car, with a balaclava over my face and four UDA[1] men sat with their feet on me. The journey from Laugharne to Belfast takes about half an hour and that journey was one of the longest times I have ever had in my life. In the back of the car that night I believed they were going to shoot me dead. I was going to get killed. I remember lying there thinking how I'd spent the last four years—from when I was 14 to when I was 18. I'd never had any life whatsoever. I'd been in borstal, I'd joined the UDA at 16 and life was always a worry and a hassle, and I never enjoyed anything.

The reason I was in the car was because I tried to break away from the UDA and in Northern Ireland when you join the paramilitaries, this is not possible to do. I joined as a paramilitary and that was me for life. But this started to get hold of me and I didn't want it any more. I didn't want to be committed to something for the rest of my life. I thought 'What if I was married and had children and the UDA came to the door and asked me to do something?' So I'd tried to break away from it.

I remember asking myself what life was all about—because to me that was the end of life that night. I remember the thoughts I had for my parents, the way that I'd treated them, the way that I'd put them down and caused my mother to have nervous breakdowns. And I remember saying 'If you're there, Jesus, take me into Heaven, forgive me for all the wrong things I've done.'

They took me to a dump in Belfast. It was freezing cold and I remember the four of them got out of the car. I was lying in the back so feared I couldn't move and one of them shouted 'Get out here now!' When I stood on my feet I had a quick look round. One was keeping deck over on the hill and the other one was at the front of the dump. Then two of them started beating me with their baseball bats, from the ankles to start with. The pain was unbelievable. I'd never experienced pain like that in my life. They continued to beat me with the baseball

---

[1] Ulster Defence Association

bats from my toes up to my ankles, but they never went above my knees. I remember putting my arms down to cover my legs and my arms got that smashed that I couldn't use them any more. And I remember screaming like mad and one of the blokes saying to me 'If you don't stop your screaming I'll do your head and all! Shut your mouth and take it as you're getting it!' I remember one of them taking an absolute mad fit and starting to go nuts on me and the other bloke had to stop him. I don't think they were supposed to go as far as they went.

Then I remember them picking me up and starting to carry me further up the dump. I couldn't walk because my legs were bashed to bits. Then they all jumped in the car and I'm left standing in the middle of this dump, and I'm feared of the dark as it is. It was freezing, it was eleven o'clock at night—I'd been taken away at nine and I was covered in blood and I was in absolute pain. But I remember getting the strength to climb under the trees. I crawled across a fence, crawled across a road, got to a house and knocked on a woman's door. She got the ambulance and I remember her next door neighbour coming in and saying to me 'You're lucky, son, because the last person that was found in that dump was found with a bullet through his head.'

• • •

From a young age, I'd say from the age of 13 on, I'd always wanted to be in the UDA. I had a friend who was in it but they wouldn't let me join because I was too young. When I became the right age, I remember meeting a commander of the UDA of Laugharne in a pub and going and talking to him about joining the UDA, and then going to a flat on a Sunday night and walking in and signing allegiance. I put my hand on the Bible and said I would fight for God and Ulster. I promised I would never marry a Catholic and I would never go into a Catholic chapel and I would be committed to the UDA. At that time I absolutely loved the UDA. I loved everything about it and at that time I wanted to die as a hero for my country.

A lot of my attitude came from the people that I ran about with. I was born and brought up in The Troubles, brought up as a Protestant on a Catholic estate in Laugharne in County Antrim, about 20 miles from Belfast. As a little boy I used to look over the fence and see the Protestant estate across the road and I used to think I'd love to be over there, I'd love to be running about with people there.

From a very young age I felt I didn't fit in. I didn't fit into the family, and I never felt part of things at primary school. I never felt very confident in anything I ever did from an early age. My lack of self-esteem was caused by certain things at home, and I always felt I wanted to be part of a different family. I don't know why, because this was even before things went wrong in my family. I battled with that for years upon years, all my life. I think I had a lot of ability, but low self-esteem and low self-confidence hindered me a lot, because the way that I felt about myself influenced the way that I did my school work.

I always remember my first day at secondary school. I really looked forward to it, getting that new uniform, getting in there. I was always looking for acceptance, I wanted to be accepted by people.

By the second and third year I became quite a loudmouth in the class, and everything at school seemed to go wrong for me. I used to be late all the time. I used to get the bat—out the front, touch my toes and the teacher went at me with the bat.

Then the other pupils in the class started to reject me quite a bit. I was the class reject. They used to send me notes in the class: 'Don't be speaking to any of us—you're the reject'. I couldn't tell anybody about this, I couldn't go home and tell my parents—I had to pretend to my parents everything was OK at school, everything was brilliant. But at times I wouldn't go to school for a month. Not because I didn't want to go but because I wasn't accepted at that school or the class I was in. And I found it very difficult. I loved to play football but again, because of this non-acceptance, I didn't have the confidence. Some of the lads who ran the football team were in my class, and I was thinking everybody was talking about me, and I just wasn't able to get involved.

After the second and third year at school I decided I would fight somebody in school who was hard, to get a name for myself. So I fought this bloke, and though he beat me, from then on I started running about with the lads who got into trouble at school because I felt accepted in there. My problems started from there.

I wouldn't say there was much sectarian stuff going on actually in the school, because in Northern Ireland you go to completely different schools: Protestants go to one school and Catholics go to another. There used to be a Catholic school not far from our school and now and again some of our lads would fight the lads out of that school.

At the age of 13 I started sniffing glue. It gave me a sense of achievement in my life. I had the same dream every time I sniffed glue: I dreamed I was lord of the manor and nobody told me what to do. Glue used to make me very violent. Me and my mate used to sniff glue all the time and we used to fight each other when we were sniffing.

I moved on from glue sniffing to alcohol. I liked alcohol. It gave me a feeling of contentment and release, and it gave me the confidence that I'd never had from a young age. I remember the first time I ever drunk it. It was the twelfth of July and we always collected things for bonfires. That's a tradition of Northern Ireland: Protestants collect for the eleventh night bonfire and then on the twelfth of July the bands march. That first time I drank a can of Tennants and my mother caught me and slapped me across the face in front of about 200 people—but it didn't deter me.

I passed no exams at school—none at all. I got taken out of my school and sent to borstal when I was fourteen and a half. And that was the start of everything.

• • •

I was eleven years old when I first broke the law, climbing up onto the roof of an industrial estate to steal the lead. I got caught by the police but I got away with it because I said I was looking for a tennis ball and they believed me. I'd definitely been taught a sense of right and wrong because my father was quite a law-abiding citizen and so was my mother. But I wasn't happy with just doing what my mates were doing, camping and that. I always wanted to have more excitement, and I think I thought of stealing as excitement. It was just curiosity, I wanted to see what it was like.

Nobody really influenced me—I did what I wanted to do, and it ended up with violence, assaults, fighting all the time. I always remember one incident which happened when I was sniffing glue. We wanted to steal a motorbike from the school and we had to scale a 30 foot wall with it! I couldn't have done this when I was ordinary, only with the strength the glue gave me. We built a scaffold on the inside of the school wall and as we built it up we carried this motorbike up the scaffold, then dropped it down the other side of the wall, and took it on to the main road. My mate got caught by the police but I cleared off and I never got caught.

I was 14 the first time I went to borstal, for criminal damage with another of my mates from school. We got given a month in the summer of 1983. I loved borstal from the word go—I absolutely loved the place because it gave me freedom away from home. It gave me freedom away from the struggles I had at school and everything.

When I came out I had loads of charges against me, that I was waiting to go to court for. But because I liked the place so much I couldn't wait for that. So I decided to get myself put in borstal for good. I committed loads of offences in a period of two weeks so that I would get sentenced and sent back there. I came out at the end of July and was back in the September doing what was called a 'one to three'.[2]

When I was 16 I was let out and the borstal got me a job so I could go back home and work on a youth training programme restoring trains. But I only stayed outside a matter of four weeks before I was back again doing another one to three.

Borstal gave me an identity because I was able to be Jack the Lad. I fought my way up to the top in it. From the very start I used to fight

---

[2] Months

quite a bit—when I first went in with my mates to do the month we ruled the place. Then when I went back in on my own, I thought I'd just carry on fighting.

I was four weeks into that sentence when the RUC came in one day and in the end I was put into a cage. I'll never forget the day—my mother was supposed to be coming to visit me—and I remember the RUC coming in and putting handcuffs on me. I wasn't allowed in a room with anybody else. I had to sleep in this cage on my own at night-time.

Then when I was 15, I was taken out and sent to the young offenders' centre in Belfast, and given what they called a 'five week order'. This was five weeks in an ordinary prison to try and deter you from the behaviour you were committing at the borstal. But it didn't deter me because when I was in the YO centre, I spent the whole time, night and day, in solitary confinement because of my behaviour in the prison. I got back to the borstal again after doing this five week order and continued to fight. Then they put me in another unit where you were treated well. You were given the best trainers, the best jeans and it was like a one-to-one sort of thing to try and sort your life out. But it just made me worse and worse all the time. The point is, borstal just gave me something that outside didn't give me. It made me feel good.

● ● ●

I served six custodial sentences, from the age of 14 till the age of 23. The longest was two and a half years for burning a shop and rioting during The Troubles. It was at the time of the protest called 'Ulster Says No' and it was a protest against shops and businesses opening up. One bloke opened his shop and someone threw a match into the store and set it alight. But I want to stress now, and I've always stressed it, that I never actually committed the crime that I did the time for.

I was part of the mob because I loved it, I got a buzz from rioting. I loved to riot. At that time I'd never taken drugs—my buzz came from rioting with the police. My adrenaline came from rioting—I loved it. But when that store was burnt I wasn't actually there. I'd been caught by the police swinging on the chapel bells. The reason why I was swinging on the bells was because that makes the Catholics think somebody's died and they all come out of their front doors. So I got up and climbed on their chapel and started swinging their bells to get all the Catholics out. Just to annoy them like, to get them away from watching TV. And the police caught me and my mate that night on the bells, and they took my name in the book. But when I was interviewed by the police, they still charged me with the crime of setting fire to the shop.

At that time I was very much involved with the UDA. I felt quite accepted when I was in the UDA. I first joined it when I was 16 and a half, 17. I'd never liked the Catholics, especially the Catholics from Belfast, and I used to fight with them a lot. I just hated them. To me they were dirt. I just hated them as stinking—they were filth to me and that was it. I didn't actually hate ordinary Catholics on the street, I just hated that sort of Catholics—IRA Catholics.

You used to have to pay a pound a week to the UDA if you were working and 50p a week if you were on the dole. What I used to do sometimes (and this is why I eventually tried to get out of the UDA) was I used to have to go round the pubs with a box collecting for the LPA—the Loyalist Prisoners' Association. So everybody was starting to get to know that I was involved with the UDA because I was going round to each pub and shaking these boxes in front of people's faces, Catholics as well as Protestants, to get money for the LPA. They were funded in that way at that time, and I suppose they were funded by people doing burglaries as well. It depended how much a person was committed to it. The IRA would have been funded in much the same way.

I'm still a bit scared of reprisals from talking out about all this. But because of my faith I believe it's right that I should—though I don't want to mention anything that I got involved with. I loved the UDA at one time but when I got more involved, because I was known in my town as being game to do anything, I found they were starting to exploit that. I realised I'd soon be used for something that I really didn't want to do, and the more I thought about it, the more I didn't want to get involved in it any more.

It came to the twelfth of July 1986—the marching day—and I'd gone to a different estate to collect for the bonfire. One of the UDA commanders came up and said to me 'Could you come down and see us? You owe us dues and we want to see you at the meeting'. But I knew they were going to beat me up so I wasn't going to turn up.

The reason I was worried was because I'd been stupid. I was drinking a lot at that time. I used to drink all weekend and get totally stupid, and I used to lose my memory quite a bit because I was drinking—I used to have quite a lot of blackouts. And when I was having blackouts, I was always mouthing out about the UDA, about the battalion that I was in, and telling the young lads that were in it to go and tell the commanders I couldn't care less what they did. I thought I was Jack the Lad. But this was causing them a lot of flack. It was like me against 40,000 men and I used to wake up on a Monday morning and be really, really scared at what I might have said.

Then one night in October that year I was in a club. In the town that I come from, the UDA would run discos on a Friday night, and we used to collect the money at the door—it was a pound to get in and the money went towards the UDA. This Friday night, a bloke came to sit at my table. He was a UDA person, and by this time I didn't want anything to do with them whatsoever. So I said 'Look, just leave'. So he left the table without saying anything. I was standing out in the hall later and he started arguing with me. The next thing I knew I was on the ground. He'd hit me in the face with a pint glass and smashed it and nearly cut my throat. He only just missed my windpipe—I've got a lot of stitches straight across my throat.

He got arrested and he signed his own statement. The UDA wanted me to retract the statement against him, and I was going to do it but that wasn't possible because he had signed it himself.

The following year, 31 January 1987, it was a Sunday night and I was in a house with about ten mates playing cards, when a knock came to the door. There was a girl in the house and she went and opened the door. I heard this scuffle in the hall, and four men come into the living room with balaclavas on. They were carrying baseball bats, and they said 'Is there a guy called Tommy here?' I knew it was me they were looking for and I just felt like melting where I was.

One of the blokes sitting there said it was a set-up—they had set me up. They wanted me reprimanded in case the rest of the lads in the UDA thought that if I could get away with saying things then they could get away with it too.

They took me out into the hall. I went with them like a little lamb. One of them started head-butting me in the hall—it was just a small, square hall—and I thought 'How am I ever going to get out of this?'

I dived back into the living room and that gave them a chance to swing their baseball bats, and they started smashing my head with the bats. Then one stuck his hand in his inside pocket and said 'Look, if you don't move now I'm going to blow your head off!' So I said, 'OK—I'll go with you'.

They put a balaclava over my head and they carried me out the door. They had turned off all the street lights. What they used to do was to throw a wire up over the mains down at the bottom of the estate and that cut out the electricity on the whole estate. They did that so they couldn't be identified carrying me out and putting me in the back on their estate car. Then they drove me off to the dump and beat me.

• • •

I spent quite a bit of time in the hospital recuperating from that. You'll maybe not believe this, but it's the gospel truth: only one bone got broken in my body. Those blokes beat my legs—you can still see the marks all up my legs. Both my legs are dented up both sides. When I first went into the hospital the doctor reckoned my body was smashed to pieces—my legs were swollen out here somewhere, and my arms were as big as my thighs and my head was split open, so I had to have stitches in it. My face was all right, I never got touched on my face. The doctor said to me 'You must have bones on you like breeze blocks, because any man who gets their body beat for 15 to 30 minutes with baseball bats and comes out with only one broken bone, it's a miracle'.

But the psychological side of it was unbelievable—the nightmares that I had after it, the pain that I had after it. Three months later I got two and a half years in jail for that shop being burnt, and it was the biggest relief I ever had in my life to get taken off the streets. Because in that period of three months after I came out of hospital I had to stay in many different houses. I couldn't stay in my own house in case these blokes returned to get me.

I remember a specific point: I went to stay in my granny's house one day, though I never usually stayed much at my granny's at this time. It was a Thursday night, just near Easter. We had a local paper and there was a fellow who wrote in it called Robert Small. He served 16 years in prison for paramilitary murders in the early days of The Troubles, but he's now a born-again Christian. I remember he put a piece in the paper, trying to deter young lads from getting involved in the paramilitary, and to persuade them to get a purpose in their lives. I remember reading this that night.

I was going through a lot of psychological pain from the beating, and after I read this article I remember bending on my knees in my granny's house and saying 'Lord Jesus, come into my life again'. This was the second time I'd asked the Lord into my life, but the first time was really only because I was in severe trouble and I needed help.

I ended up getting two and a half years in jail and like I said, it was such a relief to get into jail away from all this hassle and shifting from house to house and the worrying and the pain. So even though I didn't do the crime, I didn't fight against that sentence. I just accepted it because it was like somebody lifting the Grand Canyon off my back.

• • •

After I got let out, I got deeply involved in drugs. At the age of 21 I moved to London to work on the building sites. I was working on Canary Wharf at the time it was being built, and I started taking speed to help me do my work better. Then I got involved with drug dealers and had to do a runner back to Northern Ireland. I ended up with another prison sentence—five years this time—and I had to come back to England to serve it. I did five days in Brixton then they sent me to Camp Hill prison on the Isle of Wight.

It was there that my life started to change. Because I really hated this prison sentence. Although I'd done all the borstal and prison sentences in Northern Ireland this was all new to me. I never got any visits and I found it really, really hard. I got even more involved in drugs and I took heroin for the first time. For the eight months I spent at Camp Hill I would say that I was stoned most of the time.

The change in my life came through my faith in Jesus Christ. I had a mate back at home who had lived something of the same life as me. He had done 12 years for conspiracy to murder and he became a Christian when he was in the jail. He sent me a book called *A Long Way to Paradise*. I remember I was really depressed when I read this book. The writer had made a promise to God: he promised that if God got him out of the situation he was in, he would give his life back to him. I remember lying in that prison bed on the Isle of Wight and I said 'Lord, if you get me out of this prison to accumulated visits[3] in Northern Ireland, I'll give my life back to you'.

I put in for accumulated visits and—this is no word of a lie—I got them, plus a weekend parole leave, back in Northern Ireland. They paid my train fare back and everything.

I was sent to a prison called Maghaberry, in County Antrim. On the four landings that were allowed to congregate together, there were at least 25 Christians. These Christian blokes used to come into my cell and give me wee books—I was reading them on the sly. And this is where I really started to search my life and see what life was all about.

I still didn't find it easy to do my sentence. I went to see a psychiatrist because one of the lads in the prison told me you could con them and tell them you were going nuts and get drugs off them—drugs weren't as available in Maghaberry as they were in England. So I went to the psychiatrist and told him that if he didn't give me some drugs I was going to do myself in. He put me on a drug called Melleril which is used for geriatrics. It meant I could sleep when I wanted and when I did get a joint to go with it I was just in cloud cuckoo land. But this drug was starting to make me very angry, not towards prisoners but towards myself, and towards my family when they used to come and visit.

My mother came to visit me just before my birthday in March. A mate of mine was supposed to come with her on the visit, but he didn't come and my brother came instead. That made me so angry that I started effing and blinding at my mother on the visit. I remember watching my mother walk out the visits room crying her eyes out and this started to make me think. I thought 'My mother's stuck by me all these years and yet I'm treating her like pure rubbish'.

When it came to my birthday on March 12 I got no birthday cards for the first time in my life. To some people that may seem trivial, but to me it meant a lot. I remember on March 17—St Patrick's Day—

---

[3] Visits saved up to be taken all together in prison near home

getting on my knees and saying 'Lord, I can't do it any more'. And I was able to come off those drugs straight away, and I became a Christian.

• • •

On my release I applied to go to a half-way house. I got in touch with a mate called Billy who was working for the Prison Fellowship[4] in Belfast and I told him I didn't want to stay in Northern Ireland. I said, 'I'm a Christian now, I believe I've made a true commitment. If I go back home I'm never going to make it because I can't live among my mates, and I'm going to end up inside prison all my life. I need to break free from all this'.

So he got me into a half-way house in Preston. But unfortunately there wasn't any real discipline there and I went night-clubbing and doing everything that I wanted. I kept moving between England and Scotland and I went back on the drink and drugs. I was on the fringes of being an alcoholic—my head was totally messed up from the lifestyle I'd lived through paranoia and everything else.

In the end it took a year in a drugs rehab for me to sort myself out. I went down to Wales for the interview to this rehab. I remember walking in there and a peace came over my life like I'd never had before—I was 24 years old, and in all those 24 years I'd never felt like that before. I was desperate to get in there because at that time I was at the point where I just wanted my life to be changed. To me that was a real answer to my prayer. I knew it was right that I went there because of the peace that I felt for the first time ever in my life.

I went through the drug rehab for a year and the discipline of it was really hard. You had to be up at half seven in the morning and do a routine right through till half nine at night. Or else you could leave, because it was voluntary. I went through it, graduated from there, came out and held down a job. That was the start of my rehabilitation.

• • •

Up until that time I didn't realise that I was institutionalised. I'd always depended on institutions one way or another from the age of 14. At 26 years old for the first time ever I learned how to live on my own. After the rehab I worked on the motorways for two-and-a-half years and it was one of the hardest struggles I ever had in my life, to get my life together. I went back to work in the drug rehab again for a year,

---

[4] International Christian ministry to prisoners, ex-prisoners and their families, offering practical and spiritual support.

then I moved down to the West Country where I've been running a market business of my own until recently.

• • •

Since then I've been back into many different prisons sharing my testimony. I go round schools, youth clubs and young people's groups, sharing my story of how my life was changed. I'm involved as a youth worker on a voluntary basis helping to run a youth café for young people who are involved in drugs and alcohol. Now I've applied for a job to work in prisons as a pre-release worker. In future I hope to work with ex-offenders, to be an asset to them. I want to work with people who get in trouble, especially young people.

A lot of what I have done I regret—the pain and the hurt that I put people through. The things that led me to commit offences were rejection, not being accepted, feeling like a square in a circle. I don't feel that now, not at all. From my own point of view, I can look at my past offending as a bonus. It's a plus to me, because it means I can go and talk to young people. I can relate to others who are leading the same lifestyle as I did. I hope that in the future I can be both a deterrent and an encouragement for young people like this, and show them there is hope at the end of the line.

I've got hope, I've got faith, I've got Jesus Christ in my life, even though I have my ups and downs. My relationship with the Lord Jesus Christ is definitely what helps me stay away from offending. Nothing whatsoever could make me return to crime.

On the estate where I lived, the gospel people used to come round in the summer time and from a very young age I always remember looking into a woman's eyes and seeing a love coming from her that I'd never seen in anybody else's eyes in my life before. That always stuck in my mind. Now that I'm a born-again Christian, I tell myself that it says in the Bible that in the Lord Jesus Christ we all become one—whether we're Jew, Catholic or Protestant, no matter what we are. I would like to think that Catholics and Protestants could actually become friends one day.

Carole

Carole is 49. Sexually abused as a child, she became an arsonist—a crime commonly linked with childhood sexual abuse. She spent 20 years, from the age of 21 to the age of 41, in Broadmoor, the secure hospital for the criminally insane. She was released in 1991 and since then has spent her time learning to live independently, writing and acting. She has written poems and plays and is working on her autobiography. Because of the stigma still sadly associated with mental illness, Carole has asked for her name to be changed.

I don't remember much about the journey to Broadmoor. I recall my grandmother coming up with a big bunch of flowers. My parents were told not to tell me I was going to Broadmoor, but to a nice hospital in the country. That was in 1971: Friday the thirteenth of August—perhaps that was an omen. I was 21—my twenty-second birthday was on the thirteenth of November—and I stayed in Broadmoor until 1991—20 years from the age of 21 to the age of 41. You are sent there for an indefinite period. There was no court case or anything.

When I arrived I noticed the bars at the windows. I just felt numb. The doctor gave me an examination and then he said I had to have a bath. I said 'I don't want a bath, I had one before I came'. He said 'I can see she's going to be stroppy' and the nurse said 'She needs a dose of Douglas!' So I was dragged straight off to Douglas, which was the punishment block.

I was put in a single cell with a concrete floor and a canvas mattress and a pot in the corner. There was an inspection slot and a window with wooden shutters against it. Overhead there was a dim orange light. I was put in a strip gown and there was just this canvas bedding. No explanation was given to me and I saw no other patients. I'll always remember the nurse saying to me 'You're lucky, you've arrived just in time for dinner', and I was given a paper plate with stew on it. I had to eat it with my fingers because they said they couldn't even give me a plastic spoon because they didn't know what I'd do with it.

I was in this punishment block off and on for the next eight years because I was a rebel and I wouldn't conform. I wouldn't let them break my spirit. I see it now, how they were trying to make us conform. We had to wear certain clothes—we were forced to wear dresses which I hated—we had to put on makeup and we had to have a boyfriend. Where could we get a boyfriend? From among the male patients of course! The nurses would say 'You've got to wear a dress, you've got to have a boyfriend, or you'll never get out'.

• • •

I came from a caring home and I had a good childhood. Apart from the abuse. Dad's Canadian. He worked for the Home Office as a catering officer in an approved school. Mum never worked. They used to row a bit and Mum would say 'If it wasn't for the kids I'd be off'. It hurt me at the time I heard it, but then I'd forget about it.

Every summer holidays I used to go to stay with my grandparents in Brighton. This was my mum's mother and stepfather. They had no television so we used to play Scrabble. I loved it and that's where I think I got my love of words. My grandmother used to read me *Noddy* books—I had a whole set of them.

But this all stopped when I was about ten and my step-grandfather started sexually abusing me. He started feeling my breasts and saying I was getting to be a big girl, things like that. I told my grandmother and she believed me and told me I'd better not come and stay with them any more now that I was getting older. I told my mother too but she just dismissed it as if it was not a big issue. I think I just accepted that I couldn't go there any more.

I had one brother, four years older than me. I used to be very close to my brother till I was 11 and he was 15, when—just like my grandfather—he started sexually abusing me too. He used to come into my bedroom at night when my parents were watching TV. This went on for about a year. I couldn't tell my parents: I didn't have the guts. So I just used to leave little notes round my room. The notes said my brother was playing with me sexually, things like that. But nothing happened: my parents thought I was just going through a pre-adolescent phase. They were angry with me and they swept the whole thing under the carpet, so the abuse still went on. Then my periods started and I told my brother I could now have a baby and that frightened him so the abuse stopped.

• • •

I was always a loner at school—it was a kind of intellectual loneliness. My grandmother had taught me the alphabet and a few words. Because I could read a bit, I think I felt superior to the others in my class and I was bored by the work. I thought 'I don't want to do this, it's boring'. Making friends never came easily to me. The girls wanted to play with dolls and I wanted boys' games. I had this one brother, and next door on one side there were five boys, and on the other side one boy, and I played with all these boys and was always a tomboy. So I felt alienated and this continued throughout primary school.

I had to excel in everything I did. I had to give it 100 per cent. Even now I don't do things by halves—I'm a perfectionist. I was quite athletic. I liked team games and I loved running and jumping. I had good school reports and my parents praised me for that. I was always good at English because I had a gift for it.

I went to the same secondary school that my brother had just left, and I was put in the A form. I took on my brother's legacy—he had started a chess club for example—and some of his mates became my mates. I was happy there and I knuckled down and studied hard. I did well at that school. I got five 'O' levels and six RSAs. As well as running the chess club I became assistant head librarian and a prefect. I also played the violin.

I went on to a local college and studied for my A levels. But I didn't pass them because that's when I became ill. When I was 16, I felt these strange sensations in my hands and I told the GP and my parents and was taken to hospital. I was diagnosed as having epilepsy, given medication and sent back to college.

But then I have a total blank about those years between the ages of 16 and 19.

It seems I was in a psychiatric hospital. I've been told I started fires at the college, so I was taken straight from the college to this hospital. I have also been told that while I was in the psychiatric hospital, I set fire to the laundry room and the day room and to a padded cell, though I can't understand how I could have got the matches to do that. But I don't remember anything about it. That's the reason I was taken to Broadmoor, because as an arsonist you are seen as a potential mass murderer.

I have thought a lot about why I could have done all this, and I've often wondered if it was triggered by my brother getting married that year. He married a girl with the same name as me.

• • •

In Broadmoor we were forced to do work. I worked in the hospital shop which was called the canteen like prison shops are. There was also ward work—we'd be polishing the floors. Then there was occupational therapy—knitting, sewing, making teddy bears. Or we might be sent to work in the mini-hangar, which was packing work. That work was mixed—you mixed with the male patients there and some of them were sex offenders. Then there was handicrafts—things like pewter work—that was mixed as well.

I will say I did feel quite safe from any fear of attack by the men. The gardens were mixed work too and the men didn't attack the women—they attacked each other if anything. But they were all controlled by drugs, as we were. Most people were on the drug Largactil, which is an appetite inducer, which is why so many of them were very overweight.

There were a lot of petty rules. For instance, one day—I suppose I must have been in my 30s by then—I didn't want to eat anything. I wasn't on Largactil at that time and I wasn't hungry. So I got a banana out of my locker and I didn't go to the dining room. I just stayed and ate my banana. When the bell rang for meals a nurse came along and said, 'What are you doing here?' and I said 'I don't fancy anything'. At mealtimes we used to get counted out, so you had to go. This nurse grabbed me by the scruff of my neck and pushed me down the stairs. I hit the metal banisters and my ankle was broken. But all I got was bed rest. They did get a doctor but he just said 'No bones broken'. Then my ankle swelled right up and they did X-ray it in the end and it was fractured. But in the meantime I was just put in a secure cell and left, with no painkillers, plaster or bandages.

While I was in that cell I just lost interest in eating because of having to eat in seclusion. There was no light in the room and I just lost my appetite. They said I was anorexic but I wasn't—I just couldn't eat if I was on my own. I went right down to five stones. One of the few good nurses there finally allowed me to eat in the dining hall with other people and then I went back to eating normally again.

● ● ●

For the first seven years I was in Broadmoor, till I was about 28 years old, my parents used to come to visit me. They used to bring me in things like cigarettes, pop and clothes. Once when they visited me I remember telling them how badly I had been treated in the punishment block, and how the nurses had rubbed my face in urine. I was overheard by the screws—that's what we used to call the nurses—and that night, after my parents had left, two of these same nurses came to give me night sedation. I was complaining that I was constipated. As a punishment for speaking to my parents about my treatment, they gave me a handful of laxatives and the male nurse said 'Who told Mummy then?' As a result I had terrible diarrhoea.

After those first seven years, my parents suddenly said they wouldn't be coming to see me any more. They said they'd got through all their savings and they were too broke to come again. Their letters stopped as well. My parents never used to say much in their letters to me anyway, only what they had for dinner and what the weather was like. But at least my mum used to write once a week and she kept this up for seven years. Then I got no more letters from them. After seven years they tried to disown me.

So I was very worried because my parents had disappeared and I had no contacts on the outside at all. You were not allowed to write to your solicitor. All your letters were censored and if you complained in any way about your treatment there, the letter would come back with the word 'RE-WRITE' scrawled across it. The screws would say you couldn't write that as it would be too upsetting to relatives and friends. A lot of the women used to cut up[1] but I never did that.

• • •

For the first ten years in Broadmoor I was too drugged up to do anything much. In fact I had no treatment for 15 years except for drugs—I got no therapy until the last five years when I got group therapy. I was on a large number of drugs: Largactil[2]—1000 ml a day, which was a very large dose; Carbamazepine[3] 100 ml; 10 mg Stelazine[4]; Valium; Haloperidol[5], Procyclidine[6] and Epanutin[7]. I also had Tuinal[8] as night sedation, but when they found out it was a barbiturate it was banned because people were getting high on it. Then I was given 2 gms of Chloral hydrate[9] instead. I became addicted to Chloral and suffered cold turkey effects when I came out of Broadmoor. Injections were given in the bum. I was told I was a paranoid schizophrenic. I had ECT[10] but just once. The drugs made me mumble and the doctor said he couldn't understand what I was saying so I had to see a speech therapist.

I had no respect for any of the doctors. One I remember was Scottish and I only saw him twice in five years. Only my sense of humour kept me going. I thought 'At least it can't get any worse'.

The male nurses used to watch us women in the bath. We were made to have cold baths and two of us would be put in the bath at the same time and the men were watching in case of aggro. The male nurses also gave us our injections in the backside. The nurses wear a uniform, a white coat, but they come in the mornings wearing peaked caps and they all carry keys—the keys are swinging around.

There were just a few good nurses in Broadmoor. They were the ones who would take you aside and have a little talk with you. They took time to sort out whether you were OK. Sometimes the nurses could be

---

1 Self-harm
2 A brand name for chlorpromazine, an anti-psychotic drug
3 A generic anti-convulsant drug
4 A brand name for trifluoperazine, an anti-psychotic drug used to treat schizophrenia
5 An anti-psychotic drug
6 An anticholinergic drug commonly used as an antidote to the side effects (shaking etc) of other drugs such as Haloperidol
7 A brand name for phenytoin, an anti-convulsant drug used to treat epilepsy
8 A brand name barbiturate sleeping drug
9 One of the oldest treatments for insomnia still in use: highly addictive
10 Electro-convulsive therapy—electric shock treatment

forced to leave because the others put pressure on them. If the good ones saw nurses beating patients they might tell.

I got beaten up myself. After many years I'd managed to get on the 'Good' block, which was the block you were put in before you reached the Parole wing, and I was coming out of the canteen.[11] You only got canteen once a week so you had to buy a week's supplies. A gang of girls came up, looked at my cigarettes and said 'We'll have three of them'. They kept doing it and the number they wanted went up to 40 then to 60. So I said 'I'll fight you for them'—though there were eight of them to one of me and I got beaten up. Then the second time it happened I said 'Come on then', and I got beaten up again. So I went to the screws for help and they turned round and beat me up themselves. They said I was a grasser. They physically beat me, badly.

I still refused to give the gang my cigarettes. I tried to keep it together and next time it happened I didn't tell the screws. I told the gang I'd lost my locker key, and I got respect after that. Like at school, I was a loner even then, in there, and when they asked me to join their gang, I said no. But after that I was OK. I made one good friend, a woman who was my friend for 14 years.

I could certainly become violent during those years. For instance I got onto the Occupational Therapy wing and I got hold of a lighter and set fire to a girl's hair. I remember thinking 'I'm in here for arson so I'll bloody well do it'. She was a black girl and I must admit I was racist at that time—I don't know why because I hadn't been brought up to be racist. Anyway I took against this black girl and set fire to her hair. The emergency bell went and I was back to square one again.

After I'd been in Broadmoor about 13 years I got very depressed, almost suicidal. I said to myself, 'I'll be here for ever'. *not going anywhere*

• • •

The event that changed my life and made me determined to get out of Broadmoor was when my grandmother died. This was the grandmother I used to stay with in Brighton as a child. Gran used to come to Broadmoor twice a year by taxi all the way from Brighton. One day we were told we were allowed to have televisions in our rooms. This was while I was still in touch with my mum and dad, and I asked them for a black and white TV set. They said they were broke and couldn't get me one. But my Gran came all the way up from Brighton in the taxi with a black and white TV on her lap. It meant the world to me that she did that. She would only get two hours visiting time and it was a room as small as this one [the living room in her present flat] and yet there were two screws there listening.

---

[11] Hospital shop

Gran was always on my side. Once I took part in a TV programme called *Madness* and I read out one of my poems. My mum and dad were ashamed of me. But Gran wasn't. She used to say 'You're in the right place. If you had a broken leg you'd go to a hospital to have it treated'. The day I heard about my grandmother's death, I had got in a fight and been sent to the punishment block. So I was locked up there when the chaplain came along and he broke the news that my grandmother had died. I was very confused. I was worried about my mother, although she had never been close to my Gran.

I was going through all these emotions, locked up in solitary. I couldn't even send flowers because she had been cremated a week before. I wanted to make some sort of memorial to my grandmother so I started writing. Gran had taught me how to write and yes, that was a moment of revelation to me. I thought 'I can write, and I can use my gift for the English language'. When I wrote my book of poems I put in it, *To Grandma, dearly loved and always sadly missed*.

That was the turning point for me. I thought how my grandma used to come and see me, and I thought about the things she said. I decided I had to look to be positive and make a clear progression upwards.

• • •

When I was in my early thirties I started to get some education. I learned a bit about computers and I took five music exams—violin exams up to Grade V—and I learned the recorder. I also did a business exam and some drama therapy. And I was in the choir too.

After I'd been in Broadmoor 15 years I got into the Parole Wing— there was a separate ward for parole patients. You began in a dormitory then went into a room. From the Parole Wing we used to be taken out on trips. I remember going to Thorpe Park and Canterbury Cathedral. I wasn't really shocked at what things were like outside because I couldn't remember what they'd been like in the first place. So to me, all these things were new, as if I'd never done them. The way I finally got out was really through a kind of blackmail. We had a new doctor, a woman, and she told me to keep my nose clean for one year and she would get me out. So I had an incentive and I kept out of trouble for a year. You have to go before a tribunal with a judge and a doctor and your brief, and at my tribunal my brief said to me 'Tell the judge how you've progressed, and your plans for the future, and how you've stayed out of trouble for a year'. I said that this woman doctor had told me that if I kept my nose clean for a year I'd get out. I had witnesses to prove it so the doctor couldn't deny it.

• • •

When I was released from Broadmoor in 1991 I went to an Interim Secure Unit in Shaftesbury and I got involved in WISH.[12] I saw their organization advertised on the notice board of the Unit and eventually I became a member of their management committee. They sent me a birthday card which really touched me. The people at WISH were very nice and helped me get my poems published and I won a prize. Then I wrote a play called *Oiks and Angels,* and I got my work published in their newsletter. When I went to management committee meetings they would send a car to the Unit and I would then come back by tube. I'd never been on a tube before, as I didn't live near London as a child. They sent me on a computer course with CAST[13] and they visited me when I got taken to hospital. I now feel I have outgrown WISH though I still have great respect for the organization. But I want to move on, away from all that.

After being in the unit in Shaftesbury I went into a hostel for the mentally ill in Wimbledon where there were about 20 people and a manager. There were four or five women and the rest were men. The women were all in one unit with their own sleeping quarters, quite separate from the men. I went there in 1993 but I only stayed there six weeks before I became psychotic. In this hostel I didn't have much support and I fell flat on my face mentally. It was all because of stress. I ran out into the traffic early one morning. I was taken by the police to a police station and left there on my own in a room with no light. The police were awful to me. My social worker heard me screaming down the phone to get me out.

So I had to be taken back to the same psychiatric hospital where I'd been all those years ago, and I stayed there from 1993 to 1995. While I was there I made contact with my mum and dad again. I rang up and I said 'I'm broke, I'm in hospital, I've been kicked out of the hostel'. My mum was OK but my dad took longer to come round. In 1995 I went back to the same hostel in Wimbledon and I was there till February 1998. Then I got this flat, provided by the Cheshire Homes.

• • •

You can never say that you won't reoffend but I don't want to be doped up on drugs like I used to be. I am self-medicating now which is a lot better.

---

12 Women in Special/Secure Hospitals: organization to help mentally disordered women in such institutions and in prisons

13 Creative and Supportive Trust for prisoners. Runs skills development courses and provides education, training and careers advice.

I like living on my own in this flat. I've been here four months. I'm never ordered about by anybody, I can do all my shopping, and now I go and visit my parents in Eastbourne.

I have my support workers, key workers, doctors, and my medication.

I used to belong to a self-help group but I outgrew it. I belong to the Church of England and I found religion helpful in Broadmoor. I also get help from the National Schizophrenia Society. I used to attend their meetings.

What matters to me now is my writing and going to drama college. I attend a drama course at Clean Break[14] three days a week. We do workshops, improvisations, and creative writing. We act out situations and learn about certain types of theatre. I love it because it gives me a structure to my life. I am still very active in Clean Break. I found out about it when I saw a notice of theirs advertised. I'd done a lot of drama in Broadmoor and I found that acting gave me confidence and raised my self-esteem. It's also taught me how to work in a team—there are eight of us in the group. I learned how to type by going on the CAST computer course once a week for about 14 weeks, as well as their creative writing course. This summer [1998] I took part in a production called *Diamonds* at the Royal Court Theatre Upstairs in London. It was a series of sketches about women's friendships. I did two of my monologues—I learned them off by heart.

I can only write when the spirit moves me so I've written nothing this year so far. I have enough to cope with, though I like to keep my hand in. I found I couldn't write about my Broadmoor experiences when I was first released—I was too close to all that and I found it too draining. It was two years before I could write about it at all. It used to knock me for six because I could only write as if it's happening in the present. Now though I can detach myself from it. I've found it good therapy to write, to get it all out of my system. I have also spoken at a seminar about special hospitals.

When I first came out I was bitter and angry but all that's water under the bridge now. When I was in Broadmoor I never allowed my spirit to be broken. They want to take away your individuality but I'd look up out of the window and see the birds flying and I'd be up there flying with them.

---

[14] A theatre company that trains women prisoners and ex-prisoners in theatre skills.

Cameron Mackenzie

Cameron was brought up on a scheme[1] near Glasgow which was steeped in sectarian violence. He began drinking at the age of 12, joined a local gang and was finally jailed for stabbing and almost killing a youth from a rival gang in a drunken brawl. Now 37, Cameron is a minister of the Church of Scotland in East Lothian.

I would have said I had a secure childhood, but thinking about it now I feel that the life I went on to live would suggest otherwise. It felt like a happy enough life as you were living it. But now I wonder. I started drinking at 12, I got involved with the police even younger. I was getting into all sorts of trouble all the way through high school, and eventually I got kicked out.

And look at the rest of my life: I get myself a sort of a job and two or three months later I go and stab somebody nearly to death and go to jail for two years. Then I come out and I'm still drinking heavily. Then I manage to get off the drink, but I get on to drugs and spend seven years on the drugs. So you might ask, well, *was* it such a happy childhood, if that was the fruit of it?

I think the fruit of my life from the age of 12 to the age of 27 when I became a Christian was pretty much a mixture of awful and no' so bad!

• • •

I'm the oldest of five children—I'm eleven years older than my youngest sister. One of my first memories is moving into a house in Paisley. I remember it being really high up, a high tenement. At the back there was a walled garden—it wasnae really a garden, it was packed earth with washing lines strung across it. But there was a very high wall on three sides of it and the fourth side was made by the back of the building. I remember cycling around there on my little trike.

Once I got to school we moved to another area. We moved down on to the scheme into a rented place. In many ways that was a bad move for us because it was down deeper in the troubled areas, further into the scheme, and it was a lot wilder down there. We had been sheltered to a certain extent, being at the top end.

My primary school was Protestant and the Catholic primary was just a little way away. The Catholic primary was on one plot of land, and we were in the next plot of land on a separate street. We knew the kids there were different but we didn't know why. So we sang songs at them:

---

[1] Housing estate

Catholic, Catholic, quack quack quack!
Go to the devil and never come back!

And then we'd fight. I remember fighting with kids who were about six or seven, the same age as me, and we didn't know why we were fighting. Though the school buildings were separate, the playgrounds backed on to each other and were only separated by a little wall. We'd get dragged apart by teachers and I'd get a telling-off from my teachers and presumably the boy I was fighting would get a telling-off from his.

But I wasnae one for fighting really. I don't remember being in any other fights. I remember punching a guy who lived in the same close, the same tenement as us, because he hurt my wee brother. But I don't remember any other fighting apart from that one incident in the whole of my childhood.

The West of Scotland's famous for sectarianism, and I didn't know any Catholics until we moved from number 1 to number 30. But when we moved down the bottom end of the scheme, that was where we met our first Catholics. Properly met them I mean. That was the family who stayed in the bottom left flat and we were in the top left. That was a new thing, to actually meet some Catholics and know them by first names.

I was protected from this sectarian stuff to a certain extent because my dad was a Celtic supporter. If my dad had been a Rangers supporter then there'd have been a lot more trouble. A lot of my mates' dads were Rangers guys and they wore the Rangers sash and their fathers wore all that jazz—and a lot of them would come for the marches and were involved in the Orange Lodge. I became a Rangers supporter in my teens, but that was because they were the best team, nothing to do with the fact that I was an Orangeman. One of my pals who was a Protestant was a Celtic supporter.

•　•　•

My mum and dad had both been married before. My dad had two kids elsewhere, my mum had two kids elsewhere—so there were these two other families out there somewhere. We didn't learn about them until much later—I was about eight or ten years old before I found out I had other brothers and sisters. It was pretty strange to think that you'd folk who your dad and mum had had before you. We didn't actually meet any of those people until about the late 'sixties, early 'seventies, and that was a whole new dimension of my life. These two girls appeared and they were calling our mum '*Mum*'. By that time my dad had moved on, but his sons came when they were young adults, 16, 17, 18-year-olds.

Dad was away by that time. He would have been about my age, about 37 probably, when he left. I was about 10. It was quite a disruptive element in my life, obviously, but I did have early memories of discord in the house. I don't think my parents had a happy relationship. I think things were getting pretty rough by then. My dad eventually went off to jail and while he was in there my mum took up with somebody else, a pal's brother—which blew things up for the pal's wife and six kids.

I think my mum probably did her best in terms of us getting our homework done or whatever. But she was not in the least academic in terms of thinking about us achieving or not achieving at school. I think the level she was at herself was low—she was literate in that she could read and write and do the basics, but I think for her school was not a priority. A woman of that class needed her kids to go out and get a job. And that's what we wanted too. I wanted a job, I wanted to work and get money. I wasnae interested in learning. I didnae equate working hard at school with getting a better job, or one with more money. So from the age of 12 I worked delivering milk every day from four o'clock in the morning till half past eight. I was a working man at the age of 12. The wages were poor but with the tips and everything I was making £15, £18 or £20 a week some weeks. So essentially I felt like a working and independent guy at the age of 12. I was self-supporting in many ways from that age.

School for me was just an irrelevance. I used to go to sleep in the biology class and the technical drawing class and any other class where they would let me. The teachers quite often let me curl up along three or four benches and go to sleep because I was so tired after doing my milk round. I dogged the school—I didnae go quite a bit. I was quite happy to go along and play the game, but I had no real interest in doing much while I was there.

I had no interest in going to the high school at all. When it came to secondary school I can remember walking up the hill the first day with this brown uniform on. I'd got the blazer just the day before and I hadnae had much time to think about wearing this horrible brown uniform. I can remember walking up the hill surrounded by total strangers. But there was worse to come because you ended up being put in classes by alphabetical order. So I wasnae put with some of the guys I would have considered friends, like Billy Porter. Billy disappeared. I don't know where Billy went. I saw him at the high school and he still stayed in the same street as me, but our paths diverged at that point. Whereas Willie McDowell and I stayed in the same group because my surname was Mackenzie and his was McDowell, and we made new pals. One of my mates called McDonald, he was from another area entirely, I'd never seen him in my life before our first day at the high school. He had a broken arm so he stood out, and he became one of our gang. In fact he became very much leader of our gang because he was a bit of a fighter, which made him the main topic of all of our admiration.

I was about 12 when I was first made aware that I was breaking the law, but of course I'd done other things before that. We'd broken into an old dairy place and smashed up a couple of milk floats. I was charged for that and went before a children's panel. But that didnae appear on my record. It was just a bunch of kids looking for something to do. Great fun at the time until the security man arrived then all hell broke loose.

I also started drinking at 12. I was introduced to alcohol by two guys who were about a year and a half older than me who said, 'We're gonna go and get a bottle of wine. D'you wanna come?' That was very much everybody's introduction to drink. Later on I would have done the same myself with folk a year and a half younger than me: 'I'm gonna go for a bottle of vodka, d'you wanna go half wi' us?' That's the way it worked. So the introduction was at 12, by guys a wee bit older, and I just carried on from there.

I continued to drink alcohol because I liked it. It made me feel good. I started with wine and beer, and then moved on to vodka and lager and super-lagers, whatever was in fashion. If it was vodka we'd drink vodka, if it was Carlsberg super-lager we'd drink ten of them and get out of our minds. Drinking always went on till you were steaming. It was never just a couple of drinks until you had a buzz. It was six or ten or 12 or 14, whatever it took to get you nigh on unconscious.

If I went into a pub it was normally to get blitzed. If you didnae get blitzed it was because you didnae have enough time or enough money. Because normally—the first two years, three years maybe—it was back street drinking. You would carry the drink out of the licensed grocers, up the park, up the railway, whatever. That was all done very much out of the public view. And then we'd just stagger up the town, drunk, and fight.

At about 15 we started getting served in the pubs. But before that we'd started going to one or two of the pubs where you could get in under age. So we'd have pints of Tennants and bottles of liqueurs, whatever, we'd just have whatever was the fashion.

• • •

We were very much living in a gang culture. We could be in separate gangs even though we stayed in the same street. But I think I must have been trying to get attention, there must have been something like that going on, because I don't think I was a particularly violent person. I mean that's the crazy thing, I don't think I was a particularly violent guy. I didn't even particularly enjoy fighting.

The violence was the main problem. There were several occasions when I was brought home by the police for fighting, steaming drunk, or because I was found lying unconscious in vomit. You'd go out dressed up to the nines and then a few hours later you'd be covered with vomit. So there were some serious health risks there. I know guys as drunk as I was that have died in their own vomit. And there'll be guys in the future who'll die as drunk as I was. The main thing was that you were getting drunk and you were getting in trouble with the police—underage drinking, breaching the peace, assaults and stuff like that.

I was done once for breaking into a car which I did in the morning when I was working. We did that a lot of times but this particular time a policeman was watching as I did it. So that was one charge for theft. All my other charges were assault and breaches of the peace.

I spent a couple of weekends in the local police station. Then I got banged up for a week and given a fine, which my mates clubbed up and actually paid for. But on the day I got banged up, by the time they found out about it, it was too late for them to go up and pay it. So I had my hair cut and was banged in a cell.

In the morning when my mates arrived I had this prison haircut and I suppose that must have got me a bit of status. I suppose that must have been quite cool.

I left school without sitting any exams. I was getting sent home for two or three days at a time, and then eventually I was expelled. I was about 15 and it was about four months before the exams. So I never sat an exam, not one. By the time I got to this stage I was pretty much out of control. I was fighting in school, fighting on the way there, fighting on the way back, fighting at lunchtimes. The fighting was in groups mostly, mainly against guys who came from the other side of town and they'd be waiting outside the school. I was also showing a lot of real disruptive behaviour in the class, making it difficult for teachers and pupils alike. At one point they tried to make me a class prefect. I suppose they only wanted me to do that because they thought it would calm me down a bit to have a bit of responsibility. But I didnae want responsibility. I felt as if I had enough responsibility outside the school without getting involved.

In some ways I think I was probably desperate for attention. Feeling inferior, feeling less able than I would like to be. And as for the fighting and the violence and that—well, there was a lot of that stuff going on at home as well.

I nearly killed my stepfather. I cracked his skull in two places, for beating up my mum and all that stuff. So violence was happening at home as well. Inside the school it was natural aggression but outside the school the violence was through drink.

Anyway, at 15 I'd been expelled from school. Higher education for me meant getting out of that place. That was what I regarded as higher education!

I'd hoped that my stepfather could get me a job in the building trade. I wanted to be a plasterer because I saw that he was making good money himself. But about that time the building trade took a dive. So I ended up working in a slaughterhouse in Paisley, in the abattoir.

I stayed there for three months then I got done for stabbing a guy and I disappeared for 16 months. In the February, I turned 17 and in the March I was jailed.

• • •

This is how it happened. I was walking along with a few mates and we met these two guys. One of them—actually it was him and his brother and another guy—had given me a bit of a kicking about two or three months before that, because two or three of my mates had given *them* a kicking. So here I am walking along the street in Paisley and I meet these three guys. They said they knew what gang I was in, and then— bang, bang, bang!

They didn't do much to me, they really didn't do much to me at all. I walked away without a mark. They could have kicked the living daylights out of me but they didn't, they just gave me a fright, I suppose they were getting their own back a wee bit.

A couple of months later I was with two of my own gang and we met one of these brothers, with another guy, in a Paisley pub, and the three of us set about the two of them. And then after we'd set about them, me in a drunken rage pulled out my knife that I had strapped to my leg and stabbed the guy.

I'd been carrying that particular knife for months. I'd never used it, but if you carry a knife, you're going to use it eventually. I started carrying a knife because we were getting into the league where we were dealing with guys who were bigger and better fighters than we were: we'd moved up from the boys' league to the men's league. And in the men's league you needed a blade. The guys we were getting involved with at that stage were tooled up and we felt we needed to be as well. Fists and feet wasnae enough—though they would have been enough for me on that particular evening because those guys were not the kind of guys that I was worried about bumping into. This guy I stabbed was just a guy that I was taking my vengeance on in a drunken rage.

He had a punctured lung and a severed artery in his thigh where I'd stabbed him. He was rushed off to hospital in an ambulance and he'd lost four pints of blood by the time they got him there. But they saved his life.

I managed to get home covered in blood—the other guy's blood— and I disposed of the knife. But the CID arrived about half past eight the next morning. By that time they'd done their investigations. Somebody who saw the thing told the police it was me who did it and they came and got me. And so I just confessed the whole thing.

I was deeply shocked by what I'd done, because I'd never stabbed anybody before. I was deeply shocked by the fact that the guy had almost died. This was a guy who I didnae really have much of a grudge against. It wasnae the kind of a grudge that you kill someone for, or anything like it. It was the kind of a grudge where you'd maybe punch the guy or stick your heed in him or whatever, but you don't want to kill him. And I'd very nearly killed him! If we'd lived anywhere else it could have taken half an hour to get him to hospital and that guy would have been dead. They couldn't have got the blood into him quick enough. But he was two minutes in the ambulance to the town centre hospital, the Royal Infirmary at Paisley. If they hadnae managed to save the guy's life I'd have been doing life. I'd have got the HMP—Her Majesty's Pleasure—and that would have been me for ten or 12 years.

I got two years eventually. The initial charge was attempted murder, then it was dropped to serious assault when he came out of the intensive care unit. I was in a drunken rage when I stabbed that guy. I was lucky—I didn't have a whole lot of charges—only about five or six —in comparison with a lot of guys who maybe had whole sheets of pages. I just had the one page. So when I was actually done for that serious assault, that went very much in my favour, because I was 17 and I only had three actual convictions.

It was gang fighting that led to me going to jail. We all caused each other to offend because we ran together in a gang, and I was mostly committing violent offences. In our gang there was a core group of about ten or 12 and there was another group of about ten or 12 who hung around us, not so deeply involved in the gang but they'd be there or thereabouts. And about six of us ended up doing time in prison. Certainly more than half of us ended up doing between two years and four years.

There was a kind of a hierarchy: my mate was the boss, but all of us were just as daft as each other. We were all just pushing the boundaries, seeing how far we could go, and a lot of us ended up behind bars.

• • •

When I actually got to jail to do my two-year sentence, that felt bad. I remember going to the old Barlinnie prison in Glasgow. It had thick, thick walls and tiny little windows high up where you couldnae see anything, just one wee patch of sky. You're sharing the room with another three guys and they're using a plastic pot under the bed and it stinks and you're in these horrible clothes and you're bashing scrap— that's your job, bashing bits of metal into small pieces, or sewing mailbags. Literally. Before I went to prison I thought that was a joke but you actually did sit and sew mailbags. Folk in Barlinnie learned to adapt, we all learned to adapt. But thankfully I didn't stay there long. I was only there about three weeks.

Then I was sent to Glenochil, which was a brand new prison at that time, with high fences and electronic doors and all that jazz. You had an individual room and you could pretty much make that your own space. You could put posters up, you could put out your model aeroplanes or whatever. I got a chance to do a hairdressing course.

• • •

I got out of prison at the age of 19. One thing I remember very well: I'd always had a special relationship with my sister eleven years younger than me, as she was the baby in the family. And I remember distinctly when I got out of the jail, coming back into the home, and my wee sister was shy. She'd be maybe nine or ten at the time and she hadnae seen me for so long. When I got home there was this stranger coming into the house that she remembered and knew—but she was still so shy with me.

I was still drinking heavily and I was still getting into trouble: I was done for three assaults and a breach of the peace about three Saturdays after I got out of jail. But the hairdresser who'd taught me in prison knew I was out and he got me a job. His family stuck by me and they gave me a good report and things were OK. They made a significant impression on my life, because they were really decent people, and they trusted me and they liked me.

I think being in the jail did help me. It didnae put a stop to the violence, but when I got out the jail and then I got done for those three assaults, I really got a big fright. I thought 'This is me, I'm going back to jail, this judge is gonna throw away the key. He's gonna think, "You're just an animal, you don't even deserve to be out on the streets."'

Then I was let off, and I think I first glimpsed mercy. I didnae deserve mercy, because I'd gone out and got drunk and done the similar sort of things I'd done before I'd gone to jail.

But it was that wee bit of mercy that made the difference, and the common sense shown by people around me, folk like the probation officer who was working with me, social services, that hairdresser's family and so on. They got me a good report. So getting to jail was a landmark. Getting out was an even bigger one.

• • •

At that stage some of my other mates had gone to jail and our sentences overlapped. They'd visited me while I was in at the start, and then they went to jail and I visited them when I got out. There was a period then when all I seemed to do was visit prisons at the weekend. Sundays were spent visiting mates in the jail.

But then I kind of moved away from it. I managed to move away from the drink. I got myself a wee car and started driving. I'd go to discos in Glasgow and Edinburgh, all sorts of places. I didnae abandon my friends or anything, but my crowd kind of changed when I got the car and I was going to different places and meeting different folk.

But then I got introduced to drugs. And so for the next seven years I wasnae drinking—I was getting stoned. At least when I was stoned I wasnae violent and I didnae go to jail. And so in some respects cannabis and even LSD and speed were actually good for me. It sounds like a contradiction in terms but they were good in the respect that I didnae go to jail when I was on them. I wasnae punching anybody or stabbing anybody. And so they were a step up for me in terms of no' getting violent and no' going to jail and no' getting involved with the police again. Although of course they were a step down as well.

The only offending I did at that time was using illegal substances and I didnae get caught doing that until very near the end just before I became a Christian. I was a taxi driver by this time, and I was caught using drugs in a public place and I lost my taxi badge as a result.

But the violent offending had really come to an end. There was still the odd night where you'd be boxing or dancing and somebody'd stand on your toe or somebody'd be looking at your girlfriend or whatever, and there'd be occasional outbursts of violence. But they were sporadic more than regular. No more knives, no more of that. And then being introduced to the drugs, driving about in my car—I was getting stoned out of my head, I was tripping, but I wasnae getting violent. So that was a big change for me.

But I stayed on drugs. It wasnae just a few months—it was seven years I stayed on drugs. I never touched heroin. I occasionally tried cocaine, but cannabis was the main drug and I was on that virtually seven days a week—practically all my waking hours, to be honest. I always worked, and I'd space it out between lunch breaks, just to keep me going.

By 1987 I was staying out of trouble with the police, I wasn't stabbing anybody, I wasnae even involved. But my life was ruled by drugs and I was living an immoral life, I was sleeping about. I was still involved in petty dishonesty, I was still involved in working and signing on at the same time, and writing off for the enterprise allowance scheme which was supposed to be for new businesses and all that kind of stuff. I was still living very much on the edge of a normal life.

● ● ●

Then I met a woman who was a spiritualist. At that stage I was going through a deep emotional crisis. I didn't realise it, but my life was getting to feel pretty empty. I was looking at the immorality, I was looking at the relationships I'd had, and they were going nowhere. I was 27 years old, I had absolutely no future prospects, I was in a dead-end job, I was doing nothing and going nowhere.

This woman got in my taxi, about four or five weeks before I lost my taxi badge because of taking drugs. She was a perfect stranger and yet she knew so much about me. Incredible. She knew more about my life than anybody should have known. And she put her finger right on it when she said 'I see a great darkness over you, and the only person that can take that away is God. You must see God'. That was Chinese to me! That was really a crazy thing to say to me, because I'd never had a religious thought in my life. In the jail I went into the church service but it was only to get out of my cell. I never listened to a word, it was just to get out of my cell.

So that was my first experience of anything supernatural. And I believe it *was* supernatural. Even though I was dead against it, I believe that that was the only way God could get to me, because there was no way I was going to go that way myself. None of my friends believed in God, none of my family believed in God, nobody I knew had any interest in faith in God or Jesus or anything.

Then a few weeks after meeting that woman, somebody gave me a Bible, a New Testament Bible. I read that wee Bible and I looked at the sections that were relevant to my life—anxiety, depression, worry, fear, addictions, looking for truth, looking for love, looking for meaning, looking for something more than you've got. And all of those things were in the Bible, all those sections were there with chapter and verse and page number and I could go and look at them and see the word of God. I didn't realise it was the word of God at the time. I just saw it as a Bible, a book. But that book, that Bible, that word of God, began to speak to my life, began to offer me new hope.

So although I'd stopped the violent behaviour around the age of 20, when I started doing the drugs, I would say that the real change came in my life at the age of 27 when my whole personality, my whole way of thinking, my whole way of living, was radically transformed. Not just to the extent that I wasnae going to jail any more, but to the extent that I was able to get off drugs without any problem. I was able to stop sleeping around. I was able to start for the first time in my life believing in a God who loved me.

• • •

When I met my first Christians in March 1987 I told them about the drugs and the drink, and prison and the immorality and all this stuff. I told them that I wanted to see God, and I told them that I'd been given the Bible. They said, 'Look, you've come a long way in these months, but we think you're getting to the stage where God wants to make Himself known to you in a new way through His Son Jesus Christ'.

I'd read about Jesus in the Bible, I'd read about His death on the cross, I'd read about His resurrection, I'd read about Him dying for sinners, of whom I felt to be one of the worst. And because I never knew anything about Him, when anyone came into my house I was desperate to talk about Jesus. I was desperate to talk about this possibility of a new life, about a whole new way of thinking.

So these Christians came and talked to me two or three times, and invited me to their meetings, and I went there on a Friday night for about two months. I found they were doing all sorts of things that I'd never had any experience of before. They were doing good work in the community. They helped a woman on the scheme who had lost her baby in a cot death; they helped a woman whose son had just gone to jail; they talked to a guy who was struggling with violence - they were doing stuff that was actually relevant to the scheme.

After going to those meetings for a couple of months, I knew that I'd come to a major crossroads, a much bigger crossroads than I'd ever come to before, where God was saying to me, 'Look Cammie, you can carry on the way you're going—that's your option. You can do that if you want. But there's another option open for you. You can follow Me and I'll give you a new life'.

So one quiet Wednesday evening in July 1987 I went home to my house and I got down on my knees next to my bed and said a very simple prayer. I surrendered my whole life, my whole being, to the Lord Jesus Christ and that was when my life was totally transformed. I began to serve God in the church and in the whole community. I began to serve God in study and I went back to school and passed O grades in religious studies and English. I began to serve God by going to do missionary work with kids up in St Andrew's and kids in Glasgow.

I started to do night school at university because I began to get a deep sense of calling to separate myself from secular work to concentrate on the work of the Gospel. And that led to me going to university.

Then I went to Romania, working in the orphanages, working as a missionary there, just for a few weeks on short-term mission work. And I went to Brazil to work with street children. I just felt like God was taking more and more of my life. More and more He was offering me, and more and more I was saying 'Yes, take me, use me, do what you want with me, I want to serve you'. Through that service and through that worship and through that commitment to Christ, my whole life has completely changed.

● ● ●

More than ten years have passed since then, and I'm now a minister of the Church of Scotland. I still have an involvement to some extent with street children in Brazil, and I still get involved in a lot of young people's lives through speaking in high schools, speaking in prisons, going and speaking to youth groups, going to speak to old ladies and women's guilds all over Scotland. I'm still involved in a lot of things but my main focus now is working as a minister of the Gospel and working for the Lord. So my life is transformed now, in a million different ways.

Sometimes I do think about my past life and I do ask myself, 'Was I ever like that?' Sometimes you forget you were like that, but I *was* like that. I was part of that because of my upbringing. I was part of that because of my social surroundings, I was part of that because of my own decisions. There are a lot of reasons for why I was like that—but I *was* like that.

Somebody asked me a few weeks ago, 'Is there anything of the old Cammie still there?' And I've got to say, 'Yes, there is'. I still act stupidly at times, I still make wrong decisions, I still commit sins, I still make mistakes. But I think it's a tenuous link between what I was then and what I am now.

I'm still the same guy —I still like a laugh, I still like a joke. I still enjoy company, I still enjoy the odd dance. I don't go to the discos any more but I enjoy a wee ceilidh and a wee Scottish dance. But essentially, looking back to those days, it's a long time now. A lot of water has run under the bridge since then. Ten years have passed since I became a Christian and ten more years have passed since that day when I stabbed that guy. So 20 years separate the guy that you see now and the guy that stabbed that guy that night in the streets of Paisley.

But I can still remember the confusion, I can still remember the anger, I can still remember the stuff that was going on in my life at that point. And occasionally, those kinds of things still arise. But thankfully, because of what God has done with my life, it's less and less so.

I see myself today as somebody who matters. It's not that I'm a minister of the church and I've got all these folk coming in and I'm baptising their babies and they want to become church members and all that. I've certainly got all these responsible positions: I'm on the education authority as a representative of East Lothian, I'm a minister of a large congregation. I've got responsibilities that stretch out in many, many different directions. But essentially in my heart I see myself as a guy whom the Lord Jesus Christ has saved. As a guy whom God has saved from an empty life, a meaningless life. Now I see myself as a guy with purpose. A guy with an important place in society. But the only reason I have that place, that important place in society or whatever you want to call it is because of Jesus. If Jesus hadnae come into my life then I would be somebody different. I don't know what I'd have been doing but I certainly wouldn't have been in the position I'm in today, with a job that I love, with a beautiful wife and a beautiful little child. I wouldnae have the joy and the peace and the happiness that I have today as a Christian.

The important things in my life today are faith, worship, service, love of my family, my wife, my child, my brothers and sisters, my mum, my friends, I've got loads of friends that I love deeply and they love me deeply—we have relationships that really are important.

I stopped committing crimes when I was 20 except for using the illegal substances. But I only stopped *being a criminal* when I was saved.

Mark Haines

Mark is 35. Between the ages of 15 and 23 he committed many violent offences because of his drinking, until he started attending self-help groups. He has now been sober for 12 years and works as a community service officer for Berkshire Probation Service.

Dad was an ex-boxer, and everybody on the estate was frightened of him. I think my dad's drinking—and his attitude—certainly affected me. I think I took on a lot of that from him. You were also socially pressured to drink. My dad—this ex-boxer—was my hero by now, and it was all very macho. It was my dad's influence on me that led me to drink and get in trouble with the law. It was more of a mates' relationship than a father-and-son relationship. We seemed to be so similar, once I became old enough to go to the pub with my dad. We just stood there, drinking pint for pint and bullshitting with the best of them and fighting together and everything.

I can't pinpoint a time when I stopped being ashamed of my dad and when he started being my hero. I think there were always two sides to it. I flitted between these two views depending on who I was round. We lived on a large council estate, and if I was on the estate, with other kids from the estate, I was proud of him. But in school it was different, and if I brought somebody home from school, that was when I felt embarrassed. If I went down town with my mum and dad I always walked about 100 yards behind them in case I bumped into anyone from school. I remember being embarrassed because my mum was—is—a very short woman. I wanted my mum to be as tall as all the other mums! At a very early age I felt very embarrassed and ashamed of my parents. I just felt that my family were different. It was silly things like my dad never bothering to tax his car—things like that.

So I flitted between being sort of proud of them—specially my dad, who did become my kind of hero—to this feeling that they were different from everyone else's parents.

The earliest recollection in my life is Mum and Dad arguing, or not talking to each other for long periods. My mum's family, lots of them, were evacuated from London and they all had much larger families than ours. Lots of them had five or six kids, and there was lots of socialising going on. So I had plenty of cousins around my age that I mixed with.

But when I started primary school I was very fearful and painfully shy, just very, very self-conscious, and this feeling stayed with me right through my schooling. It was there from the start and it got worse as I got older. There was a deep feeling of inferiority to other children, as well as this embarrassment about my parents. As with lots of things in my life and lots of feelings that I've had, I've been unable to pinpoint any cause for them—they were just there. Like the painful shyness, the blushing that goes with that: I've never been able to trace where that came from but I knew it was there and I knew it just made me feel very different.

• • •

My parents showed no interest in my schooling. My dad worked away a lot. He was a long-distance lorry driver, and they certainly weren't the type of parents that would ever go up the school. Perhaps they might have done if they went to the pub first and had nothing else to do. Mum had had no education herself and was illiterate.

I certainly think I had learning difficulties at primary school, specially with my poor concentration and a constant feeling that other people seemed to know what was going on but I was always struggling.

I remember we used to read a book around the class, and when it got to my turn, although I could read quite adequately, I would go bright red and I just could not open my mouth. I would be laughed at and often end up losing my temper, and then I'd be kept behind to read to the teachers. They could never make out why I couldn't bring myself to do it in class. It was just this awkward self-consciousness I felt.

It was in junior school, which I can remember much more clearly, that the messing around started, the class clown stuff. That was my game. I liked to do that.

I would have loved to be a good sportsman but I lacked the physical ability. I've never been any good at running. As a kid I always suffered from chest problems, bronchitis and stuff like that, and lots of my friends at school were good footballers. With cross-country running I used to become so frustrated. I really used to try my best, and I'd feel like I was going to die. I carried on my class clowning thing even in terms of sport. My way of coping was still being funny in all situations, rather than just being useless—to be funny as well as useless didn't seem to be quite as bad. I did always try my best. When it came to running at secondary school there'd be guys who were stopping for a fag and then overtaking me!

When I moved on to secondary school, again I felt very frightened though I tried not to show it. By now my way of overcoming it was to fight. I had a fight the first or second day there. By this time I was about 12 and very much getting into the macho thing and that's how so many problems started for me.

I don't think I passed many exams: I've got no bits of paper anywhere to say whether I passed or failed. It never entered my head to go on to college or anything—I just got out of school as quick as I could.

I didn't start drinking till I was well over 15, when I was due to leave school. So I wasn't one of those caught drinking in the class. I remember going to a do at the cricket club that my mate from school belonged to, then a few of us lads found a pub in the town where we could get served. Once I'd started, I went on drinking to overcome my shyness and feelings of inferiority. I was also 15 when I first got in trouble with the law. But that wasn't violence—that was just being on the back of a motorbike with no crash-helmet on, one New Year's Eve.

Alcohol certainly gave me the old fashioned Dutch courage to carry out the violence that I was later to get involved in. I certainly used alcohol to be violent. But though it may seem hard to believe now, I was violent before I started drinking—not to the extremes I was with alcohol, but I was always a punch-up merchant even without a drink, even at school.

Once I'd left school I wanted to work and my dad got me a job as a driver's mate at the wastepaper company where he worked as a driver. I used to start at 6 a.m. and work till 5 p.m. Monday to Friday, and 6 till 12 on Saturdays. I used to take home 42 quid and that was quite a lot of money in those days—plenty to get drunk on anyway. But after about three months, getting up in the mornings was killing me. So when I saw a job advertised for a trainee slaughterman working in a slaughterhouse I went and got that and I ended up staying there for about six years.

After a couple of years I'd really had enough of it. Only my feelings of being virtually unemployable kept me there. But by that time my drinking was full-blown and although lots of my mates were earning more money carrying the hod, I knew it was all I could do to get out of bed in the morning. I knew the slaughterhouse was the sort of place where I could go in with a horrendous hangover—which I always had—be physically sick, literally in the corner, and they just sort of accepted me, because they knew they'd get a reasonable day's graft out of me. The bloke I worked with always used to say I was the only bloke they'd had there who started at the bottom and worked his way *down*!

By this time my drinking was getting me in a lot of trouble: violence, ABH, drunken brawls, assaults on the police, loads of stuff. All my offences were caused by alcohol.

The first time I was arrested I was very fearful and remorseful in the morning when I was in the police cell sobering up. I was very worried and confused. Fortunately, I was never given any custodial sentences. It started off with me getting a couple of fines and bind-overs to keep the peace. I went on to do two long community service orders— 180 hours and 200 hours—as alternatives to custody. And for my last offence, when I was up for affray, I got fined 250 quid and got a nine month suspended sentence, with a two year probation order. As part of that probation order I had to attend an alcohol study group. If I'd continued offending I'd have ended up in prison—there's no doubt about that.

Though I don't blame all this only on my dad, the influence that he had on me through those years did have an effect. It really was drummed into me that if anyone anywhere wanted to fight, I should just chin 'em, just let 'em have it, and ask questions afterwards. Which was a shame really, because I wasn't that good at it. Despite all my offences and all my drunken brawling, I was certainly no hard man, and I'm certainly not proud of all those innocent people I did attack in evenings of drunken insanity that got out of hand—people that I'd never even met before, people that were just out for a quiet drink with their missis. That's the way it was.

I've never seen a psychologist. Perhaps if I did he probably might say all this was because I was so unhappy with my feelings of shyness and inferiority that it poured out like an explosion.

● ● ●

What helped me stop drinking? No particular event or person. It was various members of self-help groups who just showed me from their example that I *could* stop. It was really just seeing what life could be like with the absence of alcohol. I still get violent thoughts now when people upset me but because I'm not full of drink I'm able to think it through. That's the real difference in me—that's what I've learned from the self-help groups. When things upset me I've learned that I have to deal with it another way. I only started to change when I got honest with myself and admitted that my way of thinking and acting was really warped—that's the way I see it now.

I started to try the spiritual approach that all the self-help groups recommend. I'd been an atheist all my life and it certainly hadn't got me anywhere. So I started to try and practise spiritual principles in my life. I think the friendship of other alcoholics certainly helped to make that change. Now I was using role models other than my father.

I feel very sad about the number of people I've hurt during my drinking and offending years. It's strange, though, that it's only through my reckless past that I've got the quality of life that I've got now. It's almost like I had to do it, because in these self-help groups I found the instructions that I was subconsciously searching for all my life.

● ● ●

I can't compare my life today with the sad existence I had many years ago. I certainly have changed enough to overcome the need and the urge for drink. I just see myself now as an ordinary bloke, just this ordinary guy who tries to be a good dad and a good husband and a good worker.

What helps me stay sober and away from offending now is my relationship with God, or a higher power if you like, and with my family—those are the major things that help. The self-help group I attend is still very important to me. I'm trying to live the way of life they recommend.

Only a return to alcohol could make me reoffend. But I obviously hope to stay sober and healthy and happy, to continue to try and be a good dad to my kids. I would say that with my own kids I'm the opposite from how my parents were with me—I'm certainly trying to be anyway. Perhaps like all parents we try to do better than the way we were brought up—in every area, not only education. I go to all the parents' evenings at the school, even though my boy's only six. In the year he's been at school I've probably been up the school more times than my parents did all through my schooling.

I've been sober about 12 years now. It would have been 14, but I did drink for one day, just to make sure that I wasn't wasting my time, and I convinced myself during that day that if I drink alcohol I'm definitely a menace to society and to myself.

I've now been working in the Probation Service for about four years, and I still feel quite privileged to be working in probation, having led the life I've lived. I like my job here at the hostel. I'd like to think that I would perhaps go on to do an NVQ in probation studies, but I'm not really an ambitious sort of person. I don't think I'm anything special. I just feel very fortunate in what happened to me. I know lots of people that I drank with did end up going to prison and if they're not in prison they're out there leading lives that I wouldn't want to swap with them.

But for me—and I shall never know why—the willingness to change was there. People *can* change beyond belief. It freaks people out, even today, when I bump into people I know—especially people I haven't seen for years. When I meet people like this in town, judging by the smile on their faces, most of them haven't forgotten what I was. One of them will say 'What're you doing these days?' and when I say, 'I'm in a probation hostel over at Old Windsor' they'll smile and say, 'Oh, you're still at the drinking then!'

Jim Smith

Jim is 50. In many ways his life took a parallel course to that of our previous interviewee, Mark Haines. Jim is now a qualified social worker working with young people. But as a teenager he became addicted to alcohol after taking his first drink, just like Mark, at the age of 15. He committed thefts to fund his alcoholism, and was remanded to Brixton prison, where he made friends with criminals and moved on to yet more petty offending on release. He overdosed many times on drink and drugs and spent long periods in psychiatric and general hospitals until in his twenties—again like Mark— he began attending self-help groups and started turning his life around.

One drink changed me. When I had my first drink I felt wonderful. I thought I had found the answer to life. It was as dynamic as that. I really mean it was just one drink—my very first drink of alcohol. I was 15 and in my last year at school. It was quite a large amount of beer, and I remember it significantly changed me. I felt wonderful.

The other drugs came a bit later, when I was about 16. I found I had an inability to control my drinking from the word go. But I carried on using it, because it made me feel like the person I always felt I should have been.

There was a direct connection between my alcohol abuse and my offending behaviour—a very direct connection. Once my drinking took off, I just had to have more and more. My earning capacity wasn't great, so I would steal. I wanted and I needed more alcohol, and I didn't have any money —so I stole.

It started with items in the house, items that belonged to my parents. I stole, for instance, a copper fireside set. There was a shop in Croydon that used to buy anything—it was a swap shop. So I stole this set and took it up there and got a few pounds for it, and then I bought alcohol with the money.

I was quite conscious that I was breaking the law—but I needed to get the drink. I didn't keep the company of people who were criminally inclined at all. Quite the opposite really. For a long time, I kept the company of people who drank, but certainly they weren't into crime. So I was quite a lone offender. I stole lots of things over the years, some when I was sober, some when I was drunk. Some that would be useful to me, some that were useless. Some just to sell for alcohol. I stole any number of things.

When I was about 17, I was arrested for stealing a tailor's dummy! I kicked in a shop window and stole this dummy—that was when I was very drunk. I saw the dummy in the window and I wanted what it had on. I thought, 'Well—if I just break the plate glass', I can get it. So I kicked the window, and it smashed all around me. I was very fortunate not to be hurt. I grabbed the dummy and walked off down Croydon High Street with it. Unbeknown to me, there was a car nearby containing four CID officers who were watching me and they were laughing. Two of them walked over to me. I think our actual conversation came up in court: I said 'Who are you?' and they said 'We are police officers' (they were still laughing!). I said 'Oh, am I nicked?' and one of them said 'I think you could say this is a fair cop!' But when they took me back to Croydon police station, that was the first time I'd been inside a police station, and when I was taken in and arrested, I was quite shocked.

• • •

Why did I need to drink? I certainly remember feeling very isolated at primary school. I didn't really want to go. I always had a kind of feeling that I was different. I look back now and I wonder if that was because I was adopted.

I was adopted when I was a year old, and to my knowledge I haven't any siblings. I certainly didn't have any brothers or sisters in my adopted family. I just had my parents.

I was all right at English and maths and things like that, but I did have a kind of learning difficulty—it was hard for me to grasp concepts like telling the time, tying my shoelaces, tying my tie. Sport was the one thing I did excel in. Gymnastics, PE and things. Swimming especially. I was a very good swimmer when I was at my primary school, very fast. When I got to secondary school I still did well at swimming, but I wasn't as fast as I thought. Nobody beat me in my school, but I went to the Croydon championships and I came second. I found that very difficult to accept, that somebody actually beat me.

I'd taken the eleven plus exam in 1963 and got into technical school. But I didn't want to go. I didn't feel at all happy about moving to secondary school, leaving friends that I had known. My best friend at primary school was knocked over and killed by a car, a few months after we left. That's a significant memory of mine and perhaps it had an effect on me.

When I started at this technical school I was about seventh in the class, but I deteriorated to the bottom. My attitude in the last two years at school went right down—it really wasn't good. I just didn't feel I wanted to learn. There were expectations for me to do a lot better than I did: I took about ten O levels and only passed one. My adoptive parents didn't really understand a lot of the processes of education, and they left a lot to me. As I said, I had my first drink when I was 15 and in my last year at school, during the school holidays, but I left later that year, so there were no problems at school.

So I left school at 16, and went into a job: it was a commercial apprentice job in an engineering company, and I worked in the office. The idea was that over a few years I would learn all the different departments. I didn't stay at the job very long, only ten months—but i t turned out that this was to be my longest job for many years.

The reason for this was that I abused alcohol, because it was easily available. After that I became addicted to prescribed drugs, Valium and barbiturates.

• • •

When I was first sent into custody I felt terrible, terrible. I thought 'Good God, what's happened?' My world was turned upside down.

I only went to prison once, for theft. I'd already been placed on probation and then I committed another act of theft so I was taken to Brixton prison. That was really earth-shattering. I was only on remand for a week, but it was quite shocking in many ways. I was just 18, and in three years, I'd gone from liking a bit of sport to being on probation and then ending up in Brixton.

I think the change in my offending behaviour was only due to environmental change. Because after that week's spell in Brixton, I did keep the company. I got some odd jobs with some builders, who were petty criminals, and I think I stole from them, and did some stupid things. So things weren't looking good.

But then when I was 21, I moved areas. I went with my parents to live on a caravan site in Kent that they had retired to. I didn't know anybody there, and because of this new environment, I didn't get involved with criminals any more.

I still stole, and I got caught over the years for petty things, like shoplifting offences, but I didn't in the end go down the criminal route, I went down the psychiatric hospital route.

• • •

When I was 21 I was offered treatment by a specialist in alcoholism, a Dr Salter. He offered me a place in a treatment centre, but I wasn't ready to accept that.

But when I was 22 I went into my first psychiatric hospital in Kent. I was in that hospital many times, I suppose about 12 times, over the next four years. The periods I was in for ranged from about six weeks to two or three months on one occasion.

So for 12 years I was involved first in the criminal justice system and then going into psychiatric hospitals and general hospitals for overdosing. The pattern tended to be that I'd overdose, then the general hospital would send me on to the psychiatric hospital.

And I was still stealing of course. This was still tied up with my alcoholism, my addiction. All along the way the magistrates, the occasional policeman, all kinds of people were saying 'Don't you think you ought to look at your drinking? You may have a problem there'. All that advice wasn't wasted, but I just wasn't ready to accept it at that point.

• • •

I first went to a self-help group for alcoholism when I was about 23 years old. These groups played a significant part—in fact the most significant part—in me changing my attitude to my offending behaviour and changing my whole lifestyle—the drinking and the offending. I've been helped by the examples of other people in the groups—many people who have been down the road of crime and have spent much longer than me in prison. Their example, their role model, obviously helped me.

So my attitude began to change and this went on well into my recovery—it didn't actually stop, because theft is theft, and I think that went on for a couple more years. So during what we like to call recovery, I was still stealing! Small things, but nevertheless stealing. Like siphoning a pound's worth of petrol into my car every day when I had a driving job. It wasn't a great big crime but I was very aware of what I was doing.

I finally went into a treatment centre when I was 27. Then I went on to a half-way house, the kind they call a rehab now. Obviously I went on attending self-help meetings and I met a lot of fine individual people, as I still do today. These people actually were the people who enabled me to change my lifestyle, so that eventually I found that I *couldn't* steal, not even a pound's worth of petrol. My addictive behaviour and offending did go on for a little while: I was stealing odds and ends, but maybe that was just habitual. But then I began to feel uncomfortable—in fact I'd always felt uncomfortable about theft. I never actually felt good about stealing—especially from people I knew and loved. But I had to have the alcohol so I'd always justify it. It would all be all right when I had a drink inside me. But once I was sober, it just couldn't go on, because I just didn't feel good about what I was doing. I just didn't feel comfortable. So I stopped.

I feel now that my offending had to happen, because that's the path I was on. It was connected with the disease of addiction, alcoholism, and it was all kind of wrapped up in the way I was. Alcohol was just part and parcel of the way I was living my life. And now it's not. It has no place. It's not a question of temptation. People ask 'Aren't you tempted by drink and drugs?' and I can honestly say that I'm not.

I did have an experience in hospital that actually facilitated my stopping drinking and wanting to stay stopped. I believe it was a spiritual experience. I came to a point where I just had to surrender to the life I was leading—the drinking, the drugging, the offending—everything. And it was almost as though this experience brought about the change.

• • •

Today I see myself as a responsible person in the community. I'm a social worker—I qualified a few years ago. I still attend alcoholism groups, as I have been doing for the past 22 years this year, and I 'sponsor' a lot of newer members, specially the younger ones. But they help me too. It's not just a one-way process. I also work with adolescents for Barnardo's and I actually want to do some developmental training work on my own now. I'm also a musician—I started to play music. I'm married with three daughters, and my family is very important to me.

My life is full today. I believe I live a spiritual way of life and that suits me fine. I believe the alcoholism group's programme of recovery has helped me become a better person and to strive for values I didn't even dream possible. And now I've got some idea of a kind of spiritual power, a God. I'm not a religious man but I'm a spiritual man, and I try and enjoy my life, because life goes all too quickly.

My sobriety is the most important thing in my life today—just keeping clean and sober, living a drug-free and drink-free life, one day at a time. And trying to live a good life, along the lines of values that I aspire to, trying to help people wherever possible, and to learn from everyone I meet.

For me, a return to offending would be turning my back on my recovery, turning my back on the new way of life I've had for the last 21 years, which is what it would mean if I returned to drinking and drugging. But perhaps it's not so black and white as that. I do believe that even if I wasn't drinking or drugging, there could still be things that come up, like financial pressures, that I suppose could lead me to try to get some easy money. I don't think any human being is free of that. We live in a society where there's perks in a job. But perks could mean theft in law, and there's all kinds of little things people do. I think it's about gradually letting standards slip.

I have lots of hopes for the future. I'm coming up to my fiftieth birthday—22 years sober—but it's as though I'm having a rebirth. Perhaps it's working with young people and having young children of my own. I've got a lot of plans for the future, with my music, with my independent work as a trainer. I want to do a fitness instruction course in a couple of months. I want to do lots of things, including a little bit of travel.

So there's a lot on the horizon. There's more in front of me than has gone behind in the last 21 years, and I'm quite excited about the future.

Laureal Lawrence

Laureal is 29 and is the production manager of Prisons Video Magazine, a company making documentary films on prison issues for distribution inside prisons. She was jailed for three years for the importation of a kilo of cocaine and was released in 1994.

When I was 18 I ran away to join a circus in Italy. I was one of those dancers on ice that they call *ballerinas su ghiaccio*. We had to wear all these plumes and stuff!

What was I doing there? I needed to get away. I'd backed out of my A-levels at the last minute, on the actual examination day. I just didn't turn up, and I told my mum a lot of lies. She had high expectations for me to do well in my education—and I took them to the point where they became my worst enemy. So I felt I needed to get out of the country. I think I just couldn't face my mum and tell her I wasn't succeeding. I stayed in Italy for two years, came back and worked in nightclubs, got introduced to cocaine and ended up in Holloway prison.

● ● ●

Academically I was very good, and I think there were always high expectations for me to do well. My mother was a hard-working woman with a lot of ambition for her children. So at primary school I worked hard: it was all to please my teacher, to please my mum, to make my mum proud of us, because of the fact that though my dad wasn't around, we were going *to be something.* Mum was never pushy but she was right behind me whatever I wanted to do. I was to be the doctor and my sister wanted to be a lawyer.

My parents separated when I was seven years old—quite unusual for an African-Caribbean family. My mother left my father, taking us children with her. I remember the arguments, my dad running up the stairs. But I don't think there was any physical violence between my parents, at least not in front of us kids. Then I remember this great sort of build-up and then one day my mum kept us back from school and we all packed up and went to live with my cousins.

I'm the third of four children—two girls and two boys. Till I was seven we were pretty much together as a good family. I was born in Birmingham: my parents came to England in the early 1950s. My father was a bit of a disciplinarian—to him children should be seen and not heard. But he was a good man who loved his garden. My earliest memories are of being in the garden and eating peas straight from the pod.

My friends were all family. In the street we lived in at the time, my aunt lived over the road, my cousin lived at the top of the street, another cousin lived two blocks from us, my godmother lived next door to me—as kids we played with our cousins. It was all family.

I was quite confident about going to primary school. I was pretty bright as a young kid and I threw myself into my books. I remember one teacher in particular called John Smith. He used to encourage me so much, and I took quite a lot of pride in pleasing him. It was assumed that I'd be good at school. And I was. When it came to parents' evenings, my mum was always smiling.

But I always had this feeling of being different. At primary school it was because of my dad not being around. The cousin that my mother moved to live with was also a divorcee. She had six boys and that caused a lot of hell, living in someone else's house. We were always fighting with them, though really we got on just as much as we argued.

I just always remember my dad not being around. My mother never kept us from seeing him. She said 'If you want to go, he's there, that's fine'. But I never went. I never wanted to go and visit him. I've been to see him several times since. He doesn't live too far from where my mother lives now, in Birmingham. He tends to dig up the past a lot. He's still very bitter and twisted over that. But I don't feel that love for him like I've got for my mum.

I hold my mother in great esteem. She worked really, really hard, never took on another man. She'd hate to see another man tell us kids off. That would always make her think it was because we weren't his own children. There was never another man in the family.

My mother worked so hard, but she worked in between our schooling hours, so she was always home for us when we got back from school and then she'd go back to work for the evening. It was always nights and afternoons. She worked late evenings at a bakery. She always used to come back again in time for the ten o'clock news—just when that jingle started for *News at Ten*.

●　●　●

When I got to secondary school I suppose I was labelled a bit of a bod, a swot, because I was always reading. I was always top of the class, and that brings its own problems. I had four or five friends, who stayed my friends up to the time I left. We were the bright sparks and there was a lot of friendly competition between the girls in the group. It was always us at the top of the class, us who got top marks, us who got the best results.

I think the rest of the children treated me with distaste really. I always remember there was one girl who had a little group of friends and they were so spiteful to me. For instance there was my clothes—we were never fashionable kids. I wore my uniform throughout school. I think around the third or fourth year you were allowed to wear what you wanted, but I wore my uniform throughout because that was all I had. So I was always picked on because of that, and because I didn't have fashionable glasses or trainers or whatever it was. I wore National Health glasses till I was in my fourth year and people would say 'Look at her, she looks stupid as well!'

Throughout my schooling, all the time, I felt different. I don't honestly think there was any racism in all this, because the school I went to was quite mixed. There was one girl in particular, an Asian Muslim girl, that I sort of hung round with. She had the pressure of being in a Muslim family and she knew she was going to be made to get married, though she didn't want to. She was really trying to do well at school, to get out, to go to college, and hopefully break the mould that was meant for her.

I suppose there was a sort of subtle racism in the way I was treated in sport. I couldn't do sports so I didn't hold the flag up for the rest of the black girls in my school. I've got a sort of weird physique which means I can't run—I trip over my legs. Even now, if I run too far for a bus I trip over! That caused me a lot of problems, because black girls were supposed to be good at running.

They didn't want me in the rounders team or the netball team because I was all fingers and thumbs. When it was time to pick sides I was always the last one standing there. That happened to me a lot because I was so hopeless. You'd end up with a rounders side where there were all these black girls who were really fit and good at the game and I wasn't—and I got a lot of stigma for that from my own black peers. That was another reason why I stood out.

But academically I was doing well. I did my seven or eight O levels at school and I also did five more O levels the following year at an adult education centre. So in total I've got 13.

Between my O levels and A levels I went to work in a chemist's shop. Like I said, my mother wanted my sister to be a lawyer and me to be a doctor. I thought, 'I'm going to be a doctor so I'll work for a chemist and I'll get to know about it beforehand', though I was only ordering stock and making tea.

I left senior school for college thinking 'Right—now I'm going to do my A-levels'. I was supposed to be a doctor and I was doing chemistry, maths and biology. But it just didn't happen. After the comprehensive, it just all went wrong. I found it hard at college. I needed that friendly competition which had worked very well at secondary school. I found it very hard to concentrate or to push myself on my own.

To be honest I got myself in a real tizz over my A-levels. I can be my own worst enemy—I can fear something so much that I just can't do it. That's what happened to me with those exams. I was so scared of failing that I backed out of my A-levels at the last minute. And that's how I came to run away to Italy and join the circus.

• • •

I was in Italy for the best part of two years. In between every act they had these dancers on ice, and that's what I did. Though I can't run or anything, this was on ice—actually it was silliconed wood—and I'd just do basic routines and occasionally an attempt at a skate across the stage, and it looked good. I was there with ten others on the stage.

It was a job, it was an experience, living in a caravan, going from town to town. Soon after I got there I fell madly in love with an Italian, and stayed on for two years.

It was a break. But it was a very unrealistic break. When I came back from Italy it was very difficult to stay in any one job because the guy I was seeing was still in Italy and he kept calling me over there every other month. Because I was going there so often, I couldn't hold a job down over here.

When I first came back I started working in a nightclub. I worked behind the bar to start with. My boss saw me as being a bit too bright just to do bar work and I ended up managing the place.

I carried on working in the clubs, though there were some jobs I didn't really like. I thought 'This isn't where I want to be'. I spent all this time saying I was going to get my act together, and I never really did.

I started smoking hash when I was about 21—not very seriously. It was quite late to start, considering that my elder brother was a Rastafarian and he always used to smoke, so hash was always in the house. There's always been some hash around me—it was nothing special and I wasn't scared of it. I knew what it was all about. It wasn't until I got into the nightclub work that I started taking cocaine. I'd never used it because I'd met girls who were on crack.

But cocaine was part of the whole club lifestyle. I used to get given a lot of drugs by the punters, but it always stopped there. When my work finished I went home to bed on my own. But I knew that the next night these punters were going to be there and I'd get more free coke.

So that's how I got introduced to coke. And then you get to like it. I was living by night then. I'd start work at eight or nine o'clock in the evening. The clubs didn't finish till two or three o'clock in the morning and then we'd stay and have 'afters'—the boss would get the champagne out, we'd be there till six, seven o'clock in the morning. So I suddenly started doing this nightlife. I was drinking a lot as well as using coke: the more you shove coke up your nose the more you can drink. You don't notice the drink.

I'd gone from being at school, being part of a very small group of people who were academically the best at everything, to suddenly being 'all right' and accepted by these 'normal' people. I felt, 'Great, I'm all right, I'm part of the crew'. I found myself wanting to be part of this big group of people. I don't know the word to use but somehow I felt I was on the ground level, sort of 'common' like everyone else.

Now, for the first time, being accepted wasn't about how bright you were. These people I was with, they weren't bright. They'd really got nothing between their ears. A few of them may have been running businesses, but they were spending all their profits on drugs and drink and chasing women in big cars.

• • •

Once I started working in the clubs I also started seriously breaking the law—apart from using cocaine I mean. Working behind the bar I could double my wages on one night in tips—that was an excellent way to make money. But I could also make my wages over again by helping myself from the till. I had a quick brain for working out the figures, putting different figures in the till and then at a convenient moment, taking that money out.

So I'd say my offending all started from around that time, though if we're talking about really petty crime, it started a lot earlier. In a way I'd just drifted into breaking the law when I was still living at home. When I was about 15 or 16, we'd moved to live with my mother's best friend in another part of Birmingham. She was a divorcee with five kids, three girls and two boys. The council had just laid a beautiful garden in that area of Birmingham in the middle of a subway, and our mums would send us out of an evening with a shopping trolley, and tell us to go and nick those stones—those beautiful quartz decorative things that they use in garden layouts. We'd nick those, and some of the plants, stick them in the trolley and go back home and do up the front garden.

Then my mum's friend used to send us out and say 'There's some beer glasses over there on the corner outside the pub, go and get them!'—and we'd go and get them for her. My mum was like that too. She worked hard, but for instance when she used to work in the bakery she used to bring back cakes for us—and I suppose she shouldn't have done it. I knew all these things were wrong but they weren't *bad* stealing, you know, it was stealing for the benefit of the family.

Then a bit later on I was doing things like nicking pens and paper. I used to have a cleaning job and I'd always be nicking equipment from the offices when I was cleaning up of a night time. But the reason I was sent to prison was for the importation of drugs.

Again, it was all about wanting to be part of everyone else's lifestyle. I met this girl and we suddenly became friends. She was all the sorts of things my mother wouldn't really want me to have in a friend. She was living on her own, she had three kids by three different guys, she was on the dole and working at the same time, all the rest of it. And for some reason I just felt I wanted to be with this girl, wanted to be around her.

She said her latest boyfriend was from Jamaica, he was doing this thing with drugs, and would I do it instead of her. She said 'You're all nice and clean, there's nothing on your record'. So I said 'Yes, OK, I'll do it'. I think it was more for the acceptance side of it than the actual money. The money I thought of as being able to help my mum who was working really hard. By this time she was working as a domestic in the hospital in the afternoons, and she had a cleaning job in the evenings. The money was going to benefit her—that's where it would have gone. I'm not a flash person for clothes and cars, and I didn't like to see her working so hard.

At that time I was sort of drifting. My life wasn't happening, I wasn't actually doing anything in particular and there were all these people I wanted to please. I thought 'I'm not successful as a person, so I'll take this opportunity'.

The first time I did the run it didn't work: I went all the way to Jamaica, but the guy didn't show to give me the drugs and I had to come back. There was no customs check in the airport, there was nothing when I came back. So I thought 'Oh, this is all right, it'll be all right bringing it back through'. This same girl said she could make arrangements for me to do the run again later on. I think the first time I went was the September, then I went back in the March to try and get the stuff again. But this time I got caught.

● ● ●

When I got done for it and sent to Holloway—oh my God, I just died! My mother didn't even know I'd gone. It killed me. I just thought 'Oh my God, I've let her down, I've let the family down, I've let the extended family down and what are they going to say about me?' All those things—because, within our family group, everyone's boasting about what their kids are doing. They're always on the phone to each other: it's a subtle sort of competition amongst the family, seeing who's doing what.

I got three years for the importation of just under a kilo of cocaine. I know it was stupid running for my girlfriend as I did. She'd probably have given me three or four grand and I was thinking 'Yeah, I'll give it to my mum!' It's a very hard thing to explain.

I got a touch[1]—my barrister said I was looking at seven to nine years, but I only got three. My mum was in court. Two of my best friends were there too. I got references from people, people I've never gone back to see since. It was just the shame of it really, I just couldn't bring myself to see them again.

I did 18 months in prison and I was released in September 1994. I live in London now. I flew to Jamaica from Birmingham, but when I left prison I decided I was not going to go back to Birmingham. I didn't want to see my family, I didn't want to see my extended family, I didn't want them pointing at me and all the rest of it. I didn't want to see my friends, or anyone from school, so I moved here to London.

I am definitely not proud of having been in prison, because of all the stigmas and the stereotypes of being an ex-con. But really I suppose it's just an event, it's something that's happened in my life, like I lived in Italy for a while, or I used to work in a nightclub. Jail certainly threw me. I came out wondering 'Who am I? What do I think of myself? What do other people think of me?' I was confused, very, very confused.

●   ●   ●

I began working at *Prisons Video Magazine* in the first instance because I was allowed to go out on day release from Holloway. I was doing graphic design in prison, and my tutor was doing some freelance work for the guys at PVM. So I came for an interview. I'd finished my college course and I asked the prison to give me day release to come and work at PVM instead. I started in June 1994, and when I left prison the job was ideal. It was a reason for not going back to live in Birmingham—a new start. I thrive on the sort of pressure of this kind of job—you're in a small team with a lot to do in a short time. But even working here for PVM—it's great but it's still linked to jail. I still haven't gone out into the proper jobs field.

Even the studying I'm doing is criminal justice studies—it's all still connected with jail. I've taken on a master's degree. I want to do the course, but even now I'm scared of failing. My mum says 'Oh, you're doing the course, how's it going?' And I can't tell her that I haven't touched the books for two weeks. I should have handed in an essay four weeks ago but I haven't done it. I've got myself all anxious again about failing. I'm trying to do it as a point to prove to myself that I can see it through. I have to try and break the cycle.

It's actually a physical thing. I've got a knot in my stomach even thinking about it right now. I know I should be home tonight with my books, but I've become my own worst enemy when it comes to studying. I

---

[1] Lenient sentence

want to go forward but I just can't. I don't know what's stopping me. *I'm* stopping me and I can't put my finger on why it is.

I'm still not qualified as anything, and I feel I'm still drifting in my life—I'm not *somebody*. I want to study. I still kick myself that I didn't go to my A-level exams. I was so anxious, I didn't want to fail. I'd never failed in anything. I didn't want to tell my mum I'd failed, I didn't want to tell myself I'd failed. So I've got no qualifications after my O-levels and I hate myself for that. I really want to get some and I need to, because I know it's going to do a lot for me self-esteem-wise. Besides all the things that have happened in prison, I've taken a step down as to how I see myself.

• • •

It was really because of my mother I stopped offending. My mother supported me—I knew she would—but it was the shame and the hassle of going through it all. My mum knows why I did it and it's because of her I haven't done it again. I don't want to let her down again, put her through that again. I think now I've always got that angel on my shoulder, that conscience. It's really my mum, and even when I was breaking the law I used to think 'Gosh, if she really knew what I was doing, I know she wouldn't be happy'. The last person I want to let down again is her.

But then again, when people talk about offending behaviour, I think to myself 'Crime's crime, and if I see an opportunity, I can't honestly say I wouldn't do it again, if I could work it out and see that it made sense to do it'. I don't think you ever really change your offending behaviour.

A lot of people are criminals, if they see an opportunity that suits them, with a gain to their advantage. I'm embarrassed to have a criminal record. I don't like saying I've got one. I hate the fact that I've got one. But my attitude to taking advantages of opportunities hasn't changed. However, the opportunities aren't there now. I don't know the people, I don't have the contacts. I'm not in that circle any more, I've never been in that circle here in London. I'd have to go back into working in a nightclub where the cocaine definitely is. I was married at one point—it's a long story. The guy I was married to, he was in that set and we used to go out and everyone would be passing each other wraps of coke—there'd be six in a toilet and all the rest of it.

Another thing—the drugs nowadays are crack and heroin. This is another touch that I don't want to get involved with. I don't like that scene. In Holloway I saw girls who were really, really nice girls, and they were all on the game because of crack addiction. I'd think, 'Boy, if that's what it takes to go down that road it's best I don't'. That sort of addiction has never appealed to me. And then there's the life of the rich and famous, shoving cocaine up their noses and partying and all the rest of it. But that's a very hard circle to get into and I don't really want to get into it. It was OK working in it because it gave me an excuse to take cocaine, gave me an excuse to be part of it. There's also the short-termness of it. It's all about your looks, and how long they last.

Apart from my mum, I don't have any relationships that help me keep away from crime. Quite the opposite actually. I've been finding them all quite silently beckoning me to get into selling drugs again. My husband was very much into buying his drugs, selling them here in London. He was even saying at the time, 'Yeah, let's get another run organized'. He was saying he could get girls if I could get him a contact on the other side. But I just thought 'No, I don't want to put anybody else through that'. The money sounded good but I really don't think I could have lived with myself if someone else got caught.

I could probably go and walk right back into it. I could probably say 'Hey, introduce me to someone who wants a carrier'. But now they know me, they know who I am at the airport, so how could I pull it? Also I don't like the people I'd have to mix with to do it. And I'd probably only get two grand for it nowadays. That isn't worth the hassle because I know what the end result is if it goes wrong. I don't want to go back to prison. I'm older now and less likely to say 'Yes' to people or agree with people.

But I suppose I could still reoffend if there was something that would pay me enough, if there was—this is theoretical—but if there was that one job, an all-or-nothing job, that someone could let me in on, I think I might do it. The only thing that could make me return to offending is money—lots of it. But most important—I don't want to go back to jail. I think it's a waste of time, you're in with people I wouldn't necessarily talk to or give the time of day to in the street.

Actually I suppose keeping myself busy does help. I haven't got that much time left in my day. I find it hard to make friends in London because I work too much. I've got two jobs. After every day doing this job at *Prisons Video Magazine* I go off and do another job in the evenings, taking bookings for a company. I want to clear myself of the debt my husband left me in. And this job at PVM has spurred me on. I like the computer side of things and I'm sticking with that until I can buy my own equipment. I'm also helping my mother with a loan. She wants to go back home for good and I want to follow her. I don't want to stay in this country, but I've got to go somewhere else with something, with some qualifications.

I hope to move on from this job. I hope to be able to prove to myself that I can do something else besides this, that the skills I've got aren't just good because they're for the *Prisons Video Magazine*—but they're good because they could be of use to someone else. If I can prove that to myself then I'm quite happy to leave the country.

I'm certainly working 16 hours a day at two jobs. I'm working, working, working. My mum thinks that's a very good thing to do. But I know at the end of the day if I go on this way I'm going to be just like her. She's ended up working, working, working and still not making any massive gain from it. I'm not happy doing it that way.

It's not that I don't want the responsibility. I do want to be taken seriously. I don't think I'm taken as seriously as I should be—I don't know why. I laugh a lot—people tell me I laugh a lot. That's my coping reaction. I'm very much like this on the outside but when I go home I'll be in the depths of depression. I think I've sussed out that all the smiling, the laughing, is as if I'm saying, 'Please like me, I'm OK'.

I want to be successful. I want to have a few qualifications. I don't know if that's going to change me but I've got this feeling that I need them. I want to make up for the things I couldn't see through before. I do want to make some money, but perhaps there *is* a change in me. Maybe I haven't recognized that in myself.

Bruce Reynolds

Bruce was jailed for 25 years in 1969 for his part in the Great Train Robbery. He served ten years and was released in 1978. Four years later he was jailed again, this time for supplying amphetamines. He was released in 1985. Since that time he has made a career for himself as a writer and has recently reviewed films for *The Guardian*. He is now 66.

I was 16 and working in a London office on a top floor overlooking the Embankment. There must have been about 100 people in this office and I just hated every moment of it. All I was doing was filing invoices day in and day out, and I thought to myself 'This isn't any sort of life'. During the lunch hour I used to go out and walk along the Embankment. *The Discovery*—Shackleton and Scott's old ship—was moored just alongside. At one period in my childhood we'd lived in a flat over a shop owned by a guy who'd been with Shackleton on one of his expeditions and he'd told me stories about it. You could go on to *The Discovery* and I used to go on it sometimes in my lunch hour and just stand there and listen to the wind in the rigging and think *'This* is living!'

● ● ●

I left school at 14. When I left, I was equal top of the class when it came to anything to do with English, history and stuff like that. I never had a head for figures at all.

When I left school there was very little chance of going on to further education. It was the norm to leave school round about the age of 14 or 15 and to go straight to work. For the last two or three years of my school life I was friendly with a guy who was going to the Navy training school, so my plan was to go there too, to HMS Exmouth. But when I went for a medical at County Hall I found out that I'd got bad eyes so I couldn't go into the Navy.

My dad had come with me for the medical examination and he said, 'What're you going to do now?' and I said 'Well, I've been reading a lot about foreign correspondents lately. I'm going to be a reporter. I'll go up to Fleet Street'.

So off I went to Fleet Street. I walked into the first imposing edifice I could see—which happened to be the *Daily Mail*—and told the uniformed commissionaire that I wanted to be a reporter!

I started at the *Daily Mail* as a messenger boy, which I loved. Newspaper life was very exciting and you felt you were part of it. I met all sorts of war heroes—these were people I had patterned my whole life on. People like Douglas Bader used to visit the *Mail* quite regularly. He was pals with Courtney Edwards who was the air correspondent for the paper at the time.

I just loved the whole excitement of being involved in a newspaper. You had plenty of freedom there and I worked shift work. All the commissionaires were ex-servicemen, so I was mixing with them, listening to their war stories, how they'd all been injured. It was a real education, being with these men and listening to all these stories, which went round and round in my head with things I'd heard that happened during the war.

I worked there as a messenger boy for about two years. All the jobs at the *Daily Mail* used to come up in-house and that's how appointments were made. So I hoped that a job might come up for me in the press room, which is the first stage to becoming a reporter.

But instead a job came up in the accounts department and I was asked if I wanted it.

At the time I didn't like the idea particularly but I spoke about it to my dad. Dad was a victim of the Depression, and of course to him a steady job, a job for life, was very important. So he said to me, 'It's a job for life, you've got security, take it'. So I went into the accounts department. And that's how I ended up in that office on the top floor.

I just hated it. I missed the camaraderie of being with all the other lads, the messenger boys. That office was a prison, even though I didn't know what prison was like at the time.

It's difficult to say how my life would have gone if I hadn't got involved in crime, if I'd put my energies into something else—I suppose I might have ended up as a foreign correspondent for the *Daily Mail*!

• • •

Or I might have become a professional cyclist. I'd always had a bike, and I'd joined a cycling club and become a keen cyclist. So I started to wonder seriously if I could make a career of being a racing cyclist.

Meanwhile I was getting even more jaundiced with the whole office business at the *Daily Mail*. A friend of mine at my cycling club worked at the Middlesex Hospital and he told me all sorts of stories about the research he was doing—he was a laboratory assistant at the Institute of Pathology, and he suggested I should come and work there. I suppose I romanticised—I was quite impressed with the idea that maybe I could do something useful for society. I saw myself as another Pasteur or a Curie, so I left the *Daily Mail* and went to work in the hospital.

That was very short-lived—I didn't like the animal experiments they were doing. So I left that job and went to work for a cycle firm which also had a racing team. My whole idea was that I might be able to get into that team.

But there was too much work and not enough time for cycling, and eventually I stopped going to work altogether. Instead I'd ride down to Brighton on my bike, come back home and tell my grandmother that I'd had a hard day's work. So I soon lost the job at the cycle firm.

• • •

My grandmother was the strongest influence in my childhood. She was my father's mother, though in recent years, after my father died, we found out he'd been adopted. But Gran, she was more or less the one who brought me up. In 1944, when at the age of 12 I came back from being evacuated, I went to live with her in Battersea, rather than with my father and stepmother in Dagenham.

Everybody I've met in prison has nearly always come from some sort of disturbed background. The families have broken up, there's marital discord. There's not many of them come from happy families, and there's obviously some relevance there.

My mother died when I was very young, but I've got a very early memory of the time while she was still alive, I think it's probably my earliest memory. I must have been about four or five at the time.

Then I lost my mother and her place was really supplanted by my stepmother, who for various reasons I didn't get on with. I was the grit in the oyster in the relationship between her and my father. When they had my half-brother that distanced them even further from me because obviously the attention was placed on him, even though he was just a baby at the time. I think he was about a year old when I was evacuated in September 1939 at the age of seven.

I was very conscious, all the time I was evacuated, that I was the odd one out, and to a degree obviously I did feel rejected.

I'd always had a great affection for my father, and I think it certainly was reciprocated. There were many instances of that: at various times he walked all sorts of distances to see me when I was evacuated, and he'd take me out. At the time I just couldn't understand why I couldn't be back at home. Most of the other children I was evacuated with had gone home by then.

When I got to primary school I was always conscious that I wasn't quite of the norm. Then as an evacuee I was an outsider, in the years between 1939 to 1944—between the age of seven and 12. Then when I came back and went back into school in London, I was an outsider again there as well.

But I didn't have any real problems at school, I was OK at reading and writing and I was quite good at sport, though team sports weren't really for me. I tried desperately to fit in with the mode of being the footballer, the cricketer, but I was much better at individual sports, like swimming and running.

I think I was always very conscious of this mysterious thing called authority, and I used to question why it always seemed to me that authority seemed to be arbitrary. It didn't seem to me to make sense. And every time I tried to make sense of it, it never seemed to me to be fair or even-handed.

• • •

I was 16 when I had my first run-in with the police, which I think was a quite formative thing. Prior to this I just saw the police around and there was no enmity in my relations with them. They were just there. I'd listened to my father quite a bit. He was of the Left, he believed passionately in the rights of the working man and his views of the police were basically that they were there, they weren't your enemy, but by the same token, they were the instruments of power and generally, that's who they came down on the side of—power, not the man in the street.

All of us cycling boys used to meet every evening down by a coffee stall near Battersea Park, and we used to work out where we were going to ride that night. We'd ride for a couple of hours and come back and have a cup of coffee or tea and then go home. It was on one of these occasions, I suppose about ten o'clock at night, I was riding home from the coffee stall. I never had any lights on my bike—it was considered rather sissyish then to have things like mudguards or lights. And as I was riding home a policeman called out to me from the side of the road, 'Where's your lights?' And—I suppose in a spirit of bravado—I called out 'Bollocks!'

I thought no more about it and I suppose I'd gone about a mile down the road when a police car pulled over in front of me. Three policemen jumped out of it and held me at the side of the road. I said, 'What's this all about?' Then this other policeman who'd called out to me arrived on his bike in a very aggressive mood and started shouting at me and ended up kicking my bike. I responded by kicking his bike back. Next thing I knew, he was giving me a right-hander and there was a bit of a struggle. Then one kindly old policeman said to me, 'Come on son, get in the car. Don't worry, it's OK'. He got in the police car and I followed him in. Then he pinioned my hands and said to the others, 'It's OK, I've got him. Give it to him now!'

So they steamed into me, not terribly violent but totally out of order for what was called for in that situation. I was only 16 and it was the first time I'd had anything to do with the police. When I got down the police station there was a bit of a gavolt down there. I weighed about nine and a half stone and I was six foot one, in shorts and all covered in blood. The inspector said, 'What the fuckin' 'ell's going on?'

The officers were a little bit shamefaced about the whole thing. But I was seething with rage inside with that 'kindly' old guy, and I wasn't going to let it drop. So I picked a chair up and tried to hit that officer— but unfortunately I hit the inspector. Then he just washed his hands of me and walked out and they all laid into me again.

A couple of hours later my grandmother arrived to bail me out. The police had been round to see her and told her what had happened. She had to walk from Battersea Rise to Nine Elms—they wouldn't give her a lift in their car. I appeared next morning at South Western magistrates' court and I was fined a pound. That was my first conviction, for riding a bicycle with no lights.

The interesting adjunct to this is that John Junor, who used to write a newspaper column, wrote at the time of my arrest for the Train Robbery, 'Don't waste any time over Reynolds's sentence of 25 years, he is rotten to the core. His first conviction when he was 16 was for assaulting a policeman'. But he didn't go on to say, 'He was fined a pound for riding a bike without lights'!

• • •

After I lost the cycle firm job I went to work as an assistant fitter at a firm building radar towers. At this firm I met a guy that I'd call a wide boy: he wasn't a crook but he knew the ways of the streets. He was street-educated and when I started going out with him, he showed me how to get by on the Tube without buying a ticket, he showed me how to get into the cinemas by going in the back doors. Then we did a couple of minor robberies—we smashed a couple of kiosk windows and stole some lighters. We had a rather abortive attempt at breaking into telephone boxes for the cash. Then we tried to break open a safe in a big factory, which was more or less adjacent to where we lived.

We couldn't open the safe—I don't know how we expected to open it—we had no knowledge about how to open a safe. We were only 17 or 18 years old at the time. So we ended up breaking into the canteen and stealing the cigarettes. A couple of days afterwards, before we'd had time to sell the cigarettes, we were nicked. My first conviction came up in court, and I got probation.

Conscription was still in force at the time, and once you were conscripted, whatever firm you'd worked for had by law to re-employ you after you'd done your army service. Naturally, firms didn't want to employ you for six months then have to re-employ you in two years' time when you'd finished army service. So it was very difficult for me to find a job and I ended up doing a piecework job polishing screw-heads. I got £1 for 6000. I put up with that for exactly half a day.

So now I just fell back on the thing I knew I could do, which was smashing shop windows and stuff like that, and of course I was nicked again. I'd had three convictions in the space of two years. I was on probation so I was sent to borstal.

• • •

Me and this other guy, before we actually got to borstal, we had an abortive attempt to break out of a Black Maria van. So by the time we arrived we'd achieved the extra kudos of being on special watch. We had special uniforms and of course, that means you're Jack the Lad! You're separated from all the rest of them, you've moved up a echelon, you're not just an ordinary prisoner, you're on special watch. You were mixing with people that perhaps had escaped once already.

All the same, when I got to borstal I felt sick. I suppose if I could have been let out then, after that first week, I think it's quite possible that I wouldn't have got back into trouble again because of the shock of it. Like most people I think, you'd put on the bravado during the day and you cried into your pillow at night. But after a week you got into the routine of prison life and you started liking it. Of course you like it, because you're somebody. And it's not hard to assume the mantle of prison hero by doing something which is a bit out of the ordinary, like giving a screw a hard time, showing the other cons how tough you are.

And of course this fitted in so well with all that wartime hero thing. I think I looked on prison very much as if I was a prisoner of war! And I treated the screws as if they were Germans, and it was every man's duty to escape, or at least to give the screws a hard time.

In those days the system was a lot more aggressive than it is today. You didn't challenge authority in the way you might now. Let's say there were no restrictions on screws beating you up. No-one was really concerned particularly. I half accepted all this because I'd seen all those Humphrey Bogart films where he's sneering at screws on Devil's Island and I thought that's the way you behaved, because it was cool. I mean, when I first went away, not coming from that sort of criminal background, when you heard people talking in slang about 'get up the apples',[1] and 'I pulled out me gem[2] and put on me turtles',[3] I thought, 'I gotta learn this language!'

So that's what I did. I found my faith in prison camaraderie, and the whole lexicon of prisoners' rules that you don't do this and you don't do that. And as a creed, I accepted it. I thought it was great—you don't grass, everyone's staunch, you try to help everyone out.

---

[1] Apples and pears = stairs

[2] Gemmy

[3] Turtle doves = gloves

You could say, I suppose, that I wasn't really a criminal then, but I certainly found something that I'd never found before. I found that I belonged, that I could fit in very easily. And of course, you were somebody. You weren't just nobody out in the street. I was brighter than a lot of people that were in borstal.

As soon as I got to borstal my whole aim was to escape: because that's what you had to do. Plus there was a tremendous amount of magic with people that I'd known whose elder brothers had been on the run. That had a magic connotation to me, being on the run. *Being on the run, escape*: these words were almost like a mantra to me. Because everyone who was anyone in my pantheon of heroes—or anti-heroes— had been on the run. Virtually every major political figure in history has been imprisoned at some time or another.

So I enjoyed borstal. I enjoyed every moment—I even enjoyed the moments of desperation. I was living out my fantasies—being pursued all over London, as I imagined—the dragnets being out for this violent runaway from borstal.

But of course, I didn't realise it at the time but these early exploits were an albatross that was going to hang round my neck for many, many years; because you're mounting up convictions. On the run from borstal I was obviously committing offences to stay alive.

When I got nicked the first time, there was a punishment centre at Wandsworth Prison, what you might call a recall centre for escaped or recalcitrant borstal boys. The regime there at the time was strict. There was no talking except during Saturday afternoons and Sunday afternoon exercise—that was your hour which in fact got whittled down to something like 40 minutes. The rest of the time, even at work, you weren't allowed to talk and if you did talk you were nicked. Then it was a bread and water job.

Then books—you were only allowed three library books a week, and again the same consideration was applied, that if you got caught changing a book with someone else it was a nicking offence. There were no newspapers, no radios. The only time you heard anything about the outside world was on Sunday. Church was compulsory—it was a nicking offence if you didn't go—and at the end of the service the vicar used to read out the football results and if someone in the Royal Family had died or had been having any problems. That's the only news you got.

The whole regime was a physical one. Your exercise during the week was an hour's PT every day. And this was at the time when most of the screws in Wandsworth were ex-army. Most of them were ex-guardsmen with the old flat guards' cap with the peak pulled down. They looked very much like Colchester military prison officers. I wouldn't say that people were beaten up senselessly, but there was right-handers being thrown all the time at anyone that was a bit saucy.

The most unnatural thing was keeping you isolated from women. We were all young men, and the only time you saw anything like a woman was when they put you on chokey[4] and they used to give you *National Geographic* magazines—a big block of them—to read. And you might see a picture of a topless native woman, which obviously was a great thrill. But normally sex plays such a part in your life at that time, and you're totally cut off from it in a place like that, year in and year out.

I was sent to the first borstal in 1949 and I came out from that borstal in 1952. But in those three years I got another sentence of borstal training, another sentence of between nine months and three years as a result of escaping. Then I got 18 months in a YP[5] instead, because the judge said I'd fucked up my chance of going to borstal—they thought borstal was giving you a chance! I did my 12 months in the YP after a lot of aggro being moved from Lewes to Winchester. Then they sent me back to borstal for six months, which I now think was illegal.

Then they moved the whole organization of borstal recall from Wandsworth to Reading Prison, and I finished off my time there working in the kitchen. I had five days' home leave then I had to go into the army at 21—conscription.

● ● ●

Originally, I was quite looking forward to the army. I mean I didn't have any criminal connections. Of course I'd met people in borstal but I didn't come out of borstal with the idea that I was going to be bang at it, because I didn't know what bang at it was. All I knew was breaking into factories and smashing shop windows, that's all I'd done basically. So I thought maybe the army could be my niche. I could see that it was a development that had been left over from when I was going to go in the Navy.

I was in the Medical Corps—I thought it was great—maybe I could join the paras—it'd be a good life. But I got off on the wrong foot totally because everyone I met said 'Oh, you're the borstal boy!'

Then obviously I resented small-time authority like a corporal or somebody like that, starting telling me what to do. I was a couple of years older than someone like that, I'd been through the prison system. I didn't take very kindly to him telling me what to do.

So I had a bit of a row and then I thought 'Fuck the army, I'm going home'.

So I just left. I'd only been in there two days and I was on the run again. And of course, that's exactly where I wanted to be. It was like I'd

---

[4] Punishment cell

[5] Young offenders' institution (as it would nowadays be called)

seen in the films, like *Waterloo Road* with John Mills and Stewart Granger.

So here I am in the same situation again. I'm on the run, committing offences to stay on the run, I get nicked. And because of all this record that had been built up, with all my offences, I get three years at the age of 21. I'd only been home about three months from the three years I'd spent away in borstal.

It was a heavy sentence then, three years in 1952. And as I said in my book,[6] Wandsworth is like Oxbridge—there's more dons in Wandsworth than there is in Oxbridge or Palermo!

* * *

In 1963, at the time of the Train Robbery, I was totally irresponsible. I didn't give a damn about anybody. Having said that, I never intended that violence should be used in the robbery. I certainly do regret my actions and I stated this publicly in 1995 on the Richard and Judy show at the time my book was published. I offered my sincere apologies to the family of Jack Mills, the train driver who was injured. Although I was not the perpetrator of the injury, those actions still concern me.

The Train Robbery fell into unknown territory. From what I'd heard of other major crimes, the hue and cry usually lasted about a week. But you've got to remember this was 1963—this was really the advent of television as multi-entertainment for the masses. And of course as Vietnam was the first televised war, The Great Train Robbery was the first televised crime, because it involved the audience in it—that's most of the populace—from the moment of the robbery involving these vast amounts of money.

Then of course the story continued like a criminal soap opera. Every day there were stories of different adventures from people captured, people who fell down just like dominoes. There were vast numbers of people going out on treasure hunts—the whole country was imbued with the thing. It became almost like a lottery. People were saying, 'Let's go out in the country and see if we can find some money, let's look to see if we can find any clues anywhere'. And don't forget there was this mammoth £250,000 reward—you're talking about £2.5 million at today's values.

---

[6] Bruce Reynolds has written about the rest of his criminal career in *The Autobiography of a Thief* (Corgi,1995). It culminated in the Great Train Robbery in 1963. Much has also been written by Bruce and others about the train robbery itself. Bruce admits now that it was a very ambitious crime but he was convinced that he and the rest of the gang would get away with it. He describes the robbery and its aftermath in the same romanticising terms as his accounts of being on the run from borstal and the army.

I had supreme confidence that it was just a question of staying out of the way for a little bit and then it would all blow over. But of course it just kept going on and on and on and it's still going on and on and on. It may have been a common perception that I was the mastermind behind the Train Robbery, but I tend to think that Buster[7] and Biggsy[8] are the two names people remember.

I was OK when I was in Mexico. In retrospect of course I made a mistake: I was settled in there when I got word that Buster wanted to come out there to stay with me. He did say that if it was going to affect me in any way, he'd find somewhere else. But I saw it as being very much in my favour to have him over there because he'd got a daughter the same age as my son. I'd met Buster's wife, I liked her and I thought we could establish ourselves as a little English community over there, kind of self-sufficient. And I thought he'd got the sort of money that I'd got: I'd already begun talking about putting money into a business over there. So I thought we could make a useful partnership.

Of course, when he arrived, it turned out he wasn't there for life as I was, it was just really a stopgap as far as he was concerned and he didn't have the kind of money that I had. He'd lost most of his money along the way. You could say he'd had his money stolen off him by like-minded people the same as ourselves.[9]

• • •

When I left prison in 1978 after my time for the Train Robbery, I didn't have any intention of going back into crime. The way I saw it, I'd done the robbery and I'd done my time for it and I could see that there were other areas in my life that I wanted to explore.

What could I do? I'd always had this thing about writing, from the days when I once wanted to be a foreign correspondent. But instead I went to work for an old friend of mine who was in the metal business—it was reusable steel. I worked for him for about a year and then the steel industry went through a major crisis where there were cutbacks all the way along the line and my friend had to make cutbacks too. So that job went. I worked for someone else in the wholesale dress game, but that went to pieces as well. I worked doing a bit of labouring for someone

---

[7] Buster Edwards

[8] Ronnie Biggs (still 'on the run' since his escape from Wandworth prison in 1966)

[9] Bruce was finally captured in 1969 and remanded into Leicester prison in the maximum security unit. He was sentenced to 25 years' imprisonment, and was held in maximum security conditions in Durham, Chelmsford, Parkhurst, Maidstone and finally a hostel at Wormwood Scrubs, serving a total of nearly ten years.

who had fruit and flower pitches in the market. But I really did think that I just wasn't making it pay, working. And I certainly couldn't see any areas criminal-wise. I didn't want to be in the drug business either: the way I see it, it's just a means of making money. There's no buzz in it.

The Train Robbery—there *was* a buzz in it. It was a criminal achievement and from that point of view, as a practising criminal of course I was proud of it at the time. I'd pulled off one of the major robberies of all time. It had been called 'The Crime of the Century' and it was known right across the world—so of course it meant something to me. As a criminal it had to. That's what I'd been working for all my life. You couldn't get any higher.

• • •

I'd been out of prison five years, then in 1983 I got nicked for some amphetamines. I wasn't part of a set-up or anything. I mean it was just simply one of those things, with me delivering something to someone, which was quite common at the time. I'm not going to say I didn't know what it was. It was a sealed package. But of course me being whom I am, I got three years for it.

In a way, that sentence really did reinforce a lot of thoughts that I'd been establishing in my own mind about where I was going. When I got nicked for the amphetamines, I went to an open prison. That was a real big shock to me—going back into the prison system after all those years. Going back in there, not with the glamour of coming back in as the Train Robber, but just because I'd been involved in drugs. It seemed an odd thing to be there for amphetamines, because everyone was involved in amphetamines, whether they were prescribed or not.

• • •

I came out of prison in 1985 after that sentence for the amphetamines, so I've been out now for 14 years. What stops me returning to crime? I think that like an old soldier, you look at criminal reports in the newspapers and you think 'Is there anything to admire in that? Do you feel the buzz?' There was no magical conversion on the road to Damascus for me. It's been a steady thing all the way along the line. The game basically ain't worth the candle. The sort of time you get rules it out. I haven't got the years left to spend any more time in prison. Of course I could theoretically be interested in some sort of major coup—but what a major coup would be I don't know.

I suppose if I did get involved it would be to say to people, 'I'm still up there. Don't write me off'. But crime's a young man's game. You don't care when you're young—you're not concerned. You've got that supreme confidence in yourself where you don't think that anything'll ever go wrong—and if it does, what difference does it make anyway? You can handle it. You're big enough to do it.

There isn't anything around that excites my imagination in a criminal way that I'd want to get involved in. There's nothing on my horizons criminally that I could see that would excite me, stimulate me, to return me to crime.

And then of course there's the other side of it. I was pretty lucky all my life—you can say lucky, or you can say I had good judgement—in that I only ever worked with close friends. Most of them have been people that I've known from childhood. I mean in our particular case with The Great Train Robbery it was one of the last major robberies where no-one made statements.

It was the end of an era. Because obviously the sentences handed out to us created all sorts of Frankenstein monsters for the Establishment. By giving us 30 years, you have to ask where do you go from there? What do you give to someone who's shot a couple of people? If people think they are going to get 30 years for a robbery, they might just as well walk out with guns.

●　●　●

Without a doubt I would say my family and my friends are the most important things in my life today. Of course with the period of time that's gone by, two of my oldest friends killed themselves, Charlie[10] was murdered, and another close friend of mine died at 55. I've lost a lot of friends that meant a lot to me and they're irreplaceable because obviously you haven't got the years left to make those sorts of friends again.

There was this guy I met when I was at Leicester, and I was having quite a bad time in the security wing, for one reason or another. This guy was a probation officer, but he'd been in the RAF during the war— Pathfinder Squadron, only about three of them survived the whole thing. I was feeling particularly down this one day, and I said to him, 'What's it all about, Fred?' And he said, 'What it's all about in my opinion is relationships. That's all there is in life'. And of course you think on it, and you think, that's right. The thing is, money in today's world is the only yardstick of how successful you are. That's all everything's about today—whether you're successful financially. That's the yardstick for most people. Not what sort of a person you are.

I suppose this is one of the things about prison. When you're in prison, you're judged by who and what you are, what you *really* are. I mean, you might come in there with a big reputation, but it's got to be maintained, because there's no shit in prison and sooner or later you get

---

[10]　Charles Wilson, another of the train robbers

found out, whoever you are, whatever you are. Someone will take you down if they think you're going over the top. Doesn't matter how big you are.

The predominant thing now is that I've got the responsibility of my ex-wife. We've been back together since 1980. Integral to that is my son Nick and I've got a great relationship with him. He's 35 now and he's in the music business. He's got a baby son of his own. Nick's had eight years in the Navy, he knows what the score is in all walks of life. And it would just be a retrograde step as far as I'm concerned, for him to see me as a criminal.

I've been writing now since 1987. My hopes for the future, what I'm trying to do, is to make a success of my future as a writer. I was an active criminal, let's say from the age of 17. I came out of prison in 1978. You could say I haven't been an active criminal since then. And I feel I've got a lot to say. I'd like to be known as Bruce Reynolds the writer, not Bruce Reynolds the Great Train Robber. I'm hoping that crime pays in the literary sense!

Bob Cummines

Bob—'BC' to his friends—is 46. He is a project worker for a housing association which finds hostel accommodation for homeless people living on the streets, ex-offenders and people with mental health problems. His life now, as a happily married father in a peaceful country village, is very different from his violent past, when he was a gangland gunman who served long sentences for armed robbery and manslaughter and was constantly involved in prison riots. We also interviewed Bob's wife Lynn, who played a major part in helping him go straight after he left prison ten years ago.

I was actually very pleased when I got nicked. It was all over. I'd always lived a total lie and I hated it. It was like being in a crowd but on your own. You were popular—well, you weren't *popular* but other people all wanted to be with you because you were spending money. I think it was also fear—people feared you. And you moved right out of society. You're in a different ball game altogether. You can't trust anyone. You've picked up a gun and you've killed someone. You go out with guns and people come looking for you with guns.

And so you sleep with guns. You don't go to bed without a gun. Even in your own family you don't trust anyone, because anyone can pick up the phone, get the reward for knowing where you are, or set you up to get shot—I got shot myself once. People that you may have hurt a long time ago might set you up so they can shoot you.

So yes, I was glad when I got nicked. There's a lot of danger in prisons but you don't mind that, you can handle that. It's the loneliness of being outside that's hard to handle. In prison you're not alone—you've got everyone in there with you. This is why prisons are so ridiculous. You're in prison with the same people you've been in nightclubs with, for 'kicks, chicks and champagne' as we used to say. That was our motto, if you asked any of us what we wanted, and we'd boast how we'd spill more vodka than most people drink, because we could afford to. You're all sitting there in prison, having a laugh about what you've done, and what you're planning next. Prison's just a club.

• • •

When I was still at primary school, I wanted to learn the piano, but my father wasn't having it. He said 'No, the piano's for poofs, you're not doing that. I'd rather you go boxing'. I liked the piano, it was nice. When I was a bit older I used to go to music appreciation classes and I loved music. There was a lot of stuff I appreciated. That's why I always knew I was different from the rest of them. But all this was suppressed—music was not seen as a manly thing to do.

My dad was an aggressive man. He would break furniture though he never hit my mum. But he had a temper and he drank. He once punched a door right through the panels, and for bets he used to walk along punching the tops off those old cast-iron railings with the fleur-de-lys on top. And he did street fighting—he used to come home with black eyes because they used to fight for money.

So I started boxing quite young—I think I really did it to please my father. I was Boys' Clubs boxing champion when I was just coming up to eleven. I was always winning tea services for my mum—she had more tea services than anything!

In my third year at secondary school I came second in the whole school at Latin and I won a prize. They gave me a gold-leaf Latin book. I went home to my dad and said they'd given me a book and it was gold-leaf. He said 'What're you proud of? You didn't come first!' I think that's when I really started going the other way.

I liked poetry, I liked music, I liked art, I liked things of beauty—and yet my life was incredibly ugly. I'd surrounded myself with violence and ugliness, but inside there was this little boy that wanted things of beauty. I could have gone down that other path as easy as that, as easy as that!

• • •

I was the youngest of eight children—four girls and four boys. My dad was a builder, a stone mason by trade, and Mum was a housewife—she stayed home and looked after us. We lived near King's Cross. You'd walk down the road and there was a lot of prostitution and violence. You could play out while it was light, but then when it got dark you were in. The streets weren't safe at night because of the type of things that were happening out there—you'd get bookmakers, moneylenders—I only knew this later when I grew up. You could hear fights just outside your house.

But our street was a nice little street really. All the people living in the street were in the construction industry like my dad. He had his own company, quite a big company, and he had some good contracts. The men were all craftsmen. There was an Italian bloke living just down the road from us who used to make mosaic floors. There were a lot of people from different races: Greeks and a strong Irish community. I never thought about racism until later on in life, because we all grew up together. Everybody had their street doors open and you could go in anyone's house and get bread and butter and jam—it was a very family sort of atmosphere. We used to make soapbox carts and we played in the streets. There were a lot of bombed-out houses and we used to climb and go and make camps in them. There was plenty of crime going on, but people didn't rob each other—they always went out of the area.

At first I went to Copenhagen Street School. When you got there you met children from other areas but kids from our street stuck together. You made little gangs and defended each other.

But when I was about seven or eight we moved to a new area, Holloway, where I didn't know anyone. We moved because my dad's business went down the pan. All his building work seized up, and he had to go and work in a hospital. Holloway was a very similar area to King's Cross inasmuch as it was very cosmopolitan. But it was even more vicious than King's Cross.

It was then that the fights in the school playground really started, because it was an alien environment. I suppose the children who lived in this new area were trying to suss me out. In the playground they'd test the boundaries to see how far they could go with the new kid. You'd probably have to have a fight with three or four of them and if you could stand up for yourself you'd be accepted. But if you didn't you were swallowed up.

There was lot of bullying in schools in those days. In this new school there was this big Irish kid who was a bully. He bullied me a couple of times and I told my dad about it and said I was unhappy at the school. But my dad wasn't going to do anything about it. His attitude was 'Sort it yourself'. You couldn't go home to my dad with that sort of thing. Even if you went to him with a black eye and said 'Some kid's hit me' he'd say 'Go and sort it yourself'.

So I'd got to stand my ground. I made up my mind then that if this Irish kid bullied me again I'd get back at him. I had a little cricket bat and when he came up to me I hit him across the legs with it. He stopped bullying me then and wanted to be my friend. And everyone else wanted to be my friend too, after I'd done that. So even at that early age I realised that violence was power. Because I was too small to do it with my hands, I found that by using the bat I could control people—and that was when weapons became a big thing to me. That was the biggest turning point in my life so far: I realised that violence and weapons could get me out of trouble.

• • •

When I got to secondary school it was really good because I found the headmaster loved boxing. In those days, if the teachers saw you were a bit violent they tried to move you into boxing or some other aggressive sport. I think it was a strategy to try and defuse the violence, and it was legal. In this school the headmaster was a boxing enthusiast and he used to say boxing wasn't about violence, boxing was about discipline. If you were in the boxing team you didn't have to do detentions. I was soon in a lot of detentions for fighting in the school playground, and then for truancy, so I used to go boxing instead of serving the detention.

I was very bright and I got into the grammar stream. The first secondary school I went to was a Catholic school. My mother was a Catholic, my father was a Protestant and they'd come over from Ireland because of the problems with religion over there. This school was run by monks. They were quite perverse really—they used to whack the kids with rulers for nothing. I got slung out of there for violence—but in fact the brothers who ran the school were violent themselves. I was caught fighting in the playground and one of the monks caned me across the knuckles so I battered him. They called my dad in, and first they said I was very violent, and they were going to call the police in and have me arrested for it. But when my dad saw the marks on me he said 'Look, this can go both ways'. And then they just got rid of me. So I went to another school, an ordinary school. I never went to Catholic schools after that.

My next school was a boys' grammar school. But I still didn't like school much. Though I was scoring high marks and I won that Latin prize, I found it boring. I started truanting after that first and second year. We used to go down the caffs—we all used to meet in caffs. That's where the real criminal stuff started. Some of the blokes I met there were already going burgling. We met guys from other schools who were bunking off as well, and we'd have fights with them.

My nephew was the same age as me, and he was in the same class. A teacher hit him with flex wire which he used to carry round with him. This was when I was getting good at boxing and I jumped up in the classroom and battered the teacher. I was caned in front of everybody in the school for it.

I left school at 15, though they suggested I should stay on and do my exams, and in fact the headmaster called my dad up and said I was well capable of doing them. But my dad didn't see that as important. My dad thought we should all have trades—he was a great one for you going somewhere and learning a trade. It was the same with lots of things—like that time when I wanted to learn the piano. My mum might have wanted more for us, but she was just a quiet little lady, living in a time when women were housewives and they didn't have any say in anything. She'd got eight kids, I think she had enough on her hands.

• • •

So I left school and went and worked as a post boy, a junior office boy for HM Customs. My sister's boyfriend got me the job: he worked in the City for a shipping office and he knew I didn't want to go and work on a building site. The job only paid £9 a week but I liked it. My office was right next to the Tower of London. My mum was very proud of me but my dad resented it; he definitely resented it. He didn't see it as proper work.

I'd always been living in circles where crime was happening around me all the time. It's just that I chose not to get involved. I just didn't want to know. A lot of my friends were in borstals and detention centres. But I really liked my job and I felt good about me. I didn't use drugs. I thought drugs were for the mugs. There were people that used cough mixture, smoked a bit of grass and that sort of thing, but I was training for boxing so I didn't even drink.

But then I lost my job because I was fitted up by the police. One day, when I'd been in my job about nine months, I was over at Finsbury Park, sitting on the grass with a group of boys and some girls, and some coppers came up and asked us what we were up to. What I didn't know was that two of the boys had starting pistols in their pockets, and they'd been firing them in the park. Because I'd got into the habit of standing up for myself, I challenged these coppers. I said, 'What d'you want to know for?' Then when the police found the starting pistols and started taking these boys away, I got a bit lippy and I said, 'Shouldn't you be seeing their parents or something?' And then one of the coppers said, 'Right-o! Look what I've just found in your pocket!' And it was a cut-throat razor! I just laughed at them—I'd never seen the thing before!

They took me down the law shop[1] and they charged me with possessing a weapon. My dad was called round and I said 'The guy just put that in my pocket!' But he said, 'Oh no, they wouldn't do that!'

When we got to court I said to this policeman, 'I'm going to tell them, in court, that you put it in my pocket!' He said, in front of my dad, 'Policemen don't do that, I'd never do a thing like that, and if you tell them that you'll go to borstal'. Then he told my dad, 'If he just goes in there and puts his hand up to it, it's a ten bob fine'. My dad agreed. He said, 'Oh, it don't matter, you don't want to go to borstal. Go in and we'll pay the ten bob fine'. I was dead against it but he browbeat me into it. So I went into court and I pleaded guilty, though I'd never done anything.

I hated my father for that. I never did forgive him. It cost me my job, because I had to declare to my employers that I'd been given a fine for possession of a razor. And that's when I thought, 'Right, you wanted it this way, so you can have it'. My criminal offending started then, all because I was fitted up with a razor that wasn't mine. I broke the law

---

[1] Police station

straight after that, and when I was about 16, I got done for possession of a sawn-off shotgun. And things went crazy after that.

It was the razor incident that made me so angry and led me to commit my first crime. Some guys came to me and said 'We've got a robbery and we've got a shotgun. Are you in for it?' They'd already had the shotgun cut down, and they had the ammunition. Of course I'd got a criminal record by then, which put up my street cred a bit. So I said 'Yes, I'm up for it'. It wasn't for the money—it was nothing to do with money.

I already knew how to use a gun. We used to go shooting over in Hertfordshire when we were kids, with a couple of fathers who had shotguns. We'd do a bit of squirrelling—the idea was to get us off the streets. We'd use shotguns, then we graduated to 12-bores, so we knew our way around guns. There was also the criminal element who had illegal guns on the street which you could purchase—they weren't even that expensive.

So I went out with these guys with a gun and we held up a post office van, but it was an empty one. We had hundreds of pouches and there was only about six quid in them! The post office workers got out and we stuck 'em up. It turned out that the shotgun they'd sawn up was an antique that was worth more than the robbery! We were kids who'd seen all this on the films—films did have a lot of influence. Rod Steiger movies, Al Capone, John Dillinger, Jimmy Cagney, and now and again we'd think we were Zorro. That sort of stuff used to capture your imagination, they were your heroes, in the cheap Saturday afternoon pictures. When you got to about 14 you'd be reading gangster books as well.

And then you'd have the older chaps telling you how much they were earning—they were all liars of course. That was the thing about it. When you're young you believe the myths. Then you make those myths realities. It's the same with any violence. You do it, but you're the victim as well—you're the victim of one big myth.

Once we'd done that first crime and I got six months in a detention centre for possession of a firearm, that's when I really got into violence. It made me into a super-thug. It was basically to survive, because that detention centre was a very violent place. There were what they called 'daddies' who ran the place.

I don't think I realised the gravity of where I was. This was a senior detention centre. 'Numb' would be a good word to describe how I felt. There was no fear, there was no sense of 'Oh my God—I'm here!' I didn't comprehend at that stage what was going to happen to me. I think I was shocked—that's the only way I can describe it—it wasn't real. I think I thought, 'This is all going to go away, they're going to come and say they've made a mistake'.

Most of my offences after that involved guns, armed robberies—I even went to jail for manslaughter. It was all to do with guns, robberies, violence. I couldn't escape from it. Firstly, you couldn't get a job once you had a record. Then there was the conditioning from other criminals. The attitude was: 'You don't want to be like *them*, part of the crowds in Oxford Street. You want to be a *somebody*'.

You get used so badly when you're young as well. Older guys soon realised I was quite game to use a gun and I was quite handy with my boxing. So when I had a job collecting bad debts, they'd give me 20 quid and tell me to give some bloke a good hiding and I'd give him a good hiding not knowing that they'd been paid 200 quid to do it. I was mugged off[2] all the time until in the end as I got older, I started to suss it out what was going on. And I looked at these guys and I saw through the myth. I realised that everything they'd told me was nonsense, bullshit. It was me doing the work and them getting the takings.

So pretty soon I turned on them, and then it was their turn to work for me. And then the violence escalated.

As for my victims—it wasn't personal—they were just 'bits of work', they weren't people, they were just bits of work. I'm saying this now and my head is screaming because of the horror of it. But I'm trying to think how it was at that time—and at that time it was just *bits of work*.

Someone could have said to me, 'There's a bloke there, we want him shot in the legs. How much?' And I would think about it and make an estimate, 'So-and-so, so-and-so'. And then I would watch this man's routine: it was just like hunting. That sounds terrible and it *is* terrible. But you could detach yourself from it. If you couldn't detach yourself from it, you would have gone crazy. When I finally started to analyse myself I had to live with that nightmare, I had to live with the consequences of what I'd done. You can't undo it. The only way I can undo it is by making restitution now. It was insanity.

After that first six months in the detention centre, I did over seven years in a young offenders' prison for manslaughter, and then I did 12 years—that was my last sentence —for armed robberies.

I don't know how many different prisons I've been in—I was on the ghost train for a lot of the time.[3] I was always being slung out of prisons for being in the middle of riots. I was in prisons like Parkhurst, Albany, Bristol special control unit, Winson Green. I never got parole. I was fighting everybody the whole time.

The violence in prison was about survival. It all boiled down to being more vicious than anyone else so they didn't come on you. You

---

[2] Cheated

[3] i.e. being moved from one prison to another without warning

made your mark as 'one of the chaps' and people just stayed away from you. Nobody messed with you.

During my last sentence, the 12 year stretch, I was moved from a Category A[4] prison to Maidstone, which was Category B, and I was up to my usual tricks in there. There was this fear—everyone was saying about me, 'He's bad, this guy's bad'.

• • •

rehabe...

Then something changed me. In Maidstone prison I met a man called Maurice O'Riley, who was a senior probation officer in the jail. He came up to me on the landing and he said 'I'd like to see you in my office about parole'.

I said to him 'I don't want your parole. When I get out of here I want big bags of money which I'm gonna take off security vans—so piss off, and don't you ever come up to me again and tell me you want to see me. When I want to see you, I'll tell *you'*.

Normally everyone would walk away from me when I was like that—prison officers as well. I was very arrogant and I was very violent and I was also a very good wheeler and dealer. But Maurice didn't walk away: he challenged me. He said 'When I'm rude to you, you can be rude to me'. And it took me off guard, because I didn't expect it. Maurice was the only one who'd ever challenged me. That took a lot of bottle. He was a big guy, but sort of soft-spoken—and I got to like him.

I went down to see him. We had a chat about general things, and I thought 'You're all right'. I used to wear really dark glasses in those days, and later on he used to say to me 'I want to know the man behind the dark glasses. I know the man everybody else knows. But I want to know the real man'. That was unnerving, but it was quite exciting as well to think that someone wanted to know me for *me*—my *person*. So I started going to see him quite regularly.

When I first met Maurice I was about four or five years into that last 12 year sentence. I'd never done education in prison before. All I did in prison was drink hooch and get slung into the gym—I wasn't interested in anything else. I had *no* intention of giving up crime. In fact what I was doing in prison was making contacts. When I was convicted at the Old Bailey it was the time of the super-grasses and I and all my associates got put away. So we were all just sitting in jail planning what we were going to do when we got out.

But Maurice O'Riley made me start thinking about what I was doing, and I started to change.

---

[4] Top security

Then I met my wife. Lynn worked as the prison librarian and she used to teach as well. Since I'd met Maurice I'd begun spending a lot of time in the education department and in the library, and Lynn became a friend. When I first met her I remember thinking she had incredibly beautiful eyes.

At that time I was still planning to go back out there and rob security guards and banks. But when Lynn showed a bit of interest in my poetry I thought 'This is something else!' I was trying to publish a book of poetry at the time. I used to write poetry when they put me in the discipline blocks in various prisons. I started writing when a friend of mine hanged himself and I'd had a couple of other bad experiences. I'd seen people beaten by the guards in the punishment blocks, and I was trying to work out what was happening around me, and what was happening inside me—in my thoughts. And so I wrote it all down, in the form of poems, because I never wanted to forget what went on in there. They used to take away everything you wrote down, because they didn't want any of this information to get out of the prison. They confiscated everything I wrote, but I kept my poems in my head.

I'd seen so much hypocrisy, people pretending to be nice and decent people—like the chaplains. In one prison we came out of the block after getting into a semi-riot. The screws had beaten us pretty badly. The chaplain came in and I said 'Look what's happened to these guys! You've got to say something'. He said 'I can't get involved'. So I wrote a poem in which I said

> I've seen the chaplain give sacrament
> To men beaten beyond repair
> Kneel down and pray to Our Lord
> And pretend the blood was not there.

I'd always been able to express myself in words—I suppose it was from my schooling—I could always write what I was feeling. I'd begun writing long before I got to Maidstone jail. I'd started observing things around me, the people I was in prison with. I don't want to glorify them and I'm not condoning what they did. But there were some interesting men in with me in Parkhurst. I was on the landing with terrorists and I met people like the Krays and Charlie Richardson—they were in the next cell to me and I got on with them all right. Charlie Richardson was one of the most well-read men I'd ever met—a very interesting man to talk to. I didn't look at him like Charlie Richardson the gangster, I looked at him as an interesting bloke. When my mother was dying of leukaemia, Reggie Kray had her a little caravan made out of matchsticks. He was very kind to me. In Parkhurst everyone was violent, everyone was dangerous, everyone was a potential killer. But the strange thing I noticed was that they were all very polite and respectful to each other—it was the most respectful place I've ever been in. The screws were all right there: they didn't mess with us and we got on all right with them. They treated you with respect so they got the same coinage back. And all the time I was writing poems about what was happening to me. That's how I survived.

● ● ●

My relationships with Maurice and with Lynn were beginning to change me. But I think the biggest influence in me changing round was a guy called Bev Bingham. He was the first man who ever trusted me.

At the time I first met Maurice I wanted to call my mum, who was dying of leukaemia, and Maurice said I could use the phone in the probation office. The doctor told me she only had a limited time to live, and if I wanted to see her alive I had to go now. But I wouldn't go out in handcuffs. I refused, because once I did go from Parkhurst to see my mum. They handcuffed me with chains round my arm and leg and they took me in a special security van. They put armed police around my mum's house, they had prison officers inside and they wouldn't take the cuffs off me. It didn't do her any good to see me like that and I wasn't going to do it again.

I remember Maurice coming to me and saying 'Your mum's going to die and you're not going to see her'. So I said 'Well, I'll live with that, but I'm not going out in cuffs'. I was really angry and I think they got a bit worried because I'd already been done for inciting riots and I think they were afraid I'd really go to town on them.

Then this old guy called Bev Bingham suddenly came along and he said 'I'll take him'. He was head of the Education Department at Maidstone prison and he said to me 'If I can get permission to take you to see your mum, will you promise me you won't have a mob waiting there to take you out?' Which I certainly could have done.

I said 'What are you saying to me?' And he said, 'Give me your word'. I said 'I can't do that, because if I give you my word, I'll have to stick by it'. And oh yeah, I did think I'd walk.[5] I said to myself, 'If I see my mother in that state, I might just have to walk'.

Then I thought about it and I thought 'Hold up a minute, this guy's putting himself on the line for me'. So I went back in the afternoon and I said to Bev Bingham 'You've put the worst type of handcuff on me because if I give you my word I've got to stick by that'. That's all I'd got—my word. If you rat on your word you've got nothing.

So I gave him my word and I went out of the prison with him in his car without any cuffs or anything. As we pulled up in the street where

---

[5] Escape

my mum lived, a couple of people saw us, and as we got out the car they said 'You all right?' and I knew they were really saying, 'D'you wanna go?'

I said 'Yeah, I'm fine, we'll be going back'. And that was it. They knew then that I was going back to prison with this guy.

We went to see my mum, back in that old house where I used to live, and we were there the whole afternoon. Bev left me in the bedroom with her while he sat in the lounge with my family and had a cup of tea. He totally trusted me. I could have walked out the front door just like that. But it never entered my head, because I'd given him my word. I would never have let him down—I owed this guy too much. And at the end of the visit we drove down the bottom of my road and the stallholders gave us a load of fruit to eat on the way back.

We got in the car and he said 'Are we going back?' and I said 'Yeah, we're going back'. Then I felt a real buzz because he said 'Right, now I can tell you this: all the prison officers have been having bets in the officers' mess that I would be wrapped up and found somewhere and you'd be gone!'

Those screws all thought I would cheat on my word. They were really surprised when I got back. When I went back into that jail I just felt incredible respect for this guy who was sitting next to me. And I felt incredible respect for myself too, because I didn't let him down. I think it was then that I started getting some feeling for other people. That turned me round. It told me I could trust people. Bev was one special man.

• • •

I never went to my mum's funeral. I didn't show that kind of emotion though I loved my mum. She never visited me in prison: she was an honest lady and she couldn't handle prison—in fact I think she used to tell stories that I was working away.

Crime ruins and contaminates everyone it comes across—that's the ripple effect. And no matter how good they are, families can become contaminated by it, by greed. At first it was only me who went off the rails in our family, but then I even drew my brothers into crime. On the last sentence, which I got for being the gunman on the armed robberies, two of my brothers actually got nicked with me. I made them into bad guys. I think they wanted to come in because they saw the amount of money that was flowing about. At first I think my family were very shocked at what I did. But then they saw how well people treated them because of me. It was like their brother was a celebrity. In the area where they lived, they would go up to the fruit stalls and go to pay for their fruit and the stallholders would say 'No, it's all right, give my best to Bob'. My mum never worked that out—she always thought people were so kind, and she didn't realise what it was all about. So in a way I was criminalising the whole family.

When I went back on home leave towards the end of that final sentence, my family hired a pub in London for a party. There was a big cake with handcuffs and a cosh iced on the top.

I invited Lynn to come because she was helping me with my poetry book, and also because I'd boasted about her a bit to my family, because she was educated. We all respected educated people, so taking Lynn home with me was a bit like wearing a Rolex—there was a bit of tokenism in it.

Lynn: I'd known Bob for over a year and we'd become very fond of each other. In the build-up to his home leave, we had a conversation about it and in his blustering sort of way I detected a seed of—dare I say the word—fear, or at least apprehension, about going home. I realised how much he'd been changing, and although he didn't say it in so many words, I guessed perhaps he didn't want to be picked up outside the gate with champagne and taken straight to the party. So I offered to take him somewhere quiet, for a walk in the country or something, so he could get his head together before going off to London.

Bob: When you've decided to change it's the loneliest thing in the world. I knew I could either go back into my old world and be a somebody. Or I could come into this world—Lynn's world—and be a nobody. I didn't know anyone in this world, I didn't know their rules. It was terrifying: they might find out about my past and reject me. If I went back to my lot, they'd accept me because they're my people. I was going to be Mr Wonderful, I'd have lots of money, I'd go on my holiday—then off I'd go robbing again. Then there was this young lady, offering me *this* world I knew nothing about, with people whose language I didn't really speak or understand, whose values I wasn't too sure of—and the only person I knew in it was her.

Before I went out on that home leave, I sat down in the prison with a guy called Joe Mooney. Joe and I got 12 years on the same day. We had nothing to do with each other though we both came from North London. He got done by a supergrass and we both got the big Bs—the two biggest sentences of that day—at the Old Bailey. Joe was a very honest man for a crook, and he was a crude philosopher. He said to me 'See them gates, BC? Well, they're like your mother's womb. When you go out of there you got two ways. You can go left and back to blagging. Or you can go right into a complete new experience that you know nothing about. Because you're born again when you walk through them gates. You got a choice.' And that got me thinking. I thought, 'With all the things I've done, what did I want out of crime?' I knew I wanted a nice house, I wanted a wife, I wanted children, I wanted to have a nice lifestyle—

all those things I've got now that I'm away from crime. As criminals we all laughed at the man in the street—but we actually wanted what he's got! I've wasted so many years—talk about mugs, I'd win the prize for it!

There's been lots of times when I've thought I'd capitulate and go back to crime. For a start I wasn't worried about doing jail—I really wasn't. But there was a moment in jail when the trigger went for me, the trigger that made me want to stop being a criminal. I know that happens to everyone in jail, but if the supports aren't there it won't work.

Lynn: I met Bob out of prison on that first home leave. I think that was the first huge decision I'd made in my life because it was my job on my line. For me to meet him on home leave was a huge risk. I'd never ever done anything dishonest, and there was nobody that I could tell. I think 99 per cent of me knew that what I was doing was the right thing, a humane thing to do. But there was one per cent of me thinking he might take me off and rape me, murder me, bludgeon me to death, take me hostage. I obviously couldn't meet him at the prison gate so I met him in the town. Then I drove him to a quiet country church near a deer park. I thought it would be a nice place to go to get your balance.

Bob: I loved it. It was the most beautiful place I'd ever been to in my life. I was very shaky. I was experiencing incredible beauty and to be honest I didn't trust it—I thought it would be snatched away from me.

Lynn: We didn't talk or anything. We stayed there for an hour or so and then I said 'Do you want me to take you to the train station now? Because they'll all be waiting for you at the party in London'. But Bob said he didn't want to go! So we drove to a little village, went for a walk round there and had a cream tea. By that time it was late afternoon and I said 'Look, these people have organized the party, they're going to wonder what's happened to you'. So he went to London. Then he phoned me up in the early hours and asked me to come and meet his family. I arrived at 4 a.m.

Bob: That's when I knew I didn't belong. The party was all booze and people taking coke. I had a drink but I couldn't get drunk, and I was seeing what was going on all around me. It was my party, but I was totally alone there, and it was terrifying—absolutely terrifying. So I rang Lynn and said 'Come and meet my family'. By the time she arrived they were all drunk because the party was raving. She went to shake hands with my brother and he fell over!

I went back to prison and finished my sentence. I'd made up my mind.

All I wanted was to get back to that beauty that I'd had on that home leave. But I couldn't tell anybody about it because it would be scorned.

I was finally released on 1 June 1988. I came out the gate, and there was Lynn on one side of the gate, wearing a flowery dress, and there was my sister on the other side with a bottle of champagne. Either I went in that car with my sister and back to London, or I walked the other way with Lynn. They popped the cork, we had the champagne and I said to my family, 'Goodbye—I'm going with her'.

• • •

That first year, Lynn went through a bloody nightmare. I'd never held a job since I was 15—I'd been a robber ever since then—that was my work. So immediately I got out of prison, I had people phoning me up with bits of work, people saying 'You could go into this, you could go into that'. Bodyguard work, all that crap. I was so lonely living here, out in the country, and I kept going back to London on a pretty regular basis. The pull of what I knew, the hold of what was so familiar to me, was so great—yet I really knew I had to break away, to get away from it. Then one day Lynn laid down the law. She said 'It's either London or me—make your mind up'. And so I did make my mind up—it was Lynn.

I got my first job in a supermarket packing dog food on the shelves, nights, for £100 a week, which was a bit different from what I'd been used to. Still, I stuck it out—till a prison officer phoned the store and told them that I had form[6]. So I had to walk out of that job, otherwise they would have sacked me because I didn't declare it.

The hardest thing was this total dilemma: I wanted to be a straight guy which meant I wanted to be honest. In fact I saw myself as having to be more honest than most honest people. I hadn't got to be just 100 per cent straight, I'd got to be 110 per cent straight. I went for a couple of jobs and as soon as I declared my form—smack—the door was shut.

So in the end I created my own past—like I used to do when I was on the run. I was quite good at it, I could do my own letterheads and stuff like that. I created this history of work and soon I landed a very good job as a purchasing manager and stock control manager. From there I went into a management position with a Dutch company. I made lots of money, we got lots of presents, they really looked after us. I never declared my form. And then I was made redundant.

Lynn: Redundancy was hitting just about everybody. It was the peak of the recession. We'd got married, I'd packed up work and had our baby

---

[6] Previous convictions/usually meaning a prison record in this context

daughter. It was very, very, very difficult, that period of time—it was technically two years with a little baby, two years without full-time employment. I'd chosen to give up work but I found I had to go back to work. We were trying to move when Bob got made redundant and we'd signed contracts to buy a house but we hadn't exchanged. We owed £1,000 in solicitors' fees and had no way of paying for them, and we'd bought a car on hire purchase—so we were very, very, very poor.

I think Bob's been hugely tested. Our story may sound like a happy ever after story but we've had some huge ups and downs. My family did not welcome Bob with open arms. We had about two years of isolation which I found very difficult. But now we've been together ten years.

Bob: Though some people said we wouldn't last six months! I was out of work, just doing bits of part-time work. But I still wasn't tempted to go back to crime. It was just no longer in the equation. Then I met up with Maurice O'Riley again, and he told me there was a lot I could do helping ex-offenders. With Maurice's help I went to work for the Probation Service, and then for SOVA[7], which led to my present job.

Lynn: I don't know if I believe in destiny or fate, but in fact things have just clicked into place. When Bob and I decided we were going to be together I knew I'd have to change my career. I qualified as a teacher and got a full time post. I'd always known I wanted to teach—I don't know why I ever did anything else.

Bob: When I left prison I was given a new set of values, new beliefs. In fact, a whole new life. This is why I say it's like dying and being reborn—and I don't mean that in any religious sense. When a prisoner goes back to his environment, he'll find his people have stayed in the same place. Their clothes may have changed, they'll have got a little bit older, but they've basically got the same values and they're talking the same crap that they did when he left them. One of my family said to me 'You don't speak our language any more. You haven't got our values any more, there's something different about you'. They put it down to me being a bit stir-crazy[8], because you do go stir-crazy sometimes and some people get religion. So your friends and family think you'll get over it and you'll come back and be robbing again soon. I never got over it, and I'm still here. But if I'd gone back to that environment I feel I would have been worn down to fit in, and I would have gone back at it—there's no doubt about that.

---

[7] The Society of Voluntary Associates, which recruits, trains and places volunteers to help ex-prisoners

[8] Driven 'crazy' by prison life

I noticed that during the time I was coming out of prison, my attitude towards prison officers changed. I hated them when I first went into prison. Then I actually started making friends by talking to them. In fact I bump into a few of them in town now. We go and have a coffee.

Part of my job now is to go into prisons and visit prisoners to assess whether they are suitable to come to our hostel. I often think how my life has turned full circle. My attitude towards police officers has changed as well. They used to be my enemy, but now they're the protectors of my home and my family. My little daughter's got great respect for the police. To her, policemen are people who help us, not people who persecute us, as they were when I grew up. When I was a criminal there were some corrupt policemen taking backhanders, and I used that to justify me being a villain: we were all in the same game.

• • •

Now for the first time in my life I'm at home: I'm at peace with myself. I actually like me now—and I didn't like me when I was involved in crime. People say you've got to get a mirror and look at yourself, and I didn't like what I saw. I'd become that bully in the school playground and I detested it. I think why I was so violent wasn't because I hated the world—it was because the world hated me. Because inside me there was something nice, and that had been buried so deep I couldn't find it. But there were people like Bev Bingham and Maurice O'Riley and Lynn, the nice people of this world, who did find it. They had nothing to gain—they would have been better off without me because I was a pain in the butt. They were all putting themselves on the line for me, because I was finding my way, stumbling along, and if I went bent everybody'd say 'Told you so!' I can never repay these people for what they've done: that support system was there for me when I needed it.

What I did was insanity. I'm horrified: I can't even relate to the man I was then—it's like it was someone else doing those things. But when Lynn and I went through what I'd done, and I started getting morality back, I realised it was insanity—there's no other way I can describe it, because it's not normal to stick guns in people's heads. When I did start settling down and being normal, the same as everyone else, that's when I had to deal with the nightmares. I would wake up of a night and think about what I'd done.

Once I had a really bad experience. I was sitting in a wine bar next to a guy. His hands were shaking, and I bought him a glass of wine and we were having a chat and he began telling me his life story, and how he'd hit the bottle. I was just listening and I said 'You look like you got battered about' and he said he was a security guard that got held up. He was telling me how this robbery had messed his life up. I walked out of there and I felt like shit, I really did. It smashed me to pieces.

Because like I said, what I did was never personal, just 'a bit of work'. And now I was seeing the end result.

• • •

Now my daughter goes to a beautiful school, I work with beautiful people, I *love* what I do. I worked for SOVA for five years and I was awarded the certificate for Volunteer of the Year. I really like helping people, and I'm doing a university degree as well. I'm in my third year at university studying Housing Studies—Bachelor of Science Honours— I'm doing it part time. It'll take me five years.

I don't think anything could make me go back to crime. I've always tried to understand why I felt so different from everyone else. It was because I didn't belong. Now I've actually found where I belong, and that's why returning to crime is not in the equation. Some people would say they'd retaliate if someone attacked their family. I wouldn't do that because I've got a police force to do that for me.

I can open my door up now—there's no threats to me. When people knock on my door I know it's going to be someone I'm pleased to see. Whereas before, if I went to open my door I'd have to have a gun behind it because it might be an enemy.

If ever I was going to return to crime, it would have been when we lost my second daughter: it was a still birth. That almost destroyed me. I sat down in a park opposite the hospital and the rage was in me, all the hatred came to the surface. Catholicism came back like—wham! That old Mother Church: 'Give me the child', as the Jesuits say, 'and I will give you the man'—the programme is in you. So I said to God 'Why me? You *know* I'm doing it right—why me?' There were loads of things going round in my mind, like this was my retribution for all the bad I'd done. Some of the people who knew me, some of the prison officers, when they heard that I'd lost a daughter they said 'If at any time in his life he was liable to go out it's now'—because they knew all the anger that was in me.

But now I can see crime for what it is, and it's sad. There's no winners in that game, just nightmares, just pain.

The future's bright. I've got dreams. I've got *real* dreams now. I want to get my degree. I really want to get into putting something in place for people who get out of jail. It's so personal to me, because I feel that life—that people—have been kind to me and I would like others to have that chance I had.

Bob Cummines wrote this poem in prison

Love's Power

I have killed
It meant nothing to me
I have lived like a king
It meant nothing to me

I have been tortured
It meant nothing to me
I have dared myself to dream
It meant nothing to me

I have made my own philosophy
It meant nothing to me
I made violence my voice
It meant nothing to me

I have been a god
It meant nothing to me
I fell in love
It made me mortal.

Mark Leech

Mark is 41 and until the age of 36 spent most of his adult life in prison – 62 establishments in all. He was released four years ago. He has established himself as a talented writer and has won several awards, including the BBC Television Scriptwriters' Award in 1991. He has also studied law to degree level and has won many legal cases against the Prison Service. He is employed as full-time Prisoners' Rights consultant with the Liverpool-based solicitors, A S Law. Mark is also a journalist and broadcaster, and Editor of *The Prisons Handbook*, published annually by Waterside Press. In 1998, with Bob Turney, co-author of *Going Straight*, and actor Stephen Fry, he co-founded UNLOCK, the National Association for Ex-Offenders run by ex-offenders.

On 5 February 1966 I found my mother dead in the bedroom. I was eight years old. I didn't cry when my mother died and I didn't cry at her funeral. I don't think I have ever cried about her death since.

She died from a heart attack and thrombosis. I wasn't sad because the last two years of her life had been quite harsh for me. She used to hit me with a wooden spoon, and I clearly remember creeping down one morning and burning this wooden spoon—she used to keep it on a rack above the stove. I was about six at the time, and I took it off the stove. My dad had laid a fire in the grate before he cycled off to work, and I threw it on the fire.

I was born in Manchester, and I came along very late in my parents' life. The other children were all older, significantly older than me, between 16 and 21 years older. I was very much an accident. My mother was a very firm Catholic and therefore abortion was really not an option for her. I came along in 1957 and she was already 47 years old at that time. She was ill, nearing the end of her own life, and she was tired. My brothers and sister were already at an age when they were interested in the opposite sex and youth clubs, and two of them had their own children by then. So I came along at a time when they all had interests that didn't include me, and because my mother was ill, she kind of foisted me off onto them, and that created a bit of a barrier between us. I always remember my sister refusing to be lumbered with 'our Mark' again.

Most of my friends were made outside the home, because my mother was forever pushing me out the front door: 'Just go and play out!' So all my friends were made out on the street or at school.

I loved school. I really enjoyed it. I used to stay on after school because of the arguments between my mum and my dad. Because my mother was such a firm Irish Catholic and my father was a trenchant Irish Protestant, their marriage didn't bear the stamp 'Produce of

Heaven'—it was a really fiery relationship. There was a tree at the school, and I used to sit under this tree and stay there, long after everyone else had gone home, just putting off going home.

My mother wore the trousers in our house. My father was a very hard worker, but he was away for 12 hours every day at work, from six in the morning until six at night. He was a steel worker in Trafford Park in Manchester, and he used to cycle 14 miles there and back every day. He was a bit of a weak-willed person, but he loved his children dearly. My mother was the one who made all the decisions.

There are many questions that I would certainly like to have asked her if she'd been around. Why did she make things so difficult for me? What was so hard for her, and why couldn't she do something about it? All these questions I had in my mind, and of course now I'll never have them answered.

● ● ●

When my mum died, everything seemed to change. Because she was the one who'd made all the decisions. The family just kind of collapsed in on itself, and there was a massive void. I never seemed to have clean clothes, I started to get free school meals and kids were quite hurtful in what they said about that.

My father turned to alcohol. He used to come home singing songs he'd never have got away with if my mum was alive, covered in vomit and broken twigs and bushes. It used to be a standing joke that he was the only man in Manchester with privet rash! He used to fall into bushes in a drunken attempt to find his way home, and the lock on our front door was broken, and it stayed that way for years. A hefty shove was all it needed to get into our house.

I started to play truant, which is what ultimately got me put into care, because the truancy officer was notified that I wasn't attending school. He came round, saw the state of the place, saw my father in a drunken stupor, and within a very short time after that I was taken into care and was sent off to a boarding school run by Manchester City Council.

I never made it into secondary education, because I was in care when I was eight, and when I left care I went to an approved school. From there on it was a slippery slope through detention centre, borstals and ultimately 20 years in prison. So I never really experienced secondary school education outside of local authority care and then the penal system.

I wanted to do well. Up until that point I'd always been pushed away—'Just go out and play, just get from under my feet'. Then suddenly I went from the back streets of Manchester to this boarding school where there were horses to ride and canoes to go in and expeditions to go on and mountains to climb, and a whole different world opened up.

At the age of eight I used to kind of throw myself into my studies. I've always been blessed with an ability to pick up things quite easily. Learning has never been difficult for me. In fact I've thrived on it. But it's created its own problems in a way, because sometimes I've been seen as a bit of a boffin, and that has brought its own problems. People used to say I was a smart-arse and a bookworm.

At the boarding school there was this housemaster who was a PE teacher, and he took a shine to me. I volunteered for rugby and I used to enjoy it. One day soon after I arrived at the age of eight I damaged my back in a rugby scrum. This housemaster took me up to his flat, started to massage my back and one thing led to another and he started to fondle me. That led to three years of abuse.

I didn't want the abuse—it was painful, because the brutal reality of it was that I used to spend three nights of the week for half an hour face down on the bed while he fucked me—that's as brutal as it was. I didn't want that. I didn't like it—I detested it. But as an eight, nine, ten, eleven-year-old, the half hour of pain to me was worth the twenty-three-and-a-half hours of feeling wanted. Because I felt special with him, whereas up until that point I'd never felt special. It was always 'Go out and play and get from under my feet!' Suddenly I found myself being embraced rather than pushed away. And it was nice. It was nice to feel special every time you went out in the school bus —I used to sit in the front. And little things like that meant an awful lot to me.

During those three years, between the ages of eight and eleven, I'd built up what I thought was a kind of relationship—'our secret'. But I suddenly discovered at the age of eleven that it was nothing of the sort, when I went up to his flat one night and found him with somebody else. It wasn't a special relationship between me and him: he was having the same relationship with half a dozen others in the school. And it was in that moment of recognition, when it all came together, that I suddenly realised just what he was about.

It was a real turning point in my life. From that moment on—and I mean from that *second* on—walking into that room and finding it, and recognising what it was, my life changed completely. In that one single second my life changed and it never went back again. From that moment on, when I found that situation, all the illusions, the relationship that I thought I'd created, just fell down around my ears completely. And I swore blind that nobody in authority was ever going to do that to me again.

• • •

There's no doubt in my mind that that housemaster was the main cause of my offending behaviour. Without a doubt he was the most significant person who led me towards offending although he probably didn't realise it at the time. During the three years of the abuse, I had this illusion that I'd built up in my head that this was a special relationship, that I was actually cared for. Then I realised that I wasn't cared for after all. I was being used, I was being manipulated.

This feeling of rejection is still with me after 25 years. It comes from the abuse—that what I thought was so special in fact wasn't. I cared in a way for him, but he didn't actually care for me at all. And I felt rejected by the fact that I'd seen it with my own eyes, him with somebody else. This special thing, this one central, crucial part of my life at that age, that I thought was so important, wasn't. It was a fiction. And when I saw him with that other person I felt utter and total rejection and humiliation. Getting over that took me 20 years. Really I don't think I've got over it today. I still have problems with it.

From that point on I started to run away from the school I loved. I started to smoke. When I was 12 I stole a bicycle on one of my 'escapes' from this boarding school. I knew it was wrong at the time I was doing it. Some guy had left his bike against the railings outside the boarding school, so I hopped over the wall and I took the bike. I only got about two miles down the road before he turned up with his dad in the car and they took me off to the police station. And that was me charged.

I went to court and ended up in approved school. The boarding school refused to have me back. My home circumstances were such, with my father an alcoholic, that he couldn't really look after me. So they simply tossed me into the arms of this approved school and that's where I went.

And nobody ever stopped to ask why. Nobody ever said 'Oh, hold on, why's this guy so suddenly changed? Why's he doing all these things?' They just wrote me off and threw me into the arms of a criminal justice system that was destined not to reform my behaviour, but to make it considerably worse.

I feel that somebody at that point should have said: 'Well, hold on, this guy's behaviour has so abruptly changed that we've got to try and find a reason for it'. But nobody was interested in finding the reason for it. Nobody wanted to know why. I was a criminal in the making.

• • •

My prison career was characterised by riots, assaults, rooftop protests, legal actions, always fighting the system. And that's a damaging way for any kid to grow up. And that's the result of the sexual abuse and the way that I was used and manipulated by that housemaster.

I went to court for the theft of the bicycle—that was in June of 1969—and from there I went into an approved school where I met my first juvenile criminals. They were the people I grew up with during my teenage years. I learned their values and their skills in crime and I was already very, very anti-authority as the result of the abuse.

When I was first put into custody, I don't think it had a great effect on me, because I'd been in custody of one kind or another since I went to boarding school. It wasn't as if I was taken straight out of my home when I was 12 or 13 and locked up, because I was locked up really from the age of eight when I went into care. The boarding school wasn't a prison, but I wasn't free to run away without any consequences. I knew I was required to stay there. And the things that happened in the boarding school—apart from the abuse—were all quite pleasurable things: the horses to ride, the canoes, the expeditions, the mountains. And therefore to me, when I was taken away it wasn't the same kind of transition as for somebody who is taken out of a free home environment and locked up for the first time. It had been a kind of learning process in this boarding school. So being sent to the approved school was no great shock for me.

My most common crimes were car theft and credit card fraud, that kind of thing. I don't know how many custodial sentences I served in all—15 or 20 perhaps? The longest was 13 and a half years for robbery of a Little Chef restaurant, although it wasn't me that actually did it. The person who did is now doing 17 years for other robberies. I loaned my car to somebody who went home and committed this robbery with two of his friends and—because I wouldn't say who I'd loaned the car to—I was the one that was convicted of conspiracy to rob. I was doing a six and a half and they gave me a seven on top. I did eight and a half years of that sentence.

My time outside of prison depended on how long I could make the discharge grant last. And I never really thought that life for me held any kind of opportunity. For me, getting out of prison and staying out was not something that really entered my mind because I was so wrapped up in this hatred that I had for authority and I was always being devious and trying to fuck the system all the time. So that when I did get out, there was never really any opportunity to go straight, because I was an ex-criminal—I had a criminal record.

The first thing that happens when you want to go straight and go for a job is they say to you 'Where have you been?' And at that point you've got to make a decision. You either tell the truth—which carries with it the likelihood that you're not going to get the job—or you tell lies. And if you tell lies, then you're really on your way back to prison again.

I've had many jobs. I used to hide my criminality and get jobs on the basis of a false pass. I've done that with a whole range of things from a

bus conductor to an ambulance man, right the way up to head
for the United Kingdom for *Toys R Us*—all based on lies and
false background.

I think I've probably tried most drugs. But I wouldn't say
substance abuse forms any part of my offending behaviour. I was never
addicted to drugs in the sense that I had to go out and commit crime in
order to finance the habit. I was well into my 20s before I tried drugs a t
all. I was introduced to hash in Parkhurst, and it gave me an escape—
the chemical escape that the physical walls denied me. It was a way
of just lying back on my bed, getting stoned out of my head, and
forgetting for 12 hours the fact that I was in prison. It was a nice way to
end the day. And it does become addictive—not physically addictive,
but it became mentally addictive to the point where I wouldn't be able
to sleep if I didn't have a joint in my bed. In 1992 for the first time in my
life I tried smack for a week—not injecting it—smoking it off the foil
when I was in Glenochil. And that frightened me. I tried it for a week
and I tried so much of it that it actually made me sick and now i f
anybody does it in my presence it causes a psychological reaction in
that it makes me vomit.

I don't touch any drugs now. But actually getting off them was very
difficult. Hash damaged my memory; I couldn't remember where I put
things, my short-term memory disappeared. That's all come back, I'm
pleased to say, because I've left it alone. But there's no doubt that i t
damaged me, and I acquired those habits in prison, not outside of it.

• • •

The person who had the greatest impact on changing me was Joe
Chapman at Grendon Underwood in Buckinghamshire, which is
Britain's only therapeutic prison. Joe was my group officer at Grendon.
He's now director of the Replay Trust in Oxford—he resigned from t he
Prison Service. He was without doubt the person who made me
recognise that I did have other options, that life didn't have to consist
of crime and being in and out of prison for the rest of my life. If I just
stopped to look around, there were a whole range of options, and I had
the free power, the free will, to make a choice. Crime was one option.
But it wasn't the only one—there were others. And the choice of option
lay with me, and so did the consequences of that choice I made—which
is crucial as well. Because often, whilst you're in control of the choice
that you've made, you're not in any control at all of the consequences
that flow from it. Other people are in charge of those consequences.
That's what Grendon taught me.

Grendon gave me the opportunity to stop and think about why I was
so angry, why I had these problems coping with and dealing with
people in authority, why I kept coming back to prison. Grendon had no

magic wand. But it provided an atmosphere in which it was OK to change, whereas in the majority of our prisons, that's never really a feature. You're so locked into a polarised 'Them and Us' environment, so busy planning the next job or a bit of skullduggery and ducking and diving in the jail that you never really stop to think 'How did I end up here and what options have I got for the future?' That's why Grendon was so special for me—because it gave me that chance to stop and take stock. It worked for me and it works for many others.

I was in the therapeutic wing at Grendon for 15 months. It wasn't long enough—I could have done with a couple of years in there. There isn't a fixed length of stay at Grendon. But the evidence suggests that people who've been there over 18 months stand a far greater chance of not reoffending.

I would have stayed on if the place hadn't been shut down. They closed down the whole prison overnight because of electrical faults, and we were all moved to a prison called The Mount in Hertfordshire and then to Winchester. They closed a wing down there and opened up a wing as kind of 'Grendon in Winchester'. I was elected by the other prisoners to be the chairman of that wing.

But then Grendon moved again, this time to Wellingborough prison, in Northamptonshire, while the wiring was being done again, and I was kicked out of Wellingborough—I still think somewhat unfairly. I smoked a joint on the night that Grendon closed, and I can accept that I was wrong. I made the excuse that I was devastated. Everybody was, but that doesn't excuse what I did, because I'd entered into an agreement that I wouldn't do drugs. I spoke about it and perhaps that was my biggest error—actually speaking out about it. Because it was that which led to me being booted out of Grendon after 15 months. If I'd had a couple of years, life outside would have been an awful lot easier—I would have had more skills in order to survive.

• • •

It's been a battle being out here, particularly because I came out in the month that the first edition of *The Prisons Handbook*[1] was published, and so I've been somewhat on a pedestal. People scrutinise you and look up to you, and often it's been difficult to live up to that. Life isn't easy when you're on that pedestal because you don't like to be seen to fail. Certainly I feel that I've failed in certain things, basically because I didn't have the skills to cope.

---

[1] Originally entitled *The Prisoners' Handbook* and now in its third edition under its new name and published annually. As an indication of Mark's progress, Home Secretary Jack Straw has signified his agreement to contribute to the year 2000 edition.

I've never reoffended but I still find relationships difficult. A couple of years at Grendon might have enabled me to cope with relationships a bit more and outside would have been a little bit easier then.

I still have difficulty coping with people in authority. But Grendon at least invited me—provided the atmosphere in which it was OK—to look at why I was such an angry young man. It was 20 years before I was ever able to look at it and understand all these feelings of being used and manipulated by people in authority.

I still have difficulty dealing with them today but I know now where the feelings are coming from. It's not the person sat across the desk who's giving me a bit of a hard time—it's not him that's causing these feelings in me. It's this character 20 years back in my past. I can recognise that, but it's still very difficult to actually keep that in the front of my mind.

I still feel that people are pushing me or they're singling me out or they're making life difficult for me. It's a little bit of paranoia and it's damaging—it damages me.

● ● ●

The point is, I need never have gone to Grendon. I need never have gone to an approved school in my life. I need never have seen the inside of a prison—if only somebody at the age of eleven had stopped and said, 'Hold on, why is he behaving like this?' Today they might, because they're more attuned to recognising these kinds of abrupt changes in behaviour.

I've actually had very little help since I've been outside. What's caused me to calm down is the brutal reality that we have to exist within the system and I can't go on fighting it in the way that I did when I was inside. It's taken me the best part of four years to recognise that people will just switch off. And you need to work with these people—you have to see things from their point of view.

Even though I've been out over four years now, it's taken me that long to change modes from being a prisoner to being somebody outside in freedom, because for the best part of those four years I was still in my head a prisoner fighting the system.

Just because I'm an ex-prisoner doesn't make me an expert in crime and punishment. I just come at it from a different perspective, and I have to realise that other people have their perspectives too and they're all equally valid. And I find that if I'm as angry as I was then and all those years before, I don't actually get my point across. That for me is a loss because that's what I'm about. I'm not about being angry. What I'm about is actually beginning to change things and educate people about my perspective and where I've come from so that we can all understand. And that way I think we'll start to make some progress.

I've learned very quickly that if you bawl and shout at people, people just don't listen to you.

I've had counselling during the last ten months and this is the first time I've ever spoken about it. It's been a painful experience for me because I've had to look back at some things, realise that at times I've been arrogant—I've just not been a nice person. I've been put on this pedestal. I'm about actually changing things and the first thing I've had to do is to change things in myself. I've had to lower my tone and listen to other people and take on board their views and for two and a half years after being out I didn't do that. I don't know why. I came out perhaps with the impression that I knew everything. And quite clearly I don't.

I need to work with people in order to change things, because changing things is very important. It's what drives me. I'm not interested in debates that just don't go anywhere and don't produce anything. I want to change things.

I suppose I should say that I regret my past offending—that would be the stock answer. I certainly regret the fact that I've wasted so much of my life. I find it difficult to say honestly that I have remorse, because I feel that in one way I've been a victim throughout this too. I don't think I would have offended had it not been for the abuse.

• • •

I don't ever want to go back to crime—ever. And I never will go back to it, because to lose what I've achieved while I've been out would devastate me. That is what stops me from reoffending—and the fact that I like it out here. I've got used to it out here now, I'm gradually getting away from being institutionalised and I'm thinking as a free person, I'm listening to other people. I have a good job in a legal firm where I enjoy working. I have clients who depend on me, and a readership on both sides of the prison wall who have come to rely on *The Prisons Handbook*. With UNLOCK I just want to take it one step further.

It's a nice world out here, it's a beautiful world. We've all got our problems, but this is a million times more preferable to being locked in a cell at three o'clock on a Saturday afternoon and not getting out again until seven o'clock the next morning. That is what prevents me from ever going back again. I never will go back. I don't say I don't think about it, but whenever that comes into my head, I return to what I said before about life presenting us with options. It's my choice which option I choose. While crime will always be an option for me, as it is for everybody, I recognise that there are more options. And the more I think about those other options—as a journalist, as a writer, as a broadcaster—crime recedes into the background, and those are the things that come forward. So crime becomes less of an option with every single day that passes.

It's definitely a regret on my part that I'm not closer to my father. He's well into his 80s now and I'm missing out on something I feel I could well do with. Certainly there have been times in my life when I have wanted someone, I've needed someone I could trust to talk to. But my father was never that kind of person, never the one I could go and talk to, and I've kind of missed out on that. I've missed out on my mum too of course because she died when I was eight, and that's damaged me because I've never had that stable base of the mother and the father that you can always turn to when things get too tough. I've never had that so I've always had to kind of cope on my own. In my view parental support is crucial, because there are times in your life when you come across problems, particularly as young adults: when the chips are down, your parents are going to be the only ones who will really want to know.

I'm probably as distant as you can be from my brothers and sisters. I don't have any contact with them at all really. Last time I spoke to them was in 1978, over 20 years ago. I'm very much an embarrassment to them, because I've been involved in crime, and none of them have been. My brother's an undercover customs investigator, I've got a sister who teaches at Oxford and I've got another sister who's area manageress of a building society: so me being the criminal, they've written me off. I'm also an embarrassment to them being homosexual—they find that very difficult to cope with too. Because they are all straight, they don't understand it, and I've never been able to be close enough to them to explain what it's all about, so they have only got their own views from their heterosexual viewpoint, and that's a very narrow viewpoint. Homosexuality is a very misunderstood concept in today's Britain. In my view heterosexuality is not normal, it's just common—just like being white in this country is 'common' rather than 'normal'.

Generally I'm relatively pleased with what I've achieved, though I think I've made things difficult for myself—I could have made life a lot easier if I'd been less angry with other people and had found it easier to get on with them, particularly with those in authority in the Prison Service. It's been hard to develop relationships with them. But I have done that now, and I've got a good relationship with the Prison Service, whereas—perhaps for the first two years I was out—I didn't have. They dealt with me because they had to because I was the editor of *The Prisons Handbook*—whereas now I think they *want* to deal with me. I like that and I value it. I see myself now as somebody who has got experience, not just of being a prisoner, but of being an ex-prisoner, an ex-offender.

My life has changed beyond all recognition. There's no way I'm going back. I won't choose crime as an option. There are things I still think that I fail at. But I'm getting there. At least I recognise when I have a problem and I bite my lip now rather than speak out. I was often on the verge of throwing a punch, as I was in the last couple of years in prison. But now I won't do that. If somebody disagrees with me, that's OK—we'll just beg to differ and I won't take it personally. At one time it used to be that if I had an argument with somebody it used to become personal with me. I could never accept that *they* were entitled to *their* view—they were entitled to hold a different opinion to me. The issue got lost. It was about me defeating that person. It became personal and I *had to defeat* the person and therefore his argument. And of course that's a load of nonsense—it just doesn't work like that. Now I don't allow people to affect me in that way. I just accept that they've got a different opinion and I'm probably never going to change it, and they won't change mine. So we beg to differ and we move on.

• • •

What is really important to me now? First and foremost it's my partner—him and our two labradors, Goldie and Max. Apart from personal relationships, the other main features of my life are *The Prisons Handbook*, working with A S Law, and being Chairman of UNLOCK. These are my passions—providing information to prisoners is very crucial to me. It's something that I wanted to do, something I recognised didn't exist when I was in prison. The lack of information often led to so many frustrations, because there was no need to deny people this information. So *The Prisons Handbook* is very, very important to me.

UNLOCK is probably my greatest hope for the future. I think it's important to set a balance in debates about crime and punishment, not only to make people understand why people commit crime, but also in order to reduce the number of victims. Because we've all been victims of crime in one way and another, and it's not nice. I've been burgled, I've had my car nicked, and I've been furious. I've wanted revenge, I've wanted justice.

I've spent a lot of time blaming Michael Howard for his penal policies. But I've had to recognise that even though I disagree with what he said, he was bang on in one thing, and that's this: he accurately recognised that those types of policies are what the general public out here want. And in fact for some people those policies are probably far too tame. The general public want to send people to prison, throw away the key—they wouldn't feed you, wouldn't clothe you and they couldn't give a toss about you. These are the understandable emotions of those who have been victims of crime, but you can't base the penal policies of an entire nation on that kind of response.

Politicians are attuned to what the public want: they're very, very skilled at judging that. If you can just change the focus of what the public want, then policies will fall in line with that. So UNLOCK for me is a way of recognising that the real way to move forward is not to have a go at the politicians, but to educate the public, because it's the public who influence the politicians. There are currently 66,000 people in our prisons, and the public needs to remember one crucial fact: all but 25 of them, sooner or later, are coming back out.

It's been a painful four years being out here. It's been a learning curve and a painful one. It's had its successes but it's had its failures too.

I think if everything I valued I lost, that could make me return to offending. If I lost my partner, my dogs and *The Prisons Handbook* or my ability to write—if I had nothing left and nowhere to go—crime would be my very, very last option in order to survive, as I suppose it would be for just about everyone in that situation. But that's what it would be— the last option. The final, ultimate resort.

● ● ●

His Honour Sir Stephen Tumim, formerly HM Chief Inspector of Prisons and now President of UNLOCK, writes:

Mark Leech is an excellent autobiographer. A shortened version of his appalling life story is to be found in this book. He and Bob Turney, the co-compiler of this book and author of *I'm Still Standing*, a burglar turned probation officer, are the two most prominent founders of UNLOCK.

UNLOCK is a new organization, a national association of ex-offenders who aim to work with statutory and voluntary agencies in the criminal justice system to help reduce crime. It is an old boys' and old girls' association with very particular aims. The members use their personal experience of crime and punishment to conduct and publish research to inform political debate. They aim to advise serving and former prisoners who demonstrate a genuine commitment to lead crime-free lives. They aim to promote to the public prison policies.

There are a number of more specific aims. Around 90,000 prisoners are discharged from our prisons each year, with a discharge grant amounting to one week's income support. But it has to last at least two weeks as the discharged prisoner gets no further payment for 14 days. It is not a very good system for the discouragement of small-time crime.

The Rehabilitation of Offenders Act 1974 allows prisoners who are sentenced to a maximum of 30 months to live it down. Anything over 30 months means that the conviction is never spent. This may have been acceptable in 1974, when sentences were much lower, but hardly makes sense today if we are to rehabilitate prisoners and discourage crime.

The Act refer to this

UNLOCK presses for two direct ways of trying to reduce crime. Better pre-release courses in prison based on an informed needs assessment system must be one of them. And an increase in therapeutic and resettlement prisons must be another. The government seems to have started on this course with Marchington in the East Midlands. But there is a very long way to go.

UNLOCK is attempting to remind the public of what prisons are for. We have prisons in an attempt to bring about a safer and more law-abiding community. Punishment is a part of it. Taking away a person's liberty is a punishment in itself. But, if we meet prisoners, the great majority are young and ignorant, and badly schooled—perhaps through their own faults and often not helped by inadequate families. They need, in the view of the members of UNLOCK, who have actually lived in prison, precisely the sort of reforms referred to above.

Crime will not be abolished, but it can be substantially reduced. Unless we believe that most ex-prisoners can be redeemed, we are lost.

© Sir Stephen Tumim, 1999

Jane

In 1994, at the age of 21, Jane was convicted of the manslaughter of her boyfriend's mother, a woman of 60, and sent to prison for six years. This interview took place just four months after Jane's release. She describes the difficulties that face her as she struggles to adjust to life outside. All names have been changed to protect the identities of Jane and her family, and her victim's family.

It all started when my boyfriend Neil left me. I went to his mother for help, but instead of helping me she verbally abused me. I went into a frenzy and stabbed her. I just lashed out at her with a kitchen knife—I went on and on until I ran out of breath. I just kept going.

I didn't actually see her at all at the time—I was in a daze. When I stopped I just panicked and ran out of the house, got in the car and drove home. My three-year-old son Jack was in the back of the car—it took about ten minutes to get back to my house. I was frantic but I suppose I was driving automatically. I only know from reports what happened after I stabbed Neil's mum. I know that she died on the way to the hospital. She actually managed to phone the ambulance herself—somehow she got to the phone.

I drove back home, about eight miles, and I got Jack out of the car—I just opened the door, undid his belt and he came running in after me. The first thing I did when I got back in was to look at my answering machine. I knew that my brother was supposed to be ringing me back and I found I had a message from him, telling me somewhere to meet him. It had gone past the time I was supposed to meet him. Actually I think I was just trying to find somebody to help me, I think that's what it was. Then I changed my clothes and put them all in a bag. I remember noticing I only had a little spot of blood on my jeans. I don't know what I was thinking.

I had two cars at the time and for some reason this one I'd driven back wouldn't start. It was steaming—I don't know what I'd done to it. So I got in the other one and I drove off with Jack. It was a question of who to go to—my parents or Jack's other grandmother—the mother of my first boyfriend, David—we all lived in the same village. David's mum lived closer to my house so I ended up driving to her and I told her what I'd done. She didn't believe me at first. She'd just been talking to her daughter so she phoned her daughter back and asked her what she should do. She said to phone the police. So that's what she did. And I just sat there and waited.

When the police came I told them what I had done.

• • •

I was 21 at the time I committed the offence. Really it was about relationships and emotional problems which had been building up since I had Jack. I was 17 when I met David, Jack's dad, at college. He was the same age as me and we were both doing A-levels. I think my parents wanted me to go to university and we certainly spoke about that.

I was doing A-levels in art and design, English language and law, but I only got a few months into it, because that's when I got pregnant and I left. I went to stay with David and his mum for about a month, and I did decide to have an abortion. I didn't want one, but David was pressuring me to have one. It was all planned for me to have this abortion, but when it came to the point, I just couldn't go through with it. David had said to me 'You have this abortion or I'll leave you' and he did leave me for a few months and I went to live on my own in a bedsit. Then I went home to stay with my mum and step-dad, because David had gone and I'd decided not to have the abortion. I think my parents were glad of that, but my step-dad still wanted me to get the baby adopted. We were starting the adoption proceedings but Jack arrived nine weeks early, so nothing had gone through officially.

But as soon as I saw him he was mine. From the moment I set eyes on him I decided I was going to keep him. I had to have a Caesarian because he hadn't turned round properly. He was only three pounds at birth, but it never really occurred to me that he wouldn't be all right. He was a skinny little thing: he was in a special baby care unit for five weeks and I saw him every day. At the hospital they didn't know about the adoption. They assumed everything was quite normal. I was just 18 by this time. David was there for the birth. As soon as the baby had first started to show, things changed and he wanted us to keep it. He was still at college doing his A-levels. His mum was a bit funny about things during my pregnancy. She didn't think I'd make a good mother or anything. But as soon as Jack was born she totally changed. She loved me as well then, and everything was lovely.

After I had Jack I lived with David for about a year—we had a council house. I was happy looking after Jack for about five or six months. David had finished his A-levels. He was very bright but he wasn't really doing anything. His mum blamed me, but in fact he'd just got lazy and didn't want to work at all. His mum thought I had ruined David's life, slowed his progress down, because he'd been expected to go to university. He had two older sisters who both had university degrees and he was expected to get one as well.

I broke up with David when I was about 19. It was because of his laziness—not wanting to work or look after us. I was looking after Jack and David wasn't doing anything and I couldn't seem to budget. So David and I parted, though we were on quite friendly terms. Jack did see his dad occasionally but David kept changing his mind whether he wanted to be involved or not.

That's when I started to think about the Open University. In 1993 I did the first course—I was 20. It was hell because Jack was only about 18 months old.

• • •

By this time I was in another relationship, with Neil. I met him because his sister-in-law lived round the corner from me. He was about 21 and eventually, about eight months later, he moved in with me and Jack. But we started off on the wrong foot right away, because of problems with Neil's mum. She just wouldn't accept me. The first time I met her she totally ignored me. Neil said it was only because she didn't like him being with anybody.

Then, very briefly, I had a relationship with a married man. His wife found out about the affair and she came round and threatened me and after that I always used to carry a kitchen knife in my bag for protection. Then Neil found out too, and that caused a lot of tension. His mother had just come back from holiday and I felt that when his mum was away he wanted me, and when his mum came back he wasn't bothered about me any more. I felt he was dominated by his mother and I said so. We argued and that's how Neil ended up getting out of the car and leaving me.

So there was just a build up of emotional stuff over the period of time leading up to me committing the offence. It's very difficult to explain. I didn't feel I had anything to live for really. I didn't have any respect for myself. I didn't really care about anything. Jack was three and I'd just split up from Neil. At the time of the offence I just snapped.

I'd actually driven to his mum's house. I still don't know exactly why I did. Neil and I had been talking sitting in my car just outside the public house at the bottom of his road—there was no alcohol involved or anything—we just happened to be outside the pub. I said to Neil 'If you get out of the car now, I take it it's over'. He sat there for a few minutes then he got out of the car. I suppose I didn't expect him to do that. I didn't know how to deal with it when it did happen. Anyway, there was nothing else I could say to Neil, and I suppose that's why I drove a few yards up the road to his mum's house, with Jack still in the back of the car in his seat. I drove up to the house, left Jack in the car, went to the door and asked for her help. I was in a real state at the time and I didn't know what to do. I was just about to fall over the edge and I think Neil had just finished me off by leaving me like that.

But his mother didn't help me. She shouted at me, calling me things like 'slag' and 'whore' and everything else and she said that it wasn't surprising that David had left me. So I got out the knife I kept in my bag and I stabbed her. It was like I did it till I ran out of breath. I just kept going.

In those few months before the attack I could actually feel myself losing my mind. A few weeks before the offence—this was just after the married man's wife had threatened me—I'd gone back home one day and I'd got hold of this dining room chair and smashed it to pieces on the floor. Then I took an overdose of Paracetamol. I drove out to a garage and bought some, came home and took maybe a hundred tablets and I was sitting there waiting for something to happen but nothing did. I panicked in the end and called an ambulance. I went to hospital and had to have my stomach pumped. This was all a few weeks before the offence and I guess it was a cry for help.

I certainly felt very isolated. I wanted to get Jack into a toddlers' group but I was having problems with that: they wouldn't have him there because he wasn't toilet trained. At certain stages I did have friends I could talk to: just after I had Jack I became quite close to a girl I used to know at school and she left home and moved in with me for a while. But then she left to get married and we kind of drifted apart. Then there was Jill, Neil's sister-in-law, but when she found out I'd had an affair with that married man she disowned me. I used to go and visit my parents once a week. My step-father could see the problems and I could talk to him about them, but he was just not the right person. I didn't get the help or the care from him that I needed.

Just before I committed the offence it was as if I didn't feel I was in control of myself any more. I didn't have any power over my own mind. I was getting quite a few headaches and I remember going to my GP for some medication. I didn't think about going anywhere else for help.

• • •

I can't say I had a very happy childhood. My real dad left my mum when I was eight and my brother was about five and a half. I felt glad at the time because my dad used to hit my mum. I remember him trying to come round and see us later on, and my mum wouldn't let him. I never saw him again. Sometimes I'm still curious about him, but I haven't made any attempt to find him. At first this was because I knew it would upset the rest of the family if I did. At times more recently, maybe because I've just moved back here to the town where I lived as a small child, I've wondered whether I could find out a bit more about my father.

As my brother and I got older we tended to look after each other and stick together more. Our mum remarried and I think it was when my step-dad came along that we started to become closer. Then once I left home my relationship my brother got close again and about six months before I went to prison he actually moved in with me.

I lived here in this town till I was eleven and I went to school here. That's why I feel now I'm back here like I'm re-tracking everything. I remember doing very well at infant school. I was ahead with my work, I was always top of the class and had my work on the wall. I can't remember if I got any praise from my parents, but I did at school. So I started off very well academically and it was like that up until we moved when I was eleven.

I had problems trying to fit in with the other children at school because I wasn't allowed to go out and play with my friends like I wanted to. Mum was really strict, and as we got older she became stricter, specially when my step-dad came along—maybe it started when my dad left. My friends would come round to the house and I had to make excuses for not coming out to play and because I couldn't be with them I couldn't fit in with them. If you didn't do the things that they did, then you were excluded—like playing around the estate. There was also the problem, after my dad left, of us not having any money either, not having nice clothes like other people, things like that. After my real dad left I often used to run away from home, and sometimes I'd stay out till the early hours of the morning.

My step-dad came along about two years later, when I was about ten. The first day I met him I'd actually run away from home, and I'd just come back. I'd had a fight with this boy and I'd ended up throwing stones at him, and then I was too scared to go home. I was scared of my mum—I can remember her dragging me along by my hair and stuff like that. As far as I can remember, the longest time I stayed out was when my step-dad first moved in. I got punished, but I was so afraid of being out at night anyway, that I just sort of sat there and waited for them to come and find me, even though I knew I was going to get a beating. It was even worse for my brother.

I didn't really see my step-dad much at first. I only really saw him once he moved in with us—I must have been about eleven by then and my brother was nearly nine. What really wound me up was that one day my brother and I came home from school and my mum and step-dad were having a little celebration in the back garden with some of their friends. They had just got married—and we didn't even know! I actually asked my step-dad about that just recently—about a month or so ago—and he just said 'Well, we didn't see any need to tell you!'

I didn't get on with my step-dad at all. He was violent—my mum definitely had a tendency to pick violent blokes. I think as soon as my step-dad came along, my brother and I were just like this big huge extra baggage for my mum. We weren't loved or wanted any more. My step-dad used to run the house like a military camp. When I was 18 my half-sister was born, and three years later my half-brother came along.

The two schools I went to never bothered to ask about any problems at home, and when I was in my early teens I was too young really to comprehend or to get help. Both the schools I got into were grammar schools, taking the top ten or 15 per cent of pupils in the catchment area.

I had to struggle to keep my head above water academically. In certain areas I was OK—like in English and art—but generally I was falling behind more and more. I wasn't getting any help or anything that I needed. There were some subjects that I just could not do, like science subjects and maths—I was always at the bottom in those.

I used to skive out of those lessons and just go to the ones I liked. I'd go to the art room and draw pictures instead. I knew I'd get in trouble for it but I just didn't care. I was always on my own and I always used to go to the art room, because art was a subject I was good at and I used to get recognition for it. I thought about going into fashion design once. But nobody ever really spoke to me about what I wanted to do in the future. I got detention a couple of times for skiving off, and my step-dad was furious about that because I was late and he had to come and pick me up because I'd missed the bus. One other thing I was OK at was drama. I found I was good at improvisation: I could just get out there and act. When I was in the fifth year they let me have my own class. They let me take the first and second years for drama, with about 20 kids in each class. As time went on I found I was better at organizing other people than acting myself. I liked writing little plays for them.

But things started building up, what with all the problems at home. The final thing that happened, which got me expelled, was that I decided to pinch a bottle of my mum's wine out of the pantry and I got drunk when I was at school and wrecked the deputy head's office, turning the table over and so on. I'm not sure if this was because of problems at school or maybe it was something at home. I mean, in some ways I loved school. I liked being there, because there I was *me*. I was independent, I could do what I wanted to do. But I was also very depressed. I just hid in the toilets and I just drank this whole bottle of wine. When I look back on it, I did so many stupid things and I can't figure out why. Maybe I just wanted my mum and step-dad to pay some attention to me.

I ended up in hospital because I'd gone unconscious for a little while. But I was only there for a few hours. The deputy head was sitting beside me when I woke up, trying to comfort me. When she left, as soon as I saw my chance I was straight out the door—I ran off. But I ended up going back to the school at the end of the day and my mum and dad came in and took me home. My step-dad said 'I just give up on you'. My mum didn't say much. She was dominated by my step-dad. My mum hasn't had her own opinions for a long time.

I never went back to that school. I went to college instead and finished my GCSEs there a few months later—I got eight, though some of them weren't very good grades. Then I started on my A-levels, met David and got pregnant.

• • •

After the stabbing, the police asked me a few questions when I was still at David's mother's house. I can't remember exactly what I said. Then they took me back to the police station. I left Jack with his grandmother. I was in the police station about one and a half days and the police were kind to me. On the last night I was told that I'd been charged with murder and I think that's when I broke down and went into absolute shock. I just couldn't stop crying and the matron sat with me all night. I used to smoke then and I smoked myself silly. I spoke to a woman police officer about what I'd done, and I told her I'd been provoked.

I was remanded to a prison over a hundred miles from my home and I stayed there on remand for 13 months before the trial. I don't know why it took so long because it was pretty straightforward—I was pleading guilty after all. I saw Jack on visits every fortnight.

I was fine the first night I went into prison. I find that very strange. I was locked in this little room on the hospital wing. I think they put me down as a suicide risk. I was there for just a couple of days. I can remember the bars, and I opened the window and I breathed in the fresh air. I wrote a letter to my mum and step-dad and I wrote a poem. I was really organized. I wasn't thinking about anything: I was just getting on with things. I'd got to survive I suppose—it was just survival.

Then I was put into one of the dormitories. The other two women there were OK to me—in fact I still keep in contact with one of them who was there for murder. She's at Durham prison now. She was in her 40s and she was nice to me. The other woman was supposed to have killed her boyfriend and she got life imprisonment. I remember that evening they had a little party in the room of the woman next door. I was frightened because of what I'd done. The woman I killed was 60 and *because* she was an older woman, somebody actually called me a nonce[1] in the first few days I was there. I didn't understand that at

---

[1] Prison slang for someone convicted of an offence against a child, an old person, or of any sex offence

first, but someone must have told me that it meant someone who everybody hates because they've killed children or old people, because I actually said to her 'I'm not a nonce, so don't call me one'. I had a few more problems when I was transferred to my next prison, because there were articles in the papers and magazines which had found their way into the prison. The governor called me to see him and asked if I wanted to go on Rule 43.[2] But I refused. I said I'd just be cautious and not go round on my own, and in fact I never did get attacked by any of the other women.

But when I was still on remand in 1995 and was in a single cell in that first prison I was raped by a senior officer. He came to my cell one night and told me he was coming back the following night to have his way with me. The next night I was asleep in my cell when he used his master key to come in, and he raped me. Next morning the woman in the next cell said she'd heard my cell door open and she asked me if I was all right.

I was sent to see the prison doctor and told him what had happened, but I wasn't internally examined or anything. I realised later that this was because I was going to be transferred from that prison to a different one, and in fact, the afternoon after the rape I actually was transferred to this new prison. I was told to pack and assumed I was moving to the hospital wing, but then I heard one officer tell the other to take me to reception and I immediately knew what was happening—I was being moved to another prison, which was where I stayed up until my trial. I reported the incident to another officer and asked to see my solicitor. But it was two days before I managed to speak to my solicitor, and by that time I was in a different prison. The solicitor called the police, and I was examined by a police doctor. But by then I'd had several showers and baths so there was no physical evidence. I had no witnesses either—the woman in the next cell was afraid to come forward and say what she'd heard for fear of reprisals. A doctor at my new prison told me he assumed I'd decided to drop my charges, and I said I certainly had not. But nothing came of it in the end.

When the trial came I was charged with murder. I pleaded guilty to manslaughter with the defence of provocation. The trial lasted three days. I remember the witnesses. Neil was one of them. He tried to apportion all the blame to me and none to his mother. He said it was all my fault for not accepting her. A few months before I met Neil his father had died and I think he felt responsible for his mum. Another of

---

[2] The prison rule under which a prisoner can be placed, e.g. in a separate wing of the prison for his or her own protection, and to maintain the 'good order and discipline' in the prison.

the prosecution witnesses was David's mum, because I went to her straight after the offence. She stayed neutral—she just told the story as it was. The WPC from the police station was called as a witness for the defence and she said she remembered me saying at the time that I'd been provoked. My own mother and stepfather stuck by me right from the time I was arrested.

My QC was good. I can't remember exactly what the judge said in his summing up but I felt that he said a lot of things in my favour. But after the jury found me guilty of manslaughter he commented on the fact that after I'd left the house—after I'd stabbed Neil's mum—I didn't call an ambulance—I didn't do anything—even though, as he said, I was able to think clearly enough drive home. But in fact it wasn't like that—driving the car was automatic. When I heard the judge say that, I thought I was going to get life for manslaughter—that was going through my mind. But I got six years.

After the conviction I went to yet another prison for about nine months, and then to three more prisons. I served a total of four years before I was released four months ago.

• • •

I've worked a lot on myself while I've been in prison. I didn't have any help there and I feel very angry about that. I didn't get my first parole after serving three years, and afterwards I was told that once I left prison I should go to counselling sessions for my emotional problems. I remember saying to my probation officer 'Well, it could be too late then'.

Now I'm out here, I'm facing all these problems that could have been dealt with a long time ago. My probation officers are seeing me every week now because they're so desperate to fit everything in before my licence runs out in about two months' time.

I don't see my son Jack any more. He's seven now. After I was arrested, my brother took Jack to live with him. My brother was living with me anyway so Jack's life wasn't too disrupted. As I said, I saw him every fortnight on prison visits while I was on remand. After I'd been in prison for a year, while I was still on remand, my brother and I spoke about the future and my brother said 'I couldn't live without Jack now. I want him to be with me'. I could understand that. It made me feel good in a way. But once I was convicted, I think I saw Jack for about half a visit shortly after that, and then I didn't see him any more. We went through this stage where my brother said that he needed a residence order for Jack. I wasn't quite sure about it but I went through with it because I thought it was best for Jack to be with his uncle, for security. After that my brother just didn't talk to me any more and he didn't bring Jack to see me. After a while my mum and step-dad started to bring him to see me. But then my brother was still causing problems and we ended up having to go to the family court about it.

Now, as far as I know, Jack is actually living with his dad. My brother had him for four years, then, just before I was released, Jack went to live with David. A few months before my release, David started to write to me and he asked me what my plans were for my release and what I was going to do about Jack. I hadn't been in touch with David before that—I hadn't known where he was or anything. I said I couldn't really talk about it till my release because I'd been in prison for so long that I didn't know what I felt about anything. I got three or four more letters from David, then suddenly I didn't hear from him any more. And then I phoned my mum and step-dad up one day and they'd just had a call from my brother telling them that he'd given Jack to David, who's got a new girlfriend now. David's name is on Jack's birth certificate as his father.

I last saw Jack the Christmas before last. He knew I was his mum then, when I last saw him. He was very close to me. I found it very strange. He called me Mummy, gave me a cuddle.

But I don't really feel like a mother any more. I couldn't handle bringing Jack just partly back into my life. I feel as though I'm coping with the situation as it is now and I really don't want to mess it up.

Being in prison gave me the chance just to think about myself and focus on my future, on what I wanted. It was really a chance for me to find myself. When I was first convicted, a probation officer spoke to me a few times and just talked a little bit about my offence, but everything was still too raw in me at that stage. I'd just had my trial and I don't think I was really ready to talk. I needed to talk later on. There were courses for tackling offending behaviour on offer at the beginning of my sentence, and it was up to you whether you attended them or not. At that time I wasn't interested—I just wanted to get on with other things, to get qualifications. When I was on remand I decided that if I got convicted, which I knew I would be, I would start the Open University again, take up where I left off before, and that's what I did.

And then in the year leading up to my parole I thought I'd better start getting some courses done. But I got moved to a new prison where they didn't have any, apart from a couple which I actually took, but most were about drug and alcohol abuse, which were quite irrelevant for me and my offence.

I think by concentrating on academic studies, I was probably just trying to cover everything up, kind of building this mask over the offence, for my own protection. I had to do something to keep me going. When I first went into prison I'd see people staying in their cells all day and lounging around, and I thought, I can't do this. The OU was my way of getting through my time.

I was like that with the gym as well. I remember when I was in a Group Four security van on the way to that first prison, I said to myself 'I'm going to get really fit, I'm going to get really strong, and nobody's ever going to touch me again'. As soon as I got there, as soon as I could get into the gym I did. I hadn't really done anything like that before.

• • •

It's about four months now since I left prison. As soon as I was released, within a few days I got to the gym, just as I'd done in prison, and that's really kept me going these last few months, my first months of freedom. It's like an inner strength that appears to support me. I find that weight-lifting really helps me. I go to the gym about six times a week—four times for the weights and twice for the swimming, and that gives a structure to every day. The weights place is about five minutes down the road. When I go swimming I get the bus up there and walk back, so it takes me a whole afternoon. I do kung-fu two evenings a week.

At first I stayed with my grandparents till this flat was ready for me. Since then my grandfather's become very ill. He's 80 and he hasn't got much longer to live. My grandmother's 75—they're my mum's parents. They didn't come and see me in prison as my parents did, but we used to write to each other every week. I'm not sure if they understood why I did what I did, but I'm their granddaughter and they stuck by me. I've always been very special to them—I'm their only granddaughter.

Then I moved to this place. It's classed as a hostel but it isn't really, because these are self-contained flats—there are three separate flats. I live and sleep in this one room, the sitting room, though there's a bedroom as well. But I can't get used to going to a different room to sleep yet—it's too soon after living in one cell in prison. There's a lady living upstairs—I meet her in passing. I think she's a social worker.

Sister Mary is a nun who is really in charge of this place. She's always here if I need her, but I'm allowed to just get on with my day and I've got no restrictions or anything. I've now got onto the council list for a place of my own. They've put me in a fast track system so I could get a place at any time. But Sister Mary says I can just stay here until somewhere comes up. She helps me by just being there, specially at the beginning. I was very lonely when I first came out of prison. I'd been so used to people around me, and sometimes I just needed to talk to someone. Now she's just like a friend and we just meet up once a week regularly for a chat in the evening: we have a cup of tea and we talk and watch TV.

I found it difficult to go out in the dark at first. I couldn't bring myself to walk out of the front door after about six o'clock. I had to be locked in here, in this room, as soon as it was getting dark. I never thought about this when I was in prison, but you never are out in the dark alone when you're in jail. I'm fine now, I love being out in the dark on my own.

The first day I actually came out I drove with my parents and their children to this kind of shopping place in a lay-by and my mother got some drink out of the car and we had a cup of coffee. I was looking after the children. I was holding on to their hands and it was just so strange because there were no restrictions. I couldn't work it all out. I kept thinking I was going to be told to do something.

When you first come out of prison there's this feeling of having to get everything done as soon as possible, because there are so many things to think of. When I thought of something I had to write it down and I had a massive list of all the things I had to do. After the first few weeks I was exhausted. I'd advise anyone coming out of prison that you've got to pace it, and you've got to structure your day. Then everything gradually falls into place, if you just take your time.

I didn't realise the prices of things in the shops and I'd no idea what to get, specially when you're short of money as well. How do you put meals together and things like that? Nobody tells you. Sister Mary has given me two hampers since I've been here and she gave me the necessities like milk and coffee when I first came here. I do still remember how to cook but I can't really be bothered. The Open University term starts again in a couple of weeks and then I'll have to fit my studies in as well.

I am a religious person and I always have been—Church of England. Right at the beginning of my sentence religion helped me, and then again during the last year or so. The chaplains at three of the prisons really looked after me. I used to go to church but I don't attend so regularly since I've been released.

I believe God's forgiven me, but I feel so ashamed about what I did. When I was in prison, I couldn't believe that I did it and I was detached from it. But since I've been out, since my release, I've probably felt closer to it. Reality sets in once you're back in the real world again. I'm now in a relationship again, and I can feel the beginning of things, if you see what I mean, and it scares me. It's just little things. Like when I first slept with somebody—it's just, like, flashbacks.

I've only had bad dreams since I've been out. I was dreaming the other night about my offence but it's more about prison actually, dreams that I'm back inside prison. It's just that wherever I go prison's always there in the back of my mind. There are always little reminders of it now and then during the day—for instance when I see a bunch of keys. There's this horrible thing at the back of my local post office that reminds me of prison. All it is is a door, with a kind of frame round it, but it's just like one in my last prison. It's little things like that, reminders that I come across all the time.

Now I'm trying to take each day as it comes, steadily moving forward. That's all I ask of myself each day. I just get through that day and I make a little bit of progress. Luckily I don't wake up and feel I'm still in prison. How I feel in the morning depends what I'm going to do that day, and who I'm going to see.

Things are beginning to change a bit now. I met Steve about seven weeks ago and it's made a big difference. He's my kung-fu teacher and he's 52. He knows all about my background. I've had a lot of fears—I was frightened about things, like those things that remind me of prison, and I was frightened when I thought about the past. In a lot of ways, Steve makes me feel emotionally secure and that's what I need. I feel I've now got a good friend I can talk to about anything. It was the strangest thing to be in a relationship again after prison and I was a bit scared.

I still keep in contact with my mum and step-dad. For my first Christmas since I came out of prison I spent about three days at their house. It was a bit of a strain, seeing the house again, and I must say I was glad to get back to my flat.

I see my two probation officers a lot—there's a man and a woman, which is better because it keeps the ideas flowing. I think they are really concentrating mainly on relationships and they say if it's fine by me they'd like to see me every week so that's what I do. I go to them. I find it quite easy to talk to them and they get me thinking about things I haven't thought about before.

My Open University studies mean a lot to me—I've got two more courses to do. I've just decided to study part-time and take two more years to finish it, because I need a job to support myself. Initially I was going to finish my degree this year, but looking at it now, I can't do that and get a job as well: it would be impossible. But I do need to know what my plans are going to be in the future. I've got money to pay for the next course: I wrote an article for *Sesame*, the Open University newspaper, saying how much it had meant to me in prison to be able to do the OU courses. It was lovely because readers were impressed with what I wrote and sent money to the paper to help me pay the fees, and the Open University have helped with the funding too.

I want very much to qualify as a solicitor and work for prisoners' rights, because I know what prisoners have to go through. I still keep in touch with some of the people I knew in prison. When I write to women still in there I'm always very careful what I write. There's still a certain amount of paranoia for their sake, in case letters are read.

When a woman goes into prison she finds the system takes her voice away and if she's got a problem she's got nowhere to go for help, and I don't think that's right. I've sent off application forms to the Law Society and now I've got to put a statement together of all the events that led up to my offence, which my probation officers are going to help me with. I've got to get two references: one can be from a probation officer and the other from somebody else who knows about my offence.

As for the immediate future: I applied for a job at the local university, a secretarial job with receptionist and clerical work. There would have been a lot of training involved, but they looked at my CV and they said 'You've got all the qualifications necessary and you'd be very good at this job'. I thought it would be ideal for me, because they would train me and help me, which I need because I haven't had that kind of work experience while I was in prison—that's the only thing I'm lacking in. I got a phonecall asking me to go to the university to talk to them about my offence because apart from that everything else looked OK. I thought the interview went very well. They just asked me about the offence and what I did and I explained it to them. I just told them the truth. The interviewer said 'You can expect a letter in the post any day now, asking you to come to a proper interview and go on the shortlist'. But then two days later I got a letter saying that I wasn't shortlisted because of my offence. They said they were glad of my honesty and openness and all that, but it was something to do with the rules of the university. Because of my offence, my application couldn't go any further. I don't know if it was anything to do with there being students there who they felt would be at risk in some way.

Then I applied for another job as a fitness instructor at the local sports centre. They said I'd hear early from them in the new year but I haven't heard anything yet so I don't suppose I've got that job either. I went to the interview and it went very well, I thought. They didn't know about my offence until I told them. The man interviewing me actually told me that I shouldn't have said anything. He said 'I'll give you some advice for the future—don't mention it'.

But it's against the law not to declare your previous convictions, and if you've got a sentence as long as I had, your conviction is never spent. My probation officers have told me to give their number to any potential employers and they will talk to them and reassure them about me.

So at the moment I'm putting in a few job applications each week. I go down the Job Centre and see what there is. The people there know that I've been to prison but I'm not sure if they know what my offence is. I'm applying for clerical and secretarial work and gym work. I find people's attitudes very odd. I can understand employers being reluctant to employ me for secretarial work, because I haven't really had the work experience. But I've done a lot of gym training work with people in prison. When I went to the sports centre and looked into the gym, I felt very much at home there even though I'd never been there before. The equipment's all the same as in prison and I thought 'I know I can do this job'. I just find it very odd how employers don't see that as well. They may just think that word will get out about my offence and it'll frighten customers away.

• • •

Since I've been released I haven't felt anything like the anger I felt when I committed the offence, but I've felt the beginning of things. I can't stand emotional pain, I can't stand it when people lie to me about things, specially people that I love and I trust. In prison I was never really told about anything like anger management, though I do take deep breaths, things like that, and I will think a lot about things. I think a lot more about consequences now, rather than acting on impulse.

I think if I lost my focus on my future, lost sight of my future goals, or even if a relationship went wrong today, things could go wrong for me again. But it's really about what I want for my future: I always think about all those people in prison and I really want to help them. I'm not going to be able to do that if I'm stuck in prison myself. So I wouldn't risk going back inside for anything.

I don't feel that in prison I was told the right sort of things to prepare me for release. For instance I was told to go to the DSS to get my money when I came out of prison and it isn't the DSS that you have to go to—I was sent to the wrong place! I should have gone to the employment office—the Job Centre. I felt terrible for my step-dad, because he'd been driving around trying to find the DSS. We arrived and I sat there until it was my turn—and it was the wrong place. I got a release grant of about £47 and I had £3 left in cash which I brought out of the prison. I had to get a crisis loan which you have to pay back, because that £47 only lasts one week on the benefit system in reality, though it's supposed to last two weeks.

Luckily I have plenty of interests to keep me busy, so it's only the lack of finances that I'm finding difficult, and the need to support myself. These elements are difficult enough, and problems like this don't help if you're trying to 'go straight'. But people do need to get themselves more or less immediately into paid employment after release, not only for financial reasons but for a sense of achievement and the satisfaction you can get from work. But if my qualifications can't get me a job, after all that hard work I did in prison, what chance has any of us got?

Still, prison has been an experience which has completely turned my life around. There I built myself up both mentally and physically and made my plans and goals for the future. Now I'm back in the 'real world' it's time to make those goals a reality.

A month after this interview Jane wrote to us:

I went to yet another fruitless interview about a week ago. But I won't be disheartened. I'm just more determined to achieve my goals. I've decided to embark on my own business venture as a personal fitness instructor. This is something I've always wanted to do and now, with circumstances as they are, I think this is another way forward.

Stephen Fry

Stephen Fry is an actor of international standing and repute,[1] as well as being a prolific author of books and plays. He is a descendant of the nineteenth century penal reformer Elizabeth Fry. As a youngster he 'went on a spree' with a batch of stolen credit cards and ended up in custody. He undertakes a considerable amount of work in support of ex-offenders and is non-executive director of UNLOCK. What follows is based on an interview by *Prisons Video* magazine—and his speech—at the inaugural meeting of that organization held at HM Prison Pentonville in 1998.

It's quite bewildering the number of requests one can get to support various charities. In the end one has to be rather cynical about it and say 'I can't agree to support them all' because you'd dilute yourself to such an extent you'd just be a name on the writing paper and nothing else. So you have to say to yourself: 'I will only involve myself fully and thoroughly with things that I have some bond with, some connection with, where I feel I can genuinely make a difference'.

So when Mark Leech and Bob Turney got in touch with me about UNLOCK it was apparent that this was something that I felt I had a connection to, because as an ex-offender myself I felt that lending my name to this and trying to do what I can with it would mean more to me, and I hope more to the cause itself than the average thing, like a new brain scanner for a hospital or a 'Save the Fruit Bat in Malaya' kind of thing—all of which are no doubt incredibly worthy and need to be done. But in the end, this is something which connects to me.

One of the problems for offenders on release—and pre-release—is that the gulf between the inside and the outside is so enormous these days, whipped up by the hysteria of the press who try and make 'criminal classes' appear to be some species from another planet. The more you can make the public understand that criminals are not a different species, a different race, but just 'us' who've gone off the rails somehow—and the more you can make ex-offenders understand that the world they come out to is not a world of strangeness and cruelty and lack of understanding (which only makes them want to scamper back to the security, the warmth and the routine of life on the inside, or the propping-up of self-esteem that you get in the world of crime)—the better.

We don't want ex-offenders to turn into little schoolboys with shiny caps on, going 'Yah-boo' to everyone else who's nasty. It's not a question

---

[1] Among his many film credits, Stephen Fry played the title role in the outstanding 1998 production, *Wilde*, for which he was nominated for an Oscar.

of making everybody a little Englander with their own hedge: the world is a various and extraordinary place—some people opt out of the normal way of living and others are very happy to have a nine to five job. It's not about action, it's just about society, about helping this country be a nicer, better place to live for everybody.

What do you see yourself doing for UNLOCK?
Well I've learned through bitter experience never to be too rash in making promises, so I always try to be pessimistic. I said to Mark and Bob, 'Look, you know, I can't guarantee to turn up to everything you ask me to, but don't let that stop you from asking me, because if I can I will. It's an odd life I lead—like earlier this year I spent three months in America so I can't do much from there. Other times I might be writing a book and be completely sealed off from outside influence because I have to get the thing finished. I find I'm not the kind of author who can write on a plane or a bus and so on: I have to go and lock myself away. Other times when I'm in a sort of in-between mode, I can give more and give thought, and turn up and do some visiting and just do what I can.

People will say: 'It's OK for you—you're successful'. How is UNLOCK actually going to appeal to serving prisoners?
Well—I hope I can show that being 'successful' doesn't really mean anything other than obtaining some kind of satisfaction in life. Three years ago I was almost as low as I have been, almost like the time when I was in prison. I came very close to suicide. There's a popular idea that there is this big gap—that there's the stable, normal, happy life of somebody's who's got money and is OK; and then there's the outside world. It's not true.

The idea that 'everybody else has got life sorted' is nonsensical. I commit crimes every day—they might be parking offences, or other minor transgressions. No-one is pure, no-one is just a goody-goody. For some crimes people get chased by the police; some people get on lists; people get done for conspiracy; some people get done for real hard evidence etc. There was a time when I was inside and I was as low as you can get. I went through what I'm sure a lot of people must have experienced— (when you're young in particular) which is their parents visiting them. You know, your mother's cut out things from newspapers for weeks and weeks just to keep you entertained. There are heart-breaking moments when you feel lower than whale shit, you know, you just can't believe you're in this position.

I would say essentially there are two ways out of it. One is to achieve the false glamour of the kind of respect you get from living in a world completely *outside*—the criminal world. This doesn't work, that's the problem with it. It doesn't work, it doesn't make you happy, it doesn't make you rich, if riches is what you want, it doesn't get you real respect from anybody. It's dangerous and it's difficult.

The other way is to find some self-respect *within yourself*, which doesn't mean you have to turn your back on all the people who've been your friends or who've been in prison with you. It doesn't mean you have to become a goody-goody who's going to squeal on everybody, going to grass, who can't go back to his old neighbourhood without going 'Oh, you're all still doing that are you!' It's not about that.

Just in the practical way, the thing that got me out, the thing that tugged me, the ironic thing was that if you want to help yourself the best way to do it is to help somebody else. Part of the problem of 'offending' is that most people offend in order to help themselves—sometimes quite literally because they help themselves to things they don't own. But the effect is always the reverse. The way you really help yourself is by going round helping others—I don't mean being Mother Teresa necessarily. In my case there was this guy in a cell opposite mine who couldn't read. He wanted to write his poems and he had a mixture of songs and poems in his head. He wanted to be a musician and play the guitar a bit. He'd tap things out and he wanted to write them down. So I taught him to read. Now that experience left me thinking 'God, I can *do* something!'. Me, who was always the one getting found out, the one in trouble. Other people got in with bad people—Stephen *was* the bad person! I suddenly thought 'I've done good! This guy can read!' It wasn't like I suddenly became a goody-goody. I just said to him 'Look, this is an "A", all right? We'll go through it' and just watched it. And it was like watching a garden you'd planted. And I suddenly thought 'I'm not a hopeless piece of shit! I can do things for other people!'

That's what did it for me. That's the paradox, that's the twist you have to observe, I think: it's the way you can look after yourself by looking after others. Both prison culture and criminal culture inculcate this endless idea: 'Let's look after Number One. If I look after myself, get my head down, do my bird, then I'll be all right'. Not true. It's only by connecting to others—that's how you help yourself, that's the irony. It's a strange thing to grasp, that little twist. But once you've got it—it's not like some magic, you're suddenly in heaven—because nobody is. Life is always going to be ambiguous and complex and contingent on all kinds of things outside that can shit on you. Shit happens and will continue to happen. It's not as if you take a right turn and suddenly everything's blessed—because that doesn't happen. You can be President of the United States and worry yourself into an ulcer because you've screwed around a bit stupidly. You can be anyone and you can end up with your brains against the wall because life has lost its meaning for you. It's all about what goes on inside—about self-respect. And the irony is, self-respect comes not from looking inwards—it comes from looking outwards. You see it in other people's eyes—you don't see it in the mirror.

There's a psychological preparation for people to get out of prison. It's to teach them that the world out there *is* going to be complex and confusing, it *is* going to be strange, and in a sense they're being asked to do something which is akin to the earliest explorers, or mountaineers on Everest. They're being asked to go, with pretty much the minimum of materials, out into a world which may be very strange to them, a world that may be very hostile and alien. We don't embrace ex-offenders as we should as a society. So it's to prepare them for that, and to make them realise that *on the inside*. From the moment they arrive in the prison, it's to prepare them for the day they leave, to prepare them for the fact that they can be citizens who are as good as anyone else, and to hold their heads up.

That would be done by making them confront things within themselves, and making them realise that it's not easy, that's it's not just a question of 'We'll give you these job introductions and a thousand pounds'. How long's that going to last? You'll spend it on a few evenings with friends, on drugs—you'll be back inside in a fortnight. It's about being much tougher than that.

The point about UNLOCK is that it's run by ex-offenders—the people saying this are ex-offenders themselves, not people from the probation service who do a good job—some of them are excellent, some of them are terrible, just like any branch of human affairs. But because UNLOCK is run by ex-offenders, the only advice people get will be from people who've actually experienced prison, not just people who've watched it. I think that does make a difference.

UNLOCK will say 'We're not on the side of crime. We don't think there's anything clever about crime'. Some of the people we've talked to have done some quite terrible things that would make all of our flesh crawl. But we do believe that once the sentence is deemed to be over, then the very society that gave that sentence should be in better position to deal with ex-prisoners. And they themselves should be in a better position to deal with society.

I hope that my role—as perhaps a more public person than the others—will also be to educate not the offenders, not the pre-release prisoners, but society.

What is UNLOCK actually doing to change society's views?
There are a number of things you can do. One is, in terms of lobbying, to try and keep hammering away at the Home Office and at various political parties to extend the rights and privileges of the Rehabilitation of Offenders Act 1974, which doesn't go far enough—so that the brand, the stigma is removed from the offender.

The other thing is to educate society out of this idea that criminals are from another planet—and out of the idea that you must despise them because if you don't it means that you're on the side of 'them' and not on the side of the victim. The real victims of crime very often really are the criminals. The long-term suffering, the long-term degradation, the long-term harm is done to the person who does something bad. If you have something bad done to you, it's an awful feeling, we all know that. Even if it's something trivial like having your car radio stolen. You feel really, really bad about it. But everyone claps you on the back and says 'You poor bugger, you got robbed, if I saw that person I'd kill him!' The world comes round and supports you because this thing has happened to you. But if you're the person who's done it, you hide, you go away and hide in a corner. You don't dare tell anyone you've done it because you know everyone will despise *you* for it—or every so-called decent person will.

So it's about trying to get everyone to change this ridiculous gulf that exists: you're either for the criminal, which means you're against the victim; or you're for the victim which means you're against the criminal. It's not like that—we must at least try and become one society.

You're involved in this year's Koestler Exhibition: what is inspiring you at this time to get involved with penal issues?
I suppose it's what they used to call 'synchronicity' really! It's just one of these odd things. I wrote an autobiography[2]—of my childhood which goes up to the age of about 20-odd and really finishes just when I came out of the prison. So although I've spoken about my past, many people have read the book and this was the first inkling they had that I had been inside. And so more people have asked me to become involved—I've been asked to do more prison talks than before.

My involvement with UNLOCK grew out of the fact that I'd agreed to be at the Koestler Awards, and Mark Leech asked if I would become more involved in his new organization. He knew I was coming to Koestler and he sent me website information. I looked at it and read it carefully and thought about it. I talked to extraordinary people like Bob Turney, the world's only—well, Britain's only—ex-offender probation officer! A remarkable man. And I thought, yes, this is something I really should get involved in.

---

[2] *Moab Is My Washpot*, Hutchinson, 1997, where Stephen Fry describes himself, aged 18, as 'A petty thief who ruined people's lives with theft, betrayal, cowardice and contempt'.

What do you see as being UNLOCK'S biggest hurdle?

I think there are two things. On one side I think it is the fact that with anything founded on a huge wave of optimism and goodwill by some remarkable people, people who are leaders in the penal business, if you like—people from prisons and from the Howard League of Penal Reform, people like Frank Longford and Stephen Tumim, remarkable people who in the face of great hostility have done remarkable things, have just quietly got on with it—it's very easy to get over-excited, to think that the world's going to be conquered, that things are going to get better. The world doesn't work like that: things are done in little baby steps—it's never any better than that, particularly in this country, particularly in Britain. You're always pushing against a spring-loaded door in this country, wherever you go. You *can* get it open, but it's slow work.

The fact is, we want to see crime reduced in this country for the sake of people who would otherwise be in prison as well as for the sake of shopkeepers and householders and everybody else who feels threatened by crime—for the sake of Britain just being a nicer place to be. A nicer place for women to walk around on their own. A nicer place for people to feel that they can park their car without having to—you know, virtually pass an electric current through it! But that old Chinese phrase: 'The journey of a thousand miles begins with a single step' is never truer than in the penal world. It's like the fight against anything: look back ten years when new things were being founded and people were saying 'This is the way we deal with it'. Now ten years later the prison population has gone up even further, crime rises, people's fear of crime, their perception of crime, is even worse than it was ten years ago.

So I think that the biggest hurdle, in a sense, is that all the great things that have ever been done in the world have been done by grind, by practical people just getting on with it. It's like when you travel through the Third World and you realise that it's those women walking 20 miles with a pot on their heads who are keeping the world alive, keeping their families alive. It's not the people sitting around talking grand political ideas. It's the 'getting on with it'. Like that old story of the documentary crew that comes to interview a family and the wife says 'Oh, my husband makes all the important decisions in the household. I do all the trivial things'. The interviewer said 'What do you mean?' and she said 'Well, I decide where the children go to school, what they wear, what they eat, how much we spend on food, how many clothes they've got, how many shoes they've got, how they're cleaned. And my husband decides all the important things, like whether there should be a UN presence in Bosnia and whether Clinton should be impeached!'

That puts its finger so exactly on what UNLOCK is like: it's like the woman in that family getting on with the real stuff. It's not particularly glamorous. It's like that awful military phrase that everybody uses now: *on the ground*. It's what's going on on the ground. It's small, it's detailed and it's not glamorous particularly—and, of course, lots of people will fall foul of alcohol and drugs and their old mates and they will go back to prison and continue to. And in ten years' time people will say 'What's UNLOCK really done?'

But if we can look at just five people whose lives have been utterly transformed, that's an extraordinary thing to be able to say that one has been involved with. And my God, if anything's worth trying, it's this.

The authors acknowledge the kind assistance given by Prisons Video magazine.

Peter Cameron

Peter, 51, is a freelance artist and screen-printer who has enjoyed considerable success since his release from prison nearly seven years ago. He served two prison sentences: in 1972 he was sentenced to 18 months for cannabis dealing, but his second sentence was much longer—more than ten years for conspiracy to import cannabis.

I loved being up in the mountains in Morocco, living with the Arab families, pressing up kilos of dope, smoking dope, getting it down to the beach where it would be picked up and sailed across the Med and on to Amsterdam. We were all going off to Spain and Morocco, having a nice time, plenty of cash, plenty of excitement. This went on a few years, so there must have been ten or 12 events, loading up dope and pressing up dope and being chased by helicopters along the beaches in Tangier—it was quite fun. Well—I can say it was fun retrospectively because I got away with it, it happened. But there's obviously something more to it than that. Why do people bet on horses? They must be mad. And I suppose I must have been mad too. But there's a little bit of something in us all that doesn't mind walking a thin line now and then. I think I had such an exciting life as a kid that I needed to be sailing yachts and going to Morocco and flying round in a light aircraft—just for the buzz. My parents gave me such an exciting life as a kid that I needed this adrenaline buzz.

• • •

I was brought up in East Africa as a kid because my dad went to Tanzania after the war as a schoolteacher. I had a fantastic upbringing and I remember running around bollock-naked in Africa. So I was very lucky. It was the same with my education—it was a bit of a holiday— it was very, very nice. The event that stands out most in my memory of that time was travelling. I was always moving to a different house every six months or two years. We were always on the move in Africa because of my dad's job in the colonial civil service. He was teaching, going from school to school. He'd move from Dar es Salaam to Tanga and so on, so I was on the hoof too and it was fantastic for a young fellow.

Because we lived in Africa I was a boarder at school from about the age of six. I used to get on a train and it would take a few days to get to the school, so it was just like a holiday camp. Everything was geared to travelling and being away from home. There were other English-speaking kids coming from all over Africa to these two or three schools so I had lots of friends. There'd obviously be a teacher on the train too. I was six and my sister was eight and we'd both be on the train. It was fantastic, quite an unreal world, now that I can look back on it. But at the time it was just run-of-the mill to me.

It's very clubable going to school in those circumstances, and you all seem very similar. It's like being in a small village in a huge country. You tend to know other people's parents because you've seen them before. There were seven or eight hundred families with their kids all going to two or three schools in Tanzania.

I come from a typical middle-class family. Though my mum and dad were working-class people by background, they were in the middle-class income bracket, and when they came back to England they lived a middle-class existence, near Guildford in Surrey.

I didn't really feel comfortable about moving into secondary education because it took place in this country so I had a bit of a culture shock. I was about 12 or 13 when I came back here. Because I lived in Africa and because I did quite well at school I went to a public school in Scotland called Fettes—the same school as Tony Blair in fact—he was there while I was there. If I'd known he was going to be Prime Minister I'd have tapped him for a tenner!

I was always very much involved in sport. Sport was compulsory all through my education. I did quite well at athletics and swimming because I'd lived in Africa and I took to it. I played rugby and football—luckily I played everything—tennis, squash, all these sort of things were made available to me because I'd lived in Africa and because of the school I went to.

• • •

I was about 14 or 15 when I started stealing—just the occasional little theft. It only started when I came back to England. In the school holidays I'd nick from shops. I'd take quite expensive things like Ronson lighters—I'd try and take four or five of them. I also took bits of tom[1] from shops where it was quite easy. I quite liked the excitement of doing that. I got a bit of a kick and I would weigh it in. Though mine was a quite comfortably-off family, I didn't have lots of money myself—I didn't have disposable income. So I started being dishonest at quite an early age. It was petty, but it was certainly a mentality I had—a dishonest mentality. It was also because I got a bit of a buzz, and a little bit of kudos too. At that time maybe I didn't have much confidence and as a 14 or 15 year old I wanted to show off. I used to nick quite a lot of books when I was at school as well, and sell them in secondhand bookshops up town. I had boxes full of them from the

---

[1] Tomfoolery = jewellery.

libraries and the bookshop at school—that was the stupid sort of thing I did. Immature males suffering from an overdose of testosterone at a certain age do stupid things. I didn't need to steal—it wasn't a case of having nothing, I wasn't kicking an empty Stella can round a housing estate or anything like that. It was recreational theft. Sixties culture was the reason—the anarchy of that time led me into it, and greed and excitement in equal proportions.

I got the usual O-levels—English literature and language, French, maths, biology. Then I did A-level English, biology and geology. I didn't particularly shine because I was quite lazy, but I got enough A-levels and O-levels to go to university. Art didn't feature at all—it's funny, that. I left school at 18, went to Liverpool University and got a BSc in biology. After leaving university I started to do an MSc in tropical medicine—and that's when I first got arrested for selling drugs.

• • •

I think I've taken every drug. I've taken smack, I've taken coke, I've done acid, smoked cannabis, drunk alcohol. I never got much into the way of Ecstasy or anything like that, or solvent abuse. But I had amphetamines, all that sort of thing. I think I was part of an era when people were taking drugs to make themselves think more. We were the educated people, like the jazz players who took benzedrine and the beatniks smoking pot—they considered themselves the intelligentsia. Drugs hadn't hit the estates. We used to go to buy our dope down in London, down in the East End—it was kaftan versus Crombie. We were getting our arses kicked, people were giving us a bad time, calling us poofter hippies, that sort of thing.

That cultural shift of the 'sixties was what kicked me off—and dope was part of it, with the music and the anarchy. It was a very political shift as well because there was banning the bomb, there was marching on Vietnam, there were love-ins, peace movements. The music was Dylan, protest stuff. It was an interesting time to be young and to be at university. Drug-taking was quite political—it was the long-haired hippie thing, the anti-Vietnam mentality. We were all Lefties, sitting in at the Senate, marching, supporting the Liverpool dockers—students were very Left-wing in those days.

And a new business cropped up too, because I started making money out of dope. My smoking cannabis provided me with a job. I was a bit of an entrepreneur within the cultural confines of the 1960s. The cheapest way to get my dope in was to go down the Fulham Road and buy half a weight, cut it up, do my mates and get mine for free. The next thing you know, you've got a bit of cash involved, so you just carry on and get more.

We weren't hard-faced villainous-type criminals from a criminal background. We were all pretty middle-class students. Dealing cannabis was a service industry, basically. People wanted something and I provided it. But all the same you knew it was illegal and you were doing it for the readies. I never bought or sold anything else except cannabis, though I've taken other things.

· · ·

I went to prison because of cannabis—I got a lot of porridge for it. I first got banged up in 1972. I got 18 months for selling dope at the university, my first offence. It was for dealing—a quarter of an ounce or something stupid, but it was dealing and I did make a bit of money out of it. They were draconian in those days. I'd only get a £30 fine for that now.

I'd been to boarding schools, so I had no fear of going to the nick. I thought 'Eighteen months—a shit and a shave!' The first time I was sent to prison it seemed like a bit of a joke. I was in Liverpool prison, Risley and Haverigg and it was all right, it was a laugh. Prison was a place with stupid mindless bloody rules, just like school. People like myself and Stephen Fry knew that people do this kind of thing all the bloody time in boarding schools. But actually getting sent down was a bit of a shock all the same, and a bit of a fright too. You think you're never going to get sent down. The court case and the arrest was more of a shock than the porridge, because I didn't know exactly where I was going. Slam! What's it going to be like in the nick? When they're taking you downstairs and slinging you into the back of a van you think 'What's going on down there?' You can't get through to the officers at all, and it's just like a nightmare. But I knew people inside already so I fitted into it quite easily and I could see an end to it. I was only going to do a year.

The second sentence—the last one—was a different matter. It was ten and a half years for conspiracy to import cannabis. It's impossible to think of going out. They bang you up with somebody who's in for a fine, and you suddenly realise he's going out in three weeks. On your first visit you realise you've got hundreds more to go.

What led me to commit all those offences, all that stuff in Morocco and Spain, was a combination of greed and excitement—I wanted money, excitement, a bit of the lifestyle—and I thought it was exciting. But it wasn't *that* exciting. It's much more exciting in films, in fiction, and this is what you get seduced by, till it becomes your way of life.

· · ·

Two things made me change: my guilt towards my parents and the Koestler Award.

First was my family. My parents were getting old and I felt really bad for them because I needn't have gone to prison at all. I'm not an archetypal prisoner—I was bloody educated for Christ's sake! I was doing an MSc when I got sent down. So I felt I'd let my parents down and there was disappointment there, though they were very loyal and supportive to me the whole way through my sentence. My mum died when I was in prison and I felt bad about that. It was very hard—these were people who'd worked all their lives and thought they'd done the right thing for me and basically I'd kicked them in the bollocks by what I'd done.

The second thing that changed me was winning the Koestler Award for prison art, and seeing my picture in the *Daily Telegraph*. The painting I put into the Koestler competition was my first picture. I'd never painted anything till I entered it, and when it was in the *Telegraph* I got the same kind of buzz that I got when I was pulling off one of those stunts in Morocco. It's the same now when I get a red dot on a picture showing someone's bought it—I get the same feeling. You feel you've done something on your own, against the grain. I know it's a cliché but you feel you've won one over the establishment. Winning the Koestler Award had that effect on me. I thought it was fantastic.

It all started one day when I was sitting in the education department at Walton[2] prison. I went to the Spanish class but that was such a bloody joke because some people were illiterate, some were literate, and so the class never got started. But with an art class it's different. We'd got Stevie Best the cartoonist there, Bestie he was known as, and he said 'Here's some paints, Pete'. So I painted a picture of two chimpanzees, put them in prison uniform, gave them half an ounce of burn[3], a couple of chews and a letter I'd just copied. Then I did a still life and somebody bought it for half an ounce. I'd got a result in the nick that was real—half an ounce! I said 'Great—I'll do this art business!'

Then when I won the Koestler Award I really started to enjoy painting. I painted pictures of prison life. I came to terms with my environment by painting it: instead of smashing up the place, I was painting pictures of it. So I liked it if I had to slop out the shitty exercise yard because it made a better picture for me. You don't get overawed by your environment if you use it. And I think that's what painting did for me—it was a bit of therapy. That's why it became a turning point for me, because of the excitement side of it. I don't make

---

[2] Local name for Liverpool prison

[3] Tobacco

much money but the whole idea is enjoying your life. I realise now that if I enjoy what I'm doing it's worth all the money in the world.

About half way through my last sentence I realised that I was going to do something totally different when I got out. I'd started to paint and I knew I was going to do something different. I think I said to myself then that I wasn't going to make a criminal con. I knew I'd be 45 when I got out, and now I knew I could do other things. Again, I wanted to do this for my parents. In the nick you do tend to exaggerate things in your own mind, but I hung on to the Koestler Trust, mentally. I clung to both of those things—my painting and my family.

Stephen Tumim has been very supportive. He came to Full Sutton and he dragged me out of a visit session. He said 'I wanted to meet you: I saw your picture and it's very good, keep it up'. I thought that was good. He was a good HM Inspector, and he was very supportive to people who were painting. He didn't make any big nonsense about it: he just said 'Keep it up! Good!' and went off, wearing his bow tie. He's been a very supportive geezer and a very approachable geezer.

I won the Koestler award three times while I was in prison. I sold my pictures to people like Sir Stephen Tumim and got a £200 cheque in my private cash. I said to myself 'Bloody hell—I'm earning a bit of money here! I'm sitting in the nick beginning to earn money from painting—I shall have a go when I get home'.

You don't stop living because you go to nick—whether you're meant to or not—that's the philosophy I always had. You do have to do it for yourself. Use prison I mean. You've got to take care of time in prison. The option's yours. They shut the door, lock you up, feed you and bang you up again. The rest is up to you. I didn't just sit and wait for the door to open, like a lot of other people have done.

There was a good education department in Full Sutton. I still keep in touch with one of the people who used to teach in there. I remember he took me out for a day once. He got the governor to let me out so he could take me to some art galleries. Then he took me to the pub for a pint—the first pint I'd had for four years. He was nice and he was supportive and he was a breath of fresh air. I did an Open University degree in art history in the nick, towards the end of my sentence. It only took me three years because having a BSc they gave me a load of points already, which was quite lucky. I think Open University's good. You can really choose your own subject, choreograph it just as you want it. I liked it.

So I used my time in prison. Prison came along at the right time for me.

• • •

When I got out of prison in November 1992, just before Christmas, my house had gone, my girlfriend had gone, everything had gone. I had mates, but I had no money at all. I hadn't got a brass tack. So I knew I was going to have to do something. I was pretty unemployable. I knew my mates would give me a job—I could get a job behind the bar, I could have done some driving, but I couldn't have done much physical stuff as I was getting on, and I had a bad back.

Almost right away, people were offering to lay a few kilos for me, so I could get a few bob in for Christmas.

Just at that time, Stephen Tumim rang me up. He said 'If you've got any pictures, bring them down to the Mall Gallery—there's an exhibition, the Discerning Eye exhibition'. So I took five pictures down there and hung them on his wall—there were five walls, different people's walls, and his was one—and I sold them all. So I got 800, 900 notes before Christmas from my pictures. It was providential—it was a real stroke of luck.

When you do come out of nick you are stigmatised about getting a job and you're often forced to work for yourself. So I'd been fortunate because I'd kept all my pictures, kept all my art, brought all my sketchbooks from the nick, hundreds of sketches I'd made.

You get very philosophical about your offending. If I was down on my arse now I'd probably feel very bitter and I would probably still be offending. But I do look back at it all now and try to make it as positive as possible. If I hadn't offended and hadn't done a substantial sentence, I wouldn't have discovered another thing to do. I would certainly never have discovered art on the outside—not a chance! I literally had to go to prison to do that.

It was harder to paint when I came out than it was when I was inside. For a start you've got to pay for the paints! You're not going to be able to rob them from the education department! On the outside, people don't sympathize with you. They don't send you paints for your birthday like they do in prison. So it's just as well I had that monastic start in prison, so I could get the discipline of practice, practice, practice, and I could see it work from the safety of a prison.

My CV uses the fact that I took up art in prison. There's always a little bit of voyeurism in people who buy pictures—they're interested in the person who painted them. I sell the fact that I've been to nick, and I get exhibitions as a result of it.

Now I've got a studio and I'm surrounded by nice, interesting people in the art world. I screen-print teeshirts for people—motorbike teeshirts, classic bike teeshirts: I've got a small screen-printing business. We do all the bike shows, we go to Utrecht, set up stalls and so on. That's given me a bit of money. I do the occasional talk for the New Bridge. I go into prisons as an artist in residence. I went to the lifers in

Gartree last year, and I go to the young offenders in Glen Parva—I'll do a week or a fortnight there and it's really good.

I like to think I help more people than I used to. I'm certainly less selfish and I'd like to be able to continue on that level. I like to go into prisons, now that I understand more about people being deprived of things. I needn't have gone to prison myself, but with some people you can honestly say 'I can see why you're in prison, mate, you haven't had a bleeding hope!' I mean, I'd had *all* the hopes, and yet I ended up in prison. So I can look with a much more objective point of view and see what a shitty time some kids have, specially when I go to places like Glen Parva. These kids haven't got a family, they haven't got a parent: they're 16 years old and they're parents themselves—they've got two kids coming to visit them! Some American psychologist said it's all congenital, the criminal class. That seems a draconian thing to say but you can almost see how criminality breeds itself. I'm aware of that and I try to help anyone that I can. I write to people still in the nick, going way back to the geezers I met in Gartree and Glen Parva. At Christmas I send postcards to the ones who are doing art. I like to keep my hand in there because some people get a shitty time. There are much maligned people in the nick. They get an awfully bad press but nobody has a clue what it's really like for them. I know all the authors' royalties from this book are going to the UNLOCK charity and I'm glad to be contributing to it, because it's going to try and help prisoners on their release.

The most important thing to me these days is mental security. I feel quite financially secure because I can't be made redundant. So I feel I'll never die of starvation or exposure. As long as nobody cuts my hands off and I don't go blind I'll be all right!

It's a much quieter life now. I don't go out much, I'm not the social animal that I used to be. I'm in most nights. I still see all my old mates. You find that going to nick tells you who your real friends are. You might have thought some guy was a miserable sod, but then you found he wrote to you every month, sent you a book in and gave you 50 notes when you came out. The people you thought were going to stay with you, you heard neither hind nor hair of them. Prison's a bit of a leveller in that way. I think I value people more—I'm less flippant with people now.

I'd hate to think there's anything that would make me return to reoffending. It would have to be so serious. I keep in touch with quite a few people from the nick, and some of them still ring me up and talk to me. But they know that I'm not bothering committing any more crimes. I don't quite feel dissociated from what I did. I do wonder how I could have done all that stupid thieving stuff as a kid. But I can see how I fell into the dope-smoking: I became a smuggler and a dealer, because I was a smoker.

Now I just enjoy painting my pictures, and I'm getting to sell quite a few. As well as going to prisons I go to art colleges and give slide shows. This is more to do with art than prison, but I take prison pictures as well.

I also work for the Koestler Trust. I help them out—I do a week every month with them in the new Koestler Centre just outside Wormwood Scrubs. I've become a judge for the Koestler Award, and they've made me a trustee. I work all the time. I've never worked so hard in my bloody life!

So in fact you could say that for me the nick's been a career—a very strange career.

• • •

Peter Cameron provided the illustration for the front cover of this book.

His Honour Sir Stephen Tumim, former HM Chief Inspector of Prisons, is Chairman of the Koestler Award Trust. Here, he writes about the Trust:

> You feel you have done something on your own, against the grain. I know its a cliché, but you feel you've won one over the establishment. Winning the Koestler Award had that effect on me. I thought it was fantastic.

So wrote Peter Cameron, once a prisoner, now a professional artist, and a most valued Trustee and worker for the Koestler Award Trust.

Arthur Koestler, writer and sage, was imprisoned in Spain during the Civil War and sentenced to death. He got out, but was imprisoned in France, and when he eventually reached England, he was held in Pentonville. He came to believe that prisoners—those held not only in prisons but sometimes against their will in mental hospitals—needed the self-respect that comes from being stimulated to create. Their painting, craft, writing, music, or anything they made that was shapely, was to be publicly exhibited. Prizes were to be given. It was to be an annual event. The Koestler Awards Scheme was introduced into our prisons and special hospitals in 1961, with the active support of the then Home Secretary, Rab Butler. I have had the honour to succeed as Chairman Sir Hugh Casson and David Astor. The many competition judges give their services free. We have now extended to almost every kind of art and craft. The poetry, judged by Douglas Dunn, has a taste of its own:

In my box I will put my dad, my dog, my brothers and sisters, and my rabbit.
I will put all my favourite food and my best friend.
In my box I will put my mum, but she will go in a box within a box,
just to be there, but not next to dad because my box would become a war zone.

'It is important', write the photography judges, 'to see how people are actually living their lives. And, who knows, we might even change things!'

Prisons are noisy and overcrowded places. Prisoners are continually under stress of one kind and another. One system of improvement is the practice of the arts—theatre, drawing and painting in particular, writing, craft and music. All demand concentration and the time spent is rewarded by increasing skill. Theatre may have the most value, because teamwork, words, speech, music and visual themes are all needed. The acquisition of even a modest skill here gives satisfaction and self-respect.

So the first purpose of the arts in prison is to help with the main work of imprisonment, the reduction of future crime. Most prisoners arrive to serve their sentences bitter and confused. From practising an art they derive a sense of order.

The Koestler Award Trust has the full support of the Home Office, the Prison Service, the Probation Service, the Boards of Visitors, and all the other tentacles of the criminal justice system and the relevant hospital system. We now cover young offender institutions, youth treatment centres, secure units, and special hospitals.

© Sir Stephen Tumim, 1999

Postscript

Roger Graef

When I interviewed 14 judges and magistrates about why they sent people to prison, not one believed doing so would lead to their rehabilitation. They all agreed the majority were not dangerous and need not be there. But they simply did not know what else to do. They sent them to prison out of frustration.

These and other tales of men and women caught in a criminal lifestyle are deeply, profoundly frustrating for those of us privileged, like Angela Devlin and Bob Turney, to come to know the potential so many offenders have to offer.

It is nothing less than a criminal waste to see such people, with passions and loyalties, many with skills and sensitivities, that remain unrecognised throughout their school life and adolescence. It seems that only by offending can they command our attention.

But where does responsibility lie? Who is to blame for the ease and comfort provided by collaborators in crime, who offer security and approval apparently not available in straight society? If we ignore or neglect early warnings of trouble, can we be surprised that bigger trouble lies ahead?

It is not rocket science—though now solid criminology—to see the list of predictors of future offending: poor housing, harsh erratic parenting, one or both parents unemployed, a history of sexual abuse and/or domestic violence in the family, alcohol or drug abuse, poor physical and mental health—and learning problems, truancy, school failure and exclusion. The life stories you have just read contain all these factors in abundance and almost none of the factors have anything to do with the criminal justice system. And yet anyone experiencing one or more of them is a strong candidate for anti-social behaviour, leading to crime.

As they find themselves a place in the anti-social world, on the margins of straight society, it becomes harder for them to imagine, let alone embark on, changing their situation—finishing school, getting and holding down a job and a long-term relationship. In my experience, the simple matter of trust is a core issue.

Almost without exception, the interviewees in this book became involved in crime at an early age and only determined to leave crime behind when a degree of maturity combined with other, often quite varying, triggers. One young offender I met on a ten week intensive probation programme asked me for a job on the very first day. Luke wanted to be a video editor in television. I promised him one if he did well and stayed the course. In fact, Luke did brilliantly—attending far more than the minimum required of him, and performing outstandingly in all the workshops and exercises.

The only sign of difficulty—that suggested he might have trouble in the straight world of television—was his failure to turn up at the very end of the course in time for his beautifully executed woodwork to be delivered to his home. Although clearly his fault—he had been warned of the time the van was leaving—Luke's tantrum was intense and unreasonable. It suggested he could not handle disappointment.

Moreover, the lateness itself was a piece of self-sabotage that risked spoiling the good impression he had made over ten weeks. Both were qualities common to many offenders of my acquaintance that keep them from fitting easily into straight jobs and situations.

Nevertheless, I kept my promise and arranged to meet Luke to pursue the job. He never turned up. Nor did he contact me to apologise or explain why. Luke did the same thing twice more, leaving me waiting an hour on each occasion.

I knew of both Luke's difficulty and his talent, so I persevered, not something an ordinary prospective employer would do. I found him a place as a runner on a religious television programme, whose editor was an East Ender who knew boys like Luke well. They were pleased to help an ex-offender go straight—again not a common response from potential employers.

Finally, with a firm job offer in hand, we arranged to meet at Piccadilly Circus tube at 3 p.m. on the Friday before he was due to start. It was the fourth such appointment.

I stood in front of the ticket booth at three o'clock sharp. At 3.03 p.m. Luke ran up to me. He was furious. He had been waiting at one of the five entrances above ground and I was not there. He had planned to give up after five minutes if he had not found me by then.

At least this time we had met up. We progressed to the editing room where Luke was welcomed, and shown the ropes. It was agreed he should start that Monday at 9 a.m. in Soho, at £75 per week initially (before the advent of the minimum wage which would only have increased this marginally)—a small sum but normal in television for starter jobs as runners. For a 19 year old like Luke, it was twice the dole, and he was told he would be paid properly if he did well. He had a job, a steady girlfriend, a flat in a sheltered housing project, and a mentor (me). So the stage was set for him to progress into normal society.

Monday came and went with no sign of Luke. He rang neither the editing room nor me. I wrote to him but had no reply.

Three months later I heard he was up for trial for burglary in Knightsbridge Crown Court. I went along to give him a character reference. I told the judge how well he had done in the intensive probation programme, and how he could use the chance of yet another probation sentence to address what now emerged as a drug problem. He could also take further training courses as a carpenter, or indeed, a video editor.

The judge believed me, and gave Luke probation for one last time. When we met on the street, he was grateful but unnerved. He had expected a long stretch in Feltham, for which he was far more prepared than to be back out on the street, facing the uncertainties of normal life. I took him for coffee to find out what had happened about the job.

What Luke told me speaks to the heart of the problem of (re)integrating persistent offenders into straight society. First, he said that he had been on drugs throughout his time on the intensive probation programme. Luke had hidden it so well that not only the probation officers and I had missed it. His girlfriend did not know either. He had been selling duff Ecstasy tablets each night after the programme to pay for his habit. He saw the £75 a week from the job as not enough to keep his drug supply going.

But what clinched his reluctance to take the job was the very fact that I had arranged it. He explained matter-of-factly that the real reason he didn't go was because he could not figure out why I had helped him. No one had ever done him a favour before. He was just too suspicious and unsettled by not comprehending my motives.

It's a truism that people in Luke's situation tell you what you want to hear. It is essential to develop listening skills that go beyond the bravado that most youngsters present to find out what is really going on. I thought I had done that with Luke, and yet we had still not communicated enough for him to trust me.

Having watched many other young offenders struggle to go straight both here and in America, I realise what we need to remember is their similarity with our own children, their insecurities and needs and desires—fractured and multiplied by the damage of their past.

Their difficulties are not enough of an excuse for us to forgive them time and again—indeed research into mentoring shows they thrive in structured settings, where actions have consequences. They do least well with unstructured generalised encouragement, undirected therapy—and pure punishment. Moreover, as Luke's story illustrates, personal commitment is a more powerful agent for change than the support mechanisms which we must also put in place.

But we do need to encourage them even more than we would ourselves and our children. For their lives are steeped in failure. Failure at home, where they will most likely have been beaten and shouted at from early on, failure at school from early on, leading to exclusion—a clear mark of estrangement from which it is very hard to come back. Failure to get and hold down jobs dogs their existence from then on. Small wonder the rewards of crime and the approval of criminals offer more reliable alternatives.

But if we are to challenge the 'them and us' mentality which drives the *Daily Mail* into paroxysms of rage about those deemed 'soft' on criminals, we must make the continual effort to find common ground—to see what we want and need in our lives, and ensure we help offenders to reconceptualise their own situations in more positive ways. Then we must give them the tools to act on these new models. Raising false hopes for offenders trying to go straight can be worse than neutral. It leads to still greater despair, and potential damage to themselves and those around them.

Perhaps the greatest tragedy of prison and its overcrowding is that so little use is made of the time inside to help people rethink and prepare for a new life outside. Education budgets are slashed, and constant movement means courses are not even worth starting. When they emerge, even the dole is not available to them for several weeks—almost ensuring a return to crime.

Of course, there is a long held view that people grow out of crime. As they mature, they find the adrenaline high less attractive than a more stable relationship and children. But lest we take comfort that this will happen on its own, research now shows us that many young offenders stay in prolonged adolescence into their late twenties and even thirties. Many have become fathers in their teens, often leaving young children—boys especially—to follow tragically in their footsteps. Moreover, as unemployment—especially for ex-offenders—remains high—many do not give up a life of crime. They change the pattern of offending to areas less likely to be detected. That's the real lesson of prison—don't get caught again.

It will take far more than longer sentences and better police to change that. We all must continue to look for ways to meet people like Luke on their own terms, and build sufficient trust to convince them they are worth saving. People *can* change—if proof be needed it is to be found in the stories in this optimistic book.

© Roger Graef, 1999

Roger Graef is a distinguished documentary film-maker and author. His work with his production company Films of Record includes *Police* (BBC TV, 1982) looking at the work of Thames Valley Constabulary; *In Search of Law and Order* (Channel 4, 1999) a series about innovative American schemes to divert young people away from crime; and *The Siege of Scotland Yard* (Channel 4, 1999) which followed Sir Paul Condon, Commissioner of the Metropolitan Police, as he prepared to respond to the McPherson report on the tragic death of the black teenager Stephen Lawrence. His books include *Talking Blues: Police In Their Own Words* (Harper Collins, 1989) and *Living Dangerously: Young Offenders In Their Own Words* (Harper Collins, 1993).

The WATERSIDE PRESS Prison List - *Opening up a closed world*

The Prisons Handbook Mark Leech
'A tour de force through current penal policy and practice' *Prison Service Journal*
'A must for anyone involved with prisoners or imprisonment' *New Law Journal*
THIRD EDITION 1999. ISBN 1 872 870 72 4. £37.50 plus £2.50 p&p

Murderers and Life Imprisonment: Containment, Treatment, Safety and Risk Eric Cullen and Tim Newell. Foreword by Stephen Shaw, Director, Prison Reform Trust. 1999 ISBN 1872 870 56 2. £18 plus £1.50 p&p

Prison Patter Angela Devlin A dictionary of prison slang. 'Useful for the custody suite' *Police Journal.* 1996 ISBN 1 872 870 41 4. £12 plus £1.50 p&p

Invisible Women: What's Wrong With Women's Prisons Angela Devlin. 'What an excellent book!' *Justice of the Peace.* 1998 ISBN 1 872 870 59 7. £18 plus £1.50 p&p

Punishments of Former Days Ernest Pettifer 'A good read' *The Magistrate.* 1992 ISBN 1 872 870 05 8. £9.50 plus £1.50 p&p

Introduction to Prisons and Imprisonment Nick Flynn. Foreword by Lord Hurd of Westwell. 'A comprehensive and clear overview' *The Magistrate.* 1998 ISBN 1 872 870 37 6. £12 plus £1.50 p&p

Prisons of Promise Tessa West. Foreword by Sir David Ramsbotham, Chief Inspector of Prisons. 'Extremely well-researched . . . Should be seriously considered by the Home Secretary' *Justice of the Peace.* 1997 ISBN 1 872 870 50 3. £16 plus £1.50 p&p

Deaths of Offenders: The Hidden Side of Justice Alison Liebling (Ed.) Examines deaths in police, prison and special hospital custody—including in court and police cells. 1998 ISBN 1 872 870 61 9. £16 plus £1.50 p&p

Criminal Classes: Offenders at School Angela Devlin 'If you are in any doubt about the links between poor education, crime and recidivism, read it': Marcel Berlins *The Guardian.* 1995 ISBN 1 872 870 30 9. £16 plus £1.50 p&p

I'm Still Standing Bob Turney The autobiography of a dyslexic ex-prisoner, now a probation officer. 'A truly remarkable book' *Prison Writing.* 1997 ISBN 1 872 870 43 0. £12 plus £1.50 p&p

The Longest Injustice Alex Alexandrowicz and David Wilson. Alex spent 24 years in custody protesting his innocence. This book explains how something which began with him pleading guilty (quite wrongly but in the belief that he would get a 'short' sentence) turned into a Kafkaesque nightmare. Alex's story is placed in perspective by Dr David Wilson. ISBN 1 872 870 45 7. Price £16 plus £1.50 p&p (Scheduled for June 1999)

WATERSIDE PRESS • WINCHESTER • 01962 855567
VISA/MASTERCARD